OREGON'S SALTY COAST

BY JIM GIBBS

Rugged beauty of the Oregon coast etched in black and white.

SUPERIOR PUBLISHING COMPANY
SEATTLE

Library of Congress Cataloging in Publication Data

Gibbs, James Atwood, 1922—
Oregon's salty coast

1. Coasts—Oregon.
2. Oregon—History.
I. Title
GB458.8.G52 979.5 78-11899
ISBN 0-87564-223-3

FIRST EDITION

PRINTED AND BOUND IN THE UNITED STATES OF AMERICA

Dedication

To those who see the creative hand of God
on the fantastic Oregon coast.

"Let the sea in all its vastness roar with praise!
Let the earth and all living on it shout,
Glory to the Lord."

Psalms 98:7
The Living Bible

Special Acknowledgement

Cooperation of the Portland District Army Corps of Engineers and the U.S. Coast Guard 13th District headquarters in Seattle was greatly appreciated in the writing of this book.

CONTENTS

Introduction 1

Chapter One
  Spanish Treasure, Beeswax and Early Shipwrecks 20

Chapter Two
  Indian Skirmishes 66

Chapter Three
  The Deceptive River 94

Chapter Four
  Early Astoria and Environs 115

Chapter Five
  The Heroes and the Cowards 141

Chapter Six
  Bars, Jetties and the Army Corps of Engineers 167

Chapter Seven
  Regrettable Marine Disasters 199

Chapter Eight
  Excerpts From the War Years 219

Neah-kah-nie Mountain, the mountain of mystery, as it appeared on Jan. 31, 1915. More tales of intrigue center around this area than any other place on the Oregon coast. Tons of beeswax have been extracted from Manzanita and Nehalem beaches reputedly from Spanish galleons, and persistent tales of Spanish or pirate treasure center around the headland. In the foreground is the famous old Neah-kah-nie Tavern (resort) which burned down a few decades back. Many of the fittings inside the structure came from the wreck of the British bark *Glenesslin* wrecked below the mountain in 1913. Mayer photo.

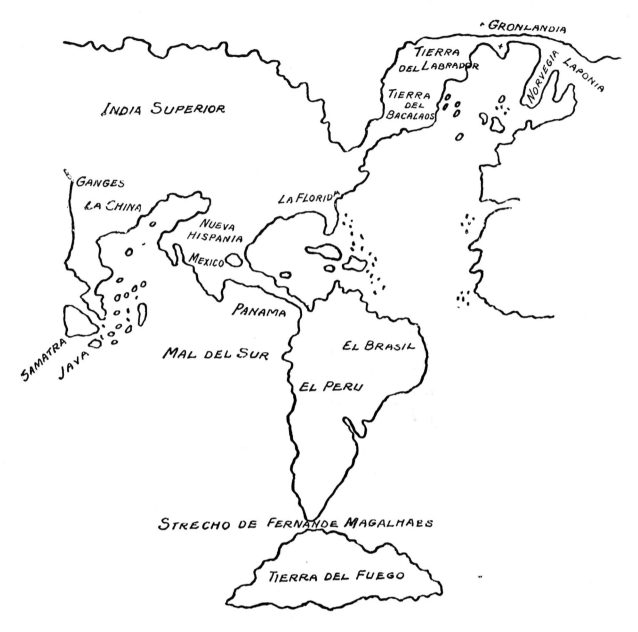

Oregon was not even a suggestion on this ancient map, (circa 1548) called Carta Marina. It shows North America as an extension of Asia.

INTRODUCTION
THE BOUNTIFUL SEACOAST

You rule the oceans when their waves arise in fearful storms;
you speak and they lie still.

—Psalms 89:9

FOR THOSE WHOSE EARS are so attuned there comes a call from the seashore down Oregon way. For precisely 363 miles, not counting coastal indentations, this salty frontier meets either in harmonious nature or vicious combat. Fantastic seascapes, iridescent tidepools, wet glistening sands and white-lipped breakers, are sights once seen, never forgotten. The undeniable forces of nature sometimes create titanic storm waves that crash against bold, rocky headlands, urged on by howling winter winds that uproot giant trees above the coastline. Worn down sea stacks standing sentinel bear scars of massive erosion from the persistence of the unrelenting combers. There are always the little marine creatures scrambling for a place to hide until the onslaught has subsided. Wet, penetrating fogs often drop their mantles as if on cat's paws. Sometimes the world completely closes down under a misty veil.

Man stands virtually helpless when voluminous liquid battering rams pound against Oregon's formidable shores, whittling away morsels of terra firma. In this hostile battleground where the land meets the sea, the latter has consistently been the victor, and will continue to be until the end of the age. As Oregon slowly shrinks, the mighty Pacific expands.

Ah, the Pacific, often peaceful, sometimes violent, an unpredictable personality so akin to a woman, and subject to change without notice.

Life in and around Oregon's Pacific rim is always fascinating, past or present. Here, the sea has a heartbeat far more enduring and infinite than that of man. The pulse of the tidal flow, the breath of the full gale or the whisper of the surf are all messages to delight the senses. Yes, here, even the seashell from its hollow in'ards has a story to tell. Awesome, placid or terrifying, this fantastic ocean front has a magnetic power. Watching a great golden orb drown itself in the western sea at day's end or following the rippling silver path of the moon's reflection can virtually cause an hypnotic spell.

Those who work the coastal waters gain a respectful fear when great liquid acclivities rise, tossing about unceremoniously the largest of floating conveyances. Solomon knew the feeling way back when, when he stated, "One of the great wonders is the way of a ship on the sea." Nor is the puniness of man ever more obvious than when his craft lies mangled on a hostile outcrop or plunges to its doom in irascible waters.

There exists an indissoluble trinity, other than that of the spiritual, between the sea, the ship and man. At times they love and reverence each other and on other occasions breed the most hostile contempt, but always, there is reconciliation. Men and ships are dependent on each other, but the ocean has been described as a mother, a mistress and a temptress.

The human element that plays its part in this continuing drama, master mariner, common sailor, artist, writer, fisherman, clam digger, rockhound or beachcomber, each have formed a deep-rooted awe and respect

Sir Francis Drake saw the Pacific from the shores of Panama in 1572. From 1577-80, he circumnavigated the world departing England with five ships, only one of which passed beyond the Strait of Magellan. In it he cruised north as far as San Francisco and Oregon's Cape Arago. He returned to England via the Cape of Good Hope. Drake was born in Devonshire, England in 1540.

of Oregon's offshore waters and its coastal ramparts. Many immortals with the pen, many geniuses with the brush, and others through the spoken word have added enduring flavor to this coastline. Symphonies composed by man have limitations, but the symphony of the sea is virtually eternal, with auras unlimited. Nor has any author, no matter how talented, ever fully captured the personality of the sea, nor artist its complete beauty.

The thought is ever present that the sea goes on and on long after ships vanish and man is reduced to ashes. And though God promised never again to flood the earth, the ocean still occupies the greater proportion of our sphere and each year accumulates more and more land for conversion into the watery kingdom.

In modern years, with his ever-increasing technology man has attempted to bridge the seas with ever larger vessels, some longer than five football fields. He has further attempted to control the undersea world with scientific submarines, but more so with the highly feared nuclear-powered submersibles armed with death-dealing missiles equipped with nuclear warheads, waiting the signal for genocide action.

The goal is no longer discovery, but control. Then there is the dread of man wantonly destroying the sea, his greatest asset, through pollution. But, polluted or not, the ocean will continue to roll against a thousand shores, not the least of which is Oregon, where the Pacific, the world's greatest water source, puts on its finest show.

Since the initial stirrings of human imagination the sea and the shore have enthralled. From the dawn of literature man has chronicled his nautical wanderings.

When man has a story to tell he will tell it in the best way he knows, be it by petroglyph or pen, and the world is richer for his efforts. Men have written of the sea and shore since 2500 B.C., when an unknown author set down on papyrus an account of his battle with a sea serpent, a document preserved in the British Museum.

The real beginning, however, goes back in the eons of time when God created the heavens and the earth, for as Genesis tells us, "God said, let there be a firmament in the midst of the waters, and let it divide the waters from the waters. And God made the firmament and divided the waters which were under the firmament from the waters which were above the firmament: and it was so. And God said; Let the waters under the heaven be gathered together unto one place and let the dry land appear: and it was so. And God called the dry land Earth; and the gathering together of the waters called he Seas: and God saw that it was good."

Oregon was formed amidst a great terrestrial revolution with vast eruptions of lava. The earth quaked violently, valleys being deeply notched and mountains formed. Long rollers broke on the coasts of a hot earth. After the creation it awaited mortal man, but man who permitted sin to creep in, caused God to repent of his works and the world was inundated. The cataclysmic wonder that would one day be known as Oregon was submerged.

From Noah's Ark down to our day some unknown ingredient has continued to pull man to the seashore and the ocean. Ironically, that elemental, ageless tow remains as strong in the nuclear age as it did in antiquity. In essence, all of us are islanders, inhabitants of the only water planet known to man in the solar system. The seas of our globe surround all the continents, making them islands in one massive ocean. Fishes live in a domain much deeper than the land's highest mountain, and more than a third larger in size than all the land mass combined.

The sea even breeds the weather and dominates the climate. The seafarer on seeing a storm building only has two alternatives, either to run for safe haven ashore or to ride it out. The safe havens are relatively few and far between along the Oregon coast, and rough bar entrances in adverse conditions will neither permit marine traffic to enter or to depart. Melville said that the sea "will insult and murder man and pulverize his most rugged ships," and Conrad focuses on its unfathomable cruelty. Still, its good far outweighs its bad. Even the best of humans has an occasional display of temper.

First commandment for the Oregon beachcomber is to never turn his back on the ocean. When her mood is angry, beware! Many have failed to heed the rule and many have not lived to tell the tale.

In ancient times, the sea was looked upon with a fearful eye, a treacherous place to be avoided by sane men. To get out of sight of land was not only considered foolhardy, but downright suicidal. Today the oceans are explored and charted in every corner, and modern communications keep them down to size. Still, it has an aura of incomparable excitement and attraction. Its unbridled fury is responsible each year for a heavy toll in lives and property, but that certain scintillating and intriguing ingredient coupled with mystery and surprise will never cease as long as man breathes fresh sea air.

No place on this earth, we repeat, does the ocean put on a better show than in Oregon. The Continental Shelf has a gentle slope westward to the deep troughs well offshore. On gentle days, the combers spill over like miniature waterfalls, and again, when the northerly and southerly winds blast, or a storm has occurred far out at sea, the surf becomes a mass of confused white water boiling and hissing like a witch's brew. When giant breakers lash the stern, rock-bound sectors, geysers often soar skyward or shoot jet streams out through blowholes. Deep fissures formed by the constant pounding through countless centuries are continually eroded by seas that end their long journeys by snubbing their noses against solid basalt. Walls of brine pulverize the softer earth above creating further wearing and incurable scars. Sometimes the surf is stirred into a frenzied froth, like the residue from tens of thousands of washing machines, bathing the shoreline in a foamy mass, deadening the sound of the shore breakers.

The ocean in motion is probably the most constant and dependable show on earth. We marvel at the human heart and its perpetual beat from birth to death, but consider the pulse of the ocean that has been going on in a continuing action since well before man. In a constant state of upheaval, waves, tidal action and currents team up along the shoreline to disperse the sediment that comes down from the hinterland via the many Oregon rivers and streams. In the upheaval, millions of tons of sand are shifted around constantly, supplying the numerous beaches which are divided from the more defiant rocky sections. Outcrops by the score have been cut off from the mainline of resistance standing like brave soldiers fighting a helpless cause, rotund, flat, slanted and craggy shapes, fending off the watery fusilades.

To the oceanographers and scientists we leave the technical side of the marine, but it's a comforting thought to know that God made it so that the more simple-minded can enjoy the pranks of the ocean and its shoreline every bit as much, if not more so than those who make it a profession. It doesn't take much training to learn that the tides run their course two times a day clockwise, beginning around an axis out in mid-ocean affected in their mysterious ways by the pull of the moon, the effect of the sun and of the earth itself. The cycle affords two highs and two lows, and the places where the ranges are the greatest afford the grandest probing grounds for the beachcomber and vacationer.

Square-rigged *Battle Abbey*, a British vessel being towed across the Columbia River bar, behind a mammoth bar swell in the early 1900's.

Some of the unusual seashore creatures endure the dry spells until covered by the incoming tides while others scramble for the water when their habitats become landlocked, nestle down deep in the sand or hold out on their rocky perches. The moon, some 239,000 miles out in space, unaffected by the junk left by our spacemen, continues its undeniable pull at the surface of our earth. Though rocks are immovable, the ocean responds to the pull, and as oceanographers say, humps up liquidly. On the other side of the world, a similar situation takes place due to the opposing centrifugal force of the earth curving in its orbit, which in a way of speaking almost matches the pull of the moon.

Way, way out in space, some 93 million miles, ol' Sol exerts its slight but definite influence with a pull reinforcing the effect of the moon when the two bodies are aligned. The moon which appears to be of little use to our traditional way of life, is in actuality a vital part of our existence and should it ever be blasted out of space could have a deadly effect on our world. Its irregular orbit around planet earth causes the extreme tides, when it comes the closest. Man should remember this when he enjoys the fascination of the minus tides or watches the watery onslaught of the flood tides inundating acres of previously attainable shorelands.

Though many maritime areas such as Hawaii and the South Pacific, due to their geographical locations, are deprived of extreme tidal fluctuations, the Oregon shoreline enjoys a veritable housecleaning with each

Appearing like a voluminous liquid mountain, a swell rises to great heights on the Columbia River bar as the French ship *Col. de Villebois du Mareuil* crosses in tow of a tug. The towline is hidden, but the French tricolor can be seen flying. This well known photo was taken in 1912 by tug captain, O. Beaton.

change of tide, the extreme fluctuations running from an extreme high of plus ten to a minus three feet. And of course, when storm waves accompany high tides, the inundated area will increase appreciably, though it does not compare to Canada's Bay of Fundy with the greatest tidal fluctuations in the world. That inlet of the Atlantic has tides or bore to 70 feet, and many of its flatlands have been diked off and reclaimed.

Some of the gradual slopes along Oregon's coast cause tidal ebbing and flowing over great stretches. Most capes and headlands however, drop steep into the depths and all that is exposed at extreme ebb tide is just more rock, rocks that have been chiseled, flattened or contorted by countless years of battering. River bars, inlets and dogholes often produce strong currents on the ebb tides and especially where large rivers enter the ocean.

Oceanographers claim that if the entire Pacific Coast was as straight as an arrow with a smooth offshore shelf, the tides would advance along its entire mass with constant speeds and menacing inundation of land masses. God, however, the master creator, saw to it that our shoreline was a mixture of promontories, curving sandy beaches and pin cushions of rocky outcrops that keep the whole process pretty much in line and makes a habitable wonderland, for both the creatures of the land and the creatures of the sea.

Few there are who at one time have not pondered the mystery of the waves. This potential source of energy is not quite what it appears to be. It isn't that each wave as an entity is traveling over a long distance, but a pulsating action passing through the water. A glass fishfloat, a bottle or pieces of drift can travel long distances at the whim of current and wind, but the waves just appear to be water on the way to somewhere else—like potential energy moving in a visible form. A sizable wave can travel upward to 5,000 miles, enough to cross any ocean in the world. At the outset, the waves are created when a sea breeze blowing over the surface causes ripples to

form as a result of friction, much in the same manner as throwing a rock into a still millpond and watching it send out a series of little ripples that widen and grow until they reach the shores of the pond. Storms usually start a confused wave pattern but nearly always have a general direction. When the waves outrun the wind they settle into the regular height and spacing of open ocean swells, the pattern often leading to that old nemesis of the sea—mal de mer. Many a landlubber on testing the elevator personality of the billows has longed for terra firma.

No more of the sea, enough for me!
I'm green at the gills, despite my pills,
Oh for dry land, a step on the sand,
Oh me oh my, I think I'll die.

Sick, yes I am, please get me a pan,
The pitch and the roll is taking its toll,
Just put me ashore, and forever more,
I'll live out my days in landlubber ways.

Waves are constant at sea but when the energy stored within touches the shallow shelf leading to the beaches, surf is created and the energy uncovered in spectacular climax. The original height of the wave determines how far offshore the surf zone begins during any prevailing conditions. As the wave gets to the shallow areas its front edge slows quicker than its hind zone, the column compresses, the wave gets thinner and taller, becomes unstable and then collapses. Thus, the death of a wave.

Oceanographers tell us that gently shoaling beaches do not produce, as a rule, crashing surf, as the wave energy is spent with bottom friction being extremely lessened. Wide surf zones on the other hand produce a labyrinth of troughs and sandbars that have larger breakers on the outer bar and smaller ones on the inner side. If, on the other hand the approach to the outer bar is steep, then plunging breakers are the result. Succeeding waves are lesser but culminate in an unpredictable mixture of plunging and spilling breakers. Steep approaches to a beach will bring waves right up to the termination of life when they suddenly well up and crash down in a frightening show of violence.

One can virtually tell the topography of a beach by the following rules: Green water is deep, white water is shallow. Spilling breakers mean gentle slope, while plunging breakers designate steep slope. Three or four lines of breakers indicate several parallel sand bars with intervening troughs.

Of course, such a measuring stick is not entirely accurate because weather and sea conditions on the Oregon coast can confuse the general rule at any time. During adverse weather, the entire shoreline can become white-lipped fury from north to south, as far as the eye can see.

Knowing the topography of the sea was a science to the early Polynesian navigators who explored and settled the myriad of islands of the Pacific, as far east as Hawaii and Easter Island. But the southern ocean is not like the North Pacific. Frequent overcast days and changing cloud patterns reflect on the ocean's face. The menu of the day in in the South Pacific is generally clear, sunny skies affording the sea a steady variety of hues—blues, aquamarine, greens, each revealing the controlling depths.

Again we repeat that despite all the books that have been written about the sea, its mystery, intrigue and attraction continue to grow in the mortal mind.

The Oregon coast, often peaceful, occasionally violent, is certainly not an exception.

CAPE PERPETUA

What better place to discover the Oregon coast than at its midpoint, the crown of the central sector, Cape Perpetua. This precipitous 803-foot monolith is the highest immediately fronting the coast. Rising sharply from the sea it was forged in the furnace of the earth, spewed out as molten lava and formed as a bastion to stand for time immemorial as a warlike castle fending off the charging seas that constantly roll against its girth. Since its inception, the Eocene basalts (hard, dark colored rock of volcanic origin) have weathered the onslaught of wind, wave and torrent. For most of the eons of time it knew not the footprints of man. Long before white explorers' sails broke the horizon, occasional coastal Indian villages dotted the shoreline. Great shell mounds, residue of the ravenous feasting on shellfish and game are all that remain of a people that lived in relative peace in a happy fishing and hunting ground which in their ignorance was tantamount to Eden itself. Illiterate, yet satisfied, one generation paralleling the next, their culture remained primitive, but stable. Completely unaware of the existence of the white man and his progressive ways, and without contact from the outside world, those natives, like the early Polynesians, pursued the only kind of an existence they knew. And they found it wasn't all that bad. They fished, they hunted, they bartered, they lived, they died.

Occasionally rival tribes on the central Oregon coast would war against each other, usually when one invaded the territory of the other. Skirmishes were generally short-lived. Their eventual demise came with the white man who was to bring disease, whiskey, guns and superior power. Once under subjection, the coastal Indian was herded to the reservation under the inhumane guise of justice.

Ancient Indians revered the lands that spread out in the shadow of Perpetua, south to the Siuslaw and northward to the Alsea and Yaquina rivers. In the lee of the great promontory, flowed a myriad of streams, including the peaceful Yachats River, two miles north of the cape. In this general area lived probably no more contented red men in America. They had everything to sustain life for a primitive people—an endless abundance of game, fish, roots, berries and shellfish. The largest shell mounds found anyplace in Oregon were discovered at Yachats and on Cape Perpetua, and there is hardly a section where one cannot dig into the ground and hit layers of shells where Indians sat by the hour and gorged themselves on a continuing supply of mussels, clams and oysters.

With relatively mild weather the year-round, and a constant fresh supply of pure scintillating water, tall timber and beaches choked with driftwood, it is hard to imagine a more idyllic situation for a primitive race. Probably they had dwelled there for more than a thousand years, and had not the white man come, their simple, unchangeable way of life would have perhaps continued for countless decades just as prior to the age of exploration.

Today, the descendants of the central coast Indians are mostly settled in the Siletz area, northeast of Newport, while a ribbon of black asphalt winds along the coast, Highway 101, through their old familiar haunts. Since the early 1930's, millions of vehicles from the old Model T to the fanciest Cadillac of our day have brought countless tourists to view Oregon's seafront. Caucasian residents have occupied virtually all of the favorite haunts of the ancient Indian. The trip down the Oregon coast a half century ago demanded the crossing of the major coastal rivers by pint-sized ferryboats whose limited services were terminated with the completion of the highway bridges.

Cape Perpetua, in the extreme southwest corner of Lincoln County, is not only prominent, but historic. Discovered on March 7, 1778, by Captain James Cook, the intrepid English sea rover, explorer and navigator, it remains an eternal sentinel to his honor. Some misguided historians attribute the name of the cape to the nasty weather Cook encountered which "perpetually" kept him within its view. According to the navigator's journal, however, he named the headland for St. Perpetua, an early Christian martyr, allegedly murdered in Carthage on March 7, in the year 203. It was on that day in 1778, (celebrated in old England), that Cook sighted the cape.

It is said that the Christian saint was a noble lady of ancient Carthage, and that in the rage of religious persecution and of her father's pleading and tears for her to renege, she stood fast in her faith. Refusing to denounce her Lord and Master, Jesus Christ, she was beheaded and her body thrown to the beasts.

Thus today, the wonder of nature known as Cape Perpetua honors both Captain Cook and the martyred St. Perpetua.

Wandering through and inhabiting the wilds of the cape and of the 622,000 acre Siuslaw National Forest is a vast variety of animals: raccoons, squirrels, chipmunks, black bear, black-tailed deer and elk. On the sea front, seabirds of most every type, from the seagull to the pelican, from the cormorant to the sandpiper and from the murre to the oyster catcher, dine on fish and crustaceans and nest on the steep slopes. In the depths, live everything from the slippery little smelt to the great gray whale which travels as far as 11,000 miles annually between the Arctic Ocean and Mexico, parading off the Central Oregon coast, some leaving the migratory parade to stay on for a considerable while. These leviathans, some bettering 50 feet, weigh a ton per foot and make the longest ocean migration of any of God's whale species. Uncanny in their navigational instincts, they perform through the sea what the swallows accomplish in their annual junket to Capistrano.

There is life everywhere on the sea front. On the rocks, exposed on the ebbing of the tides, is a carpet of blue mussels by the millions, interspersed with voracious barnacles. There are starfish of virtually every color of the rainbow, and the ever present green sea anemones that close up when exposed by the tide and which open up like delicate flowers when inundated. Deceptive, they attract, anesthetize and entrap their victims in their folding petals. Some of the larger anemones live to be 150 years old, enjoying twice the life span of humans. Then there are the defiant sea palms, another strange marine plant organism, shaped almost like a miniature palm tree, shackling themselves in the most unbelievable places where the full power of the breakers smashes against exposed rock. They take the punishment of hundreds of superbowl linemen and only occasionally get decapitated.

Dotted with giant spruce which breast the howling winds of winter, Cape Perpetua stands almost as a symbol, similar to the other great headlands that front the Oregon coast. Often times the forces of nature send storm waves smashing against her girdle of rock, her trees being rudely extracted by howling blasts of wind that sometimes climb to the top of the Beaufort scale. The countless marine creatures compete for a place to dwell, and the unseen micro-organisms relentlessly turn fallen vegetation into soil while rocks pounded loose from the cliffsides, many of the agate variety, fall onto the beaches to be polished by the sluicing waves into fascinating semi-precious gems, along with bloodstones and jasper. Fissures, and sea caves as well as the ebb and flow of uneven, unpredictable breaker patterns may provide a fascination for the human, but yearly, as has been told, many are injured and sometimes killed by not using every precaution. In recent years, a teenager fell into one of the many caves between Yachats and Cape Perpetua. Barreling waves roared through the cave's mouth en-

veloping the lad time after time. Only the unusual formation of the cave permitted his ability to breath occasional air. Those who came to rescue him said his shrieks of terror could be heard two miles away. With no way to save the boy through the entrance to the cave, it was decided to lower a member of the rescue squad through a small hole at the top. The breakers were soon snapping at him as he swung like a plumbline in a gale. Though inundated several times, the brave volunteer finally reached the hysterical youth. By superhuman effort both were hoisted to safety.

One must also beware of the drift logs responsible for injury and sometimes death. Breakers can knock the unsuspecting from a log which in turn rolls over him, or catch him in a scissors-like action in conjunction with a second log.

There is a huge sea cave directly under the highest slope of Perpetua. Chiseled out of a basaltic mass by onrushing surf through countless years, the cavity, like a small amphitheatre is nearly 50 feet high and 100 feet deep. During the winter storms the effect is sensational, seas roaring to the butt end of the cave and then cascading back out, regurgitating tons of white spray in geyser-like proportions.

When it comes to sea caves, however, none is greater than the Sea Lion Caves, claimed to be the world's largest. Located ten miles south of Cape Perpetua, the place has been an official tourist attraction since 1932. With a floor area of nearly two acres and a vaulted rock dome some 125 feet high, southward from the main chamber, a low passage runs 1,000 feet to a sea level opening. Measured from another direction the cave is nearly 1,500 feet long blending in its cathedral-like ceiling, hues of greens, pinks, reds and purples. The colors reflect in the ocean water inside the cave, sometimes producing a beautiful aquamarine color not unlike the Blue Grotto on Italy's Isle of Capri.

Not in the British Isles, New Zealand or Japan has there been found a cave of comparable size and interest. But of course the cave itself is not the main attraction, it being the stellar sea lions that make it their home.

Tourists enter 320 feet above sea level, and are taken down in an elevator to the floor of the cave where they, at the right season, find hundreds of these great mammals from playful 30 pound pups to ornery and powerful one ton bulls posing a threat to any would-be trespassers. Content to stay inside or outside their unique natural habitat the year round, these cumbersome creatures have found a perfect environment. When the weather is pleasant and mild, they fish, frolic and sunbathe on the rocks outside the cave, but during adverse weather they have at their disposal the full and complete protection of perhaps the best animal hideaway in all the world. Inside the cave are three openings: two facing the sea and one "dry" entrance to the north. In 1932, a footpath and a stairway with 111 steps gave entry to the cave.

The elevator which now descends to the cave floor is a far cry from the entrance made by the adventurous seafarer who discovered the indenture in the coastal wall in 1880. His name was William Cox, a retired sea captain. As long as there are things to be discovered, mortal man will try, or die in the attempt. Captain Cox was such an individual and he was determined to find out just what was inside the deceptive entrance. Perhaps he had visions of finding some ancient Spanish treasure, loot from a captured galleon, hidden within by a band of swarthy pirates, for even back then such legends were persistent along the Oregon coast. Again, maybe he visualized a terrifying sea serpent or perhaps a mermaid fair combing her lovely locks on the slippery rocks inside the entrance. Whatever, he was intrigued by the presence of the cave and laid plans to enter it by skiff, there being no known way to gain entrance to the cave from the landside. An experienced hand with a small boat he was willing to challenge the rise and fall of the swell pulsating at the cave entrance. Sizing up the situation, Cox, his heart in his mouth, proceeded. His craft lifted and then settled in the trough. Arm and back muscles straining, he endeavored to keep from broaching to and capsizing. Through the entrance, a swell caught the boat and pushed it forward, but quick reaction straightened its course and the outside light was suddenly diffused. As his eyes adjusted, he looked about in total amazement at the size and extent of the unusual cavern. Lighting a kerosene lantern, he held it aloft and searched for a place to land the boat. Finding a gentle, sloping rock shelf, he made it fast and began his exploration of the weird shapes and shadowed corners, his heart pounding at being the first white man to enter the strange, hidden domain. If any of the coastal Indians had entered, it was a well guarded secret for they believed such places to be full of evil spirits. Perhaps Cox was the first human to explore the cave.

His fascination drew attention away from a few sea lions scattered about. Upset by the presence of this intruder, they barked to no avail. Further, Cox had paid little attention to a mounting surf, foaming and curling at the entrance. When ready to leave, his passageway out was blocked. The adventurer was trapped. Though calm on the inside, the outside weather had soured and the ocean was being whipped into a furious froth; a storm was in the making.

Pondering his seemingly foolhardy adventure, Cox resigned himself to settle down with his sea lion companions until sea conditions would permit his exit. How long, he wondered, would it be until he saw the full light of day again. The poor captain was in a bit of a predicament to say the least. His belly was getting hunger pangs and he felt damp and cold, the surf continuing to pant angrily at the cave entrance. Hours passed slowly, in fact a few days came and went before the storm died and the seas calmed. Finally, the desperate individual made his daring exit, this time heading into the surf. Hands tightly gripped on the oars, the doughty captain stubbornly pulled the craft back out into what seemed a great, big beautiful world, uninhibited by rock walls.

For such an exploit it would seem that history would have preserved the occasion by officially naming this geographic feature Cox Cave, but alas, the sea lions whose home it has been for decades were accorded the honor. But don't feel too bad for Mr. Cox, for he was not entirely overlooked, his name being applied to a prominent seamark, a mile and a half south of Heceta Head, a conical-shaped hunk of basalt. Evidently the birds have not respected Cox's sentinel as they continue to whiten its summit and sides with their droppings.

Picturesque Heceta Head, probably closer to the half-way mark on the Oregon coast than Perpetua, lies only a mile north of the Sea Lion Caves, it being named for the renowned Spanish shipmaster and explorer Bruno Heceta, commanding the corvette *Santiago*. Perhaps the most photographed and painted geographical feature on the coast, its basic popularity is attributed to the picturesque and thought-provoking lighthouse so perfectly set into the seascape that one almost feels that God put it there in the beginning.

When the *Santiago* passed the bold headland in the late summer of 1775, it was probably observed by wide-eyed Indians filled with both excitement and terror. Brer' Bruno, however, wasn't quite so impressed, scanning the misty shoreline as he did, noting shallow water for some distance off the cape, suggesting for the sake of a better name, Heceta Bank. Though the cape bears his name, he might have gained far greater fame had he ventured into the Columbia River, historians claiming that he was actually the first to recognize its existence. He saw the long sought after "River of the West" on August 17, 1775, noting an opening from which rushed a current so strong he could not enter. Had he waited for the bar to calm and crossed over, history would read considerably different. Instead, the great discovery was left to a Yankee, Robert Gray, who on May 11, 1792 entered the river and named it for his ship. Had Heceta followed up his sighting several years earlier, the name of the great river might well have become either Heceta or Santiago. But it was not meant to be. The nautical observations of the Spanish navigator placed his position within one minute of the latitude of Cape Disappointment, at the river's north entrance, which he named Cape San Roque, before breezing onward to other discoveries.

The Oregon coast, in the age of exploration and up through the coming of the white settlers, was divided by its prominent headlands. These great landmarks were the only means of locating the respective parts of the shoreline. We know them today as Tillamook Head, Mt.

Neah-kah-nie, Cape Meares, Cascade Head, Cape Foulweather, Cape Perpetua, Heceta Head, Cape Arago, Cape Blanco, Humbug Mountain, Cape Sebastian and Cape Ferrelo—all prominent and rising directly from the ocean shores. All of these natural sentinels served at one time or another as landfalls for galleons returning from the exotic east, as early as the 16th century, up through the era of the commercial sailing vessels that often had to set their courses in accordance with the winds that wafted them across the vast Pacific.

Occasionally, the similarity of these capes and headlands from the seaward side caused mistaken identity which led to many erroneous calculations in the faded past.

Under a light mantle of fog and Oregon sea mist Yaquina Head Lighthouse stands tall, towering over the rocky obstructions, bathed by a surging surf. Unconcerned, the gulls go about their daily task of searching for food.

CHAPTER ONE
SPANISH TREASURE, BEESWAX AND EARLY SHIPWRECKS

Is THERE A SUBJECT that so ignites the excitement and imagination as that of buried treasure? When one thinks of old Spain, gold, silver and precious stones immediately come to mind, and where there was Spanish treasure in olden times, not far behind were pirates and privateers thirsting for plunder in the name of lust, greed, fame, fortune or prestige. That the ships of wealthy Spain were usually the target of the marauders may seem unjustified, but when one considers that the larger share of Spain's wealth was ruthlessly extracted from the Aztecs, Incas, Indians, Southeast Asians and others, under the guise of religion, perhaps it was just retribution.

Aside from the subject of treasure, the brave, intrepid Spanish navigators of past centuries deserve much credit for opening unknown seas and lands to world commerce long before other nations dared venture far from their home waters. To pioneer the hidden corners of the world they suffered much hardship and privation. Shipwreck was common and the dreaded scurvy wiped out Spanish sailors by the score. Though they wielded a mighty sword over many of their victims, the price they paid in human life was considerable.

Though much of the discovery of the new world must properly go to the Vikings, the Portuguese, the Dutch, English, French and Russians, yet it was Spain that stood out, especially where the Pacific was concerned. Spanish sailors of old were not strangers to Oregon's prominent coastal landmarks.

Of course, due to the astounding research of New Zealand-born Bary Fell, a marine biologist, much of the accepted early history will be changed. The Harvard researcher has come up with a deciphering of an ancient language affording strong evidence that there were men and women from Europe not merely exploring, but living in North America as early as 800 B.C. They worked as miners, tanners and trappers, and are believed to have shipped their products back to Europe. Celtic and Carthaginian people, pagan worshippers of Baal, lived, worked and traded in New England and in the mid-west, their only monuments some strange haunts, one reputedly a winter solstice chamber in Vermont, believed to have been used by New England Celts for lunar observations, and a series of slabstone buildings in New Hampshire.

A great lapse in history must have occurred, and the contact between two continents was abruptly terminated, for until recent years most of our exploration type history books revolved around America's discovery by Christopher Columbus in 1492.

Whatever new historical discoveries might be uncovered, Spain will continue to remain as a Pacific pioneer, though anti-dated by the Polynesians. Unfortunately this great nation of yesteryear sought power through wealth and this ultimately helped cause her downfall. The cost of exploration had yielded little in the early 16th century. In 1519, Spanish royalty, bogged down with internal affairs enlisted the services of the intrepid Ferdinand Magellan, a renowned Portuguese navigator whose country had refused his grandiose plans for new world discovery. By royal edict, he, with a picked crew was dispatched to seek a passage around South America to the East Indies, a demanding voyage that was to end in triumph, hardship and tragedy.

Spain had rejected the magnitude of Columbus' discovery of the West Indies and the fact that he proved the world was not flat. He had unknowingly opened a whole new future world of wealth for Mother Spain, but he, one of the world's great explorers, was to die in disgrace.

Before Magellan's epic voyage, Balboa had already crossed the Isthmus to discover the Great South Sea, naming it Pacific, in 1513, while Portuguese explorers had sailed eastward terminating with the Oriental world. To Magellan fell the task of rounding for the first time the whole of South America, and clawing his way across the world's greatest ocean on a westward passage to the Indies. Thus a fleet of five small vessels, the *Santiago, Trinidad, San Antonio, Concepcion* and *Victoria* set out from Sanlucar Sept. 20, 1519, on one of the boldest voyages of the age of exploration. He was to discover an "outlet to the Moluccas." through which trade would inevitably follow, trade that would fatten the purse of Spain and outdo her immediate rival, Portugal.

It took three months for the fleet to reach Rio de Janiero, during which crude navigation instruments exchanged the North Star for the Southern Cross. Brazil, under Papal decree, belonged to Portugal, so Magellan pressed southward toward the land of Patagonia and the ice-laced Antarctic. Gripped by almost unbearable cold, the expedition faced a near mutiny, many of the men with frost-bitten hands and feet. One of the mutineers was hung and two left behind on barren shores. Then the *Santiago,* sent southward to reconnoiter, was totally wrecked in a squall. The *San Antonio* was then sent home when the expedition pilot refused to go further. The three remaining ships proceeded through what we know today as the Straits of Magellan, the high-walled desolate wastes that cut through the toe of South America. After rigorous days of terrible suffering they reached the vast Pacific, sailed along the coast of Chile and then pushed onward in the Pacific toward the Spice Islands, existing on rancid water and maggot-infested biscuits. Week after week they sailed the wide ocean until their water and food supply was exhausted, the crews subsisting on sawdust and leather strappings from the rigging. Scurvy and beri beri took their toll. Finally, an abandoned atoll was reached for temporary replenishment, but by March 5, 1521, the food supply was completely exhausted once again. Hope was gone. Then suddenly appeared the island we know today as Guam. The starving individuals could hardly believe their eyes. Hundreds of natives surrounded the ships in their praus, but the first act they performed was to steal the *Trinidad's* skiff. Then they streamed aboard like pirates stealing the ships blind. Almost too weak to resist, one

Spaniard managed to fell a native chief with his cross-bow, while his shipmates fired a broadside. As the natives retreated, Magellan rallied his men, 40 of whom he took ashore well armed, where they found a utopia—coconuts, sugar cane and bananas, the latter being the favorite, as many had lost their teeth from scurvy.

Following rest, recuperation and replenishment, Magellan named the island and the others in the area, Los Ladrones, meaning "the thieves," and then pressed onto the Philippines. A few years before, he had sailed eastward to the meridian of the Philippine archipelago in the cause of Portugal; now he had made the westward passage for Spain. This would be the crossroads where the two belligerent nations would lay their claims. Sailing through the myriad of 7,000 islands, past Leyte, he landed at tiny Limasawa. Then on to other islands, he influenced many of those pagan people to adopt the Roman Catholic faith. He, however, came up against a stubborn chief named Mactan, who firmly resisted forceful coercion, and when the great navigator landed with 50 of his men and some Philippine converts, they were surrounded. In the battle that followed, Magellan, fighting bravely, was stabbed to death.

The expedition leader, having circumnavigated the world, had opened the future ocean track that Spanish ships would follow for the next two and a half centuries.

The remaining ships, *Trinidad* and *Victoria* (the *Concepcion* had earlier burned) withdrew to East Indies spice ports, the former falling to the Portuguese. Only one ship was to make it back to Seville, Spain, her complement suffering to such an extent, that most of them perished en route. The battered, leaking *Victoria,* alone rounding Africa, made it home under the intrepid Juan Sebastian del Cano, one of those earlier involved in the

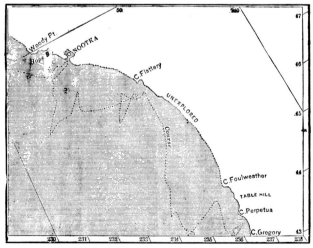

Shame on you Capt. James Cook! This is his map showing the course of his ships, and an unbroken coast from the 43rd parallel to and beyond Nootka Sound. The intrepid navigator and explorer failed in his efforts to find the bar entrances along the Oregon coast, and assumed there to be none.

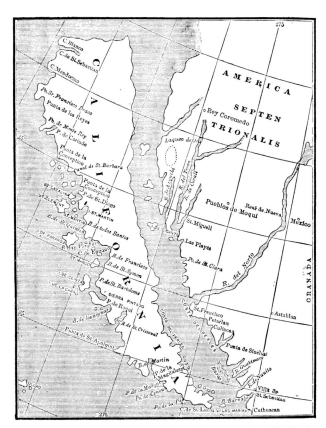

Cape Blanco and Cape Sebastian part of a California island? That's the way these two prominent Oregon landmarks were depicted on a Dutch maritime map made in 1624-25. Though it shows California as an island, the Spaniards had explored the whole Gulf of California nearly a century earlier and determined that the peninsula was part of the mainland.

mutiny, but having been pardoned. Of the original 247 man expedition, only 18 were to complete the circumnavigation of the world—a three year voyage which ended Sept. 8, 1522.

Now, the reader may ask, what does Magellan's voyage have to do with Oregon? First, it revealed the Americas as a separate continent from Asia. Secondly, and probably most important, it opened up Spanish transpacific trade, which as previously mentioned was to last for two and a half centuries, connecting the western rim of North America with the Orient, or as the Spanish put it, trade between New Spain (Mexico), the East Indies and Moluccas.

Through this period, Oregon territory was virtually unknown to the civilized world, but under the beach sands and rocky outcrops of the Oregon coast are believed to be the rotting remains of both Spanish galleons once engaged in the transpacific trade and of caravels sailing up the coast from Mexico.

For 250 years after the voyage of Magellan, Spain carried on that trade, the most important terminus ports being Acapulco and Manila. A galleon made the passage

each way annually. On the westbound trek, the cumbersome sailing vessels would fall in with the prevailing winds and current near the equator, then northward to Magellan's old anchorage in Los Ladrones (Guam), and on to Manila. On the eastward trek, the galleons would set a northerly course, catching the prevailing winds, falling in with the Japanese Current by turning east at the northerly end of the Japanese archipelago and following the great circle route across the Pacific. Though a landfall was sought along the northern California coast, usually Cape Mendocino, storm, wind and current would bring a landfall anywhere between the 30th and 45th parallel. Generally, after a long eastbound passage, any headland from northern California to northern Oregon was acceptable before working south along the coast to Acapulco or San Blas. Storm-wracked ships also found refuge at Monterey or the bays of San Francisco and San Diego. Much of their trouble came from the contrary seas and fog-shrouded coast of Oregon.

History has paid little mind to it, but it appears that Sir Francis Drake, first Englishman to circumnavigate the world, (1577-80) dropped his anchor for five days, (June 1579) in the cove on the south side of Oregon's Cape Arago. He too, complained of a "vile stinking fog," and to show his chagrin, named it "Bad Bay."

For a half century after Ferrelo's reputed sighting of Oregon, no known official exploration northward was attempted by Spain. Attention instead was directed toward the Orient where it was confidently anticipated that rich provinces might be secured by Spain, despite her direct contention with her rival, Portugal.

Ferdinando Cortez who landed in Mexico as early as 1519 had not been oblivious to the wealth of the Far East, having in 1525 sent out two ships with the object of taking the Philippine Islands. The expedition failed, but a second, under Ruy Lopez de Villabos, with the backing of a large force was successful in taking formal possession of the islands. Later, however, he was forced into relinquishing control through native reprisal. Not until 1564, some 40 years later, were the Spanish totally successful in their efforts, due much to the leadership of Miguel de Legazpi, who had sailed from Mexico with a considerable number of militiamen and a large fleet of ships. He was to enforce Spain's claim to the coveted archipelago. So successful was this thrust that Spain was to hold a sword over the islands for the next 300 years, extracting countless quantities in gold, silver and precious gems to fatten the coffers of Spanish royalty.

In Legazpi's expedition sailed one Urdanata, who, though acting as a priest was also an excellent navigator, and might easily, except for orders, have been the fleet commander. It was he who officially noted for the first time what Magellan may have suspicioned, that the tradewinds blowing always in one direction within certain limits on both sides of the equator, making it easy to sail west but not to return, might be avoided on the eastward voyage by sailing northward into a region where the winds would be more variable. On his recommendation the fleet, on its eastward track, sailed north to the 40th parallel permitting a passage with far less difficulty. This was to become the accepted route of the galleons which, with favoring winds, could usually make a landfall somewhere near Cape Mendocino before following the coast southward.

A profitable trade resulted between Manila and Acapulco. The early caravels gave way to larger more commodious, stronger built galleons. The smaller craft were used principally as coasters. Portugal was beginning to lose its trade war with its constant foe, and most maritime nations avoided head-on confrontations with Spain, desiring instead, hit and run tactics.

Spain considered the Pacific its own exclusive lake, forbidding other countries from its waters. When Dutch and English ships later defied that authority Spain labeled their people "illegitimate pirates," and when caught hung them immediately from the highest yardarm, or employed a firing squad for immediate action.

Spain had the coveted "throne" of trade, but desired an exclusive, discouraging the natural procession of mutual trade with other nations. The greed for wealth under the cloak of conquest and religion produced many unfortunate overtones, but it took a long time to dethrone the king of the seas.

Many of the salts of the old Spanish galleons gazed upon the shores of Oregon on returning from the Orient, but who actually was the first Caucasian to see that virgin coast? One must remember that in the early years, navigation instruments were crude at best, sightings were subject to question, and explorers apt to fudge a little about their accomplishments.

Was the discoverer of Oregon, d'Aguilar, Ferrelo, Flores or Viscaino? How about the old Greek mariner, Valerianos, who sailed for Spain, as Juan de Fuca? He told Michael Lok, respected English merchant living in Venice in April 1596, of having been in the West Indies of Spain 40 years and that he had sailed to and from many places in the service of the Spaniards. Further he claimed to have been in a Spanish vessel returning from the "Islands Phillippinas," toward "Nova Spania" which was plundered and taken at "Cape California" by Captain Candish (Cavendish), whereby he lost 60,000 ducats of his own goods.

Continuing his story, he said he was sent out as a pilot of three small ships which the Viceroy of Mexico dispatched from Nova Spania to discover the Strait of Anian along the coast of the South Sea and to fortify in that strait, to resist the passage and proceedings of the English nation, and, that by reason of a meeting among the soldiers for the misconduct of their captain, the voyage was overthrown, and the ship returned to Nova Spania from California without anything done in their voyage, and that after their return the captain was justifiably punished.

Also he claimed, shortly after the ill-fated voyage, the viceroy sent him out again in 1592, with only a small caravel and a pinnace, armed with mariners only, to follow the said voyage for the discovery of the Strait of Anian, and the passage thereof into the sea; and that he followed his course in that voyage west and northwest in the South Sea, (North Pacific) all along the coast of Nova Spania and California, and the Indies (along the Oregon Coast) until he came to latitude 47 degrees; and that there, finding that land trended north and northeast, with a broad inlet of sea, between 47 and 48 degrees of latitude he entered sailing therein more than 20 days. Before entering the strait, he sighted "a great headland or island (Cape Flattery) with an exceeding high pinnacle (Fuca's Pillar) or spired rock like a pillar thereupon." He also saw people clad in beast's skins and noted the land to be very fruitful. Not being armed to resist the force of the savage people, he returned to Acapulco hoping to be rewarded by the viceroy for the service he had done.

The Strait of Juan de Fuca still bears his name despite the efforts of numerous historians to discredit his claim. Neither do any documents about his alleged discovery exist in the Spanish archives, but then of course, the loosely operated government of New Spain paid little heed to the discovery aspect unless treasure was involved.

If de Fuca's account is true, he may have been the first to skirt the entire coast of Oregon, though probably by no means the first to see the Oregon Coast.

It is obvious that there was considerable Spanish maritime activity along the Pacific Northwest shores in pre-discovery times and certainly the evidences speak for themselves. In addition to early Spanish and Oriental shipwrecks in Oregon, Indian legend claims that a vessel was wrecked near the Quinault River in Washington as early as 1550, long before de Fuca's voyage of discovery.

Never did a galleon depart Manila without a cargo of treasure—gold, silver, specie, and such items as rare silks, taffeta, Cantonese crepes, costly vestments for cathedrals and missions, precious cut and uncut stones, fabulous jewelry, costly gifts from India's mogul and highly prized Gehdda wax, a beeswax common to India, utilized by the Roman church for tapers and candles. No galleon ever departed for Mexico without the substance. It has a slower burning ratio than other types of beeswax. European, Japanese, and North American wax is derived from the bee of the Apis mellifera variety while the small Indian bee is of the Apis dorsata variety. The higher melting point and slower burning qualities made it a priority item in 16th and 17th century New Spain, lighting the dwellings in Acapulco, Mexico City and Guadalajara.

Often "sized" for galleon transport, many chunks were inscribed with numerals over which historians disagree as to meaning. Were they bill of lading marks, dates, religious markings? At any rate, tons of Ghedda beeswax have been removed from the sands of Oregon, from the south entrance of the Columbia River down to and beyond Nehalem Spit. Some is still found to this day, the largest discovery in recent years having been made at Nehalem Beach near Manzanita in 1973. It was a 45 pound piece of the substance discovered in the sands by Lowell Damon.

Tons of the wax, perhaps well over 300 tons have reputedly come from at least one wreck of a Spanish vessel on Nehalem Beach. Indians told of such an incident long before the white settlers came to Oregon. Oriental junks also carried beeswax, but the quantities were not nearly so large. It is however, a fact that junks did wreck on Oregon beaches in ancient times and perhaps may have left an additional amount of the substance to help confuse the modern mind.

From the initial transpacific crossings of Manila caravels and galleons, commencing in 1565 till the final voyage in 1815, records in Spanish archives list 30 of these vessels as having been lost on westbound passages.

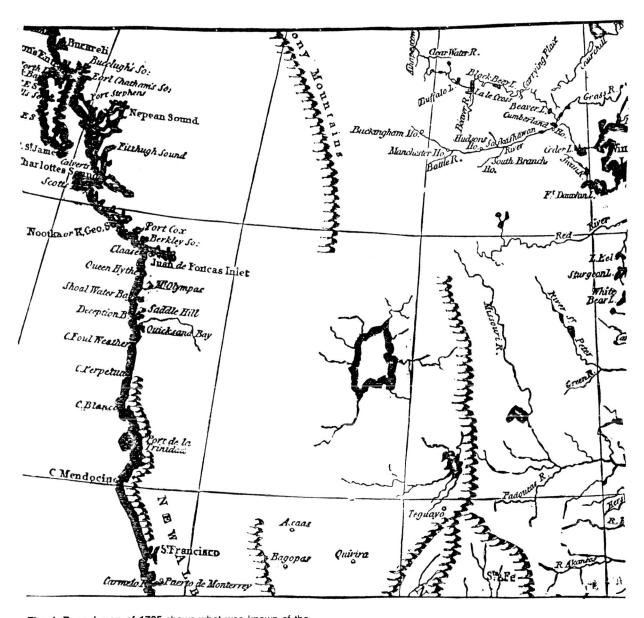

The J. Russel map of 1795 shows what was known of the Pacific Coast prior to the publication of Vancouver's report and the visit of Lewis and Clark.

Vessels of discovery. The ship *Columbia* and the sloop *Lady Washington* which figured in the discovery of the Columbia River, Tillamook Bay and Grays Harbor. The 220 ton *Columbia*, commanded by both Capt. Robert Gray and Capt. John Kendrick was a privateer during the Revolution. The *Lady Washington*, of 90 tons, was invaluable in getting into tight places where the larger vessel was unable to sail. Sketch, after an original by Robert Haswell, mate of the *Washington*, found among the private papers of Captain Gray.

Entrance to the Strait of Juan de Fuca after a print in "Voyages Made in the Years 1788-89 by Capt. John Meares," published in London.

Most of this number went to a watery grave in the fickle, often hazardous Philippine Sea and one is known to have stranded on the inhospitable rocks of a Japanese island. Still another was captured and plundered by a British privateer and two others went missing. Of the latter, one is traditionally believed to have been wrecked off San Miguel Island, (in the Channel group) off California's coast where traces of Ghedda beeswax has occasionally been found. Some believe her to have been the *San Antonio*, a treasure-laden craft which departed from Manila in 1603. Another is known to have been wrecked in Drakes Bay in California in 1595.

The other listed as missing was the *San Francisco Xavier,* claimed by many to be the wreck on Nehalem Beach near Manzanita. If so, it was cast ashore in the year 1705. Generations of Nehalem Indians extracted its beeswax from the beaches, as did the white settlers.

As New Spain dispatched smaller caravel type supply vessels up the coast to California seeking new harbors of refuge for returning galleons, as well as for establishing missions, some were swept northward to the Oregon coast by great gales, never to return to the port of departure. It is not only possible but probably quite correct to assume that some of these craft were cast ashore on remote Oregon beaches, and placed in the viceroy's ledger as, "lost without trace."

The northward movement of caravels goes back many years. Cape Ferrelo on Oregon's southern coast was reputedly named by Bartolome Ferrelo, who was Cabrillo's pilot in 1542 and 1543, a half century after Columbus crossed the ocean blue. Cabrillo died en route, but his final words to Ferrelo were to continue north. Ferrelo did just that, but the cape later named for him

may not be the one he actually saw, many historians insist. On Jan. 19, 1543, Ferrelo carried out his dying commander's instructions, sailing northward in the teeth of a gale. Gaining 42 degrees 30 minutes on March 1, supposedly Cape Blanco, the ship's food supply was nearly exhausted and many of his crew down with scurvey. Thus the ship returned home.

Some historians claim Juan Rodriguez Cabrillo had only reached the 38th parallel when he succumbed, a little north of San Francisco Bay, and that his counterpart Ferrelo got only as far as Cape Mendocino, and was not the first white explorer to see the Oregon Coast. The truth may never be known.

In compliance with his sovereign mandate, the viceroy dispatched a trio of ships from Acapulco in the spring of 1596 under the command of Sebastian Viscaino. Beyond an attempt to establish two colonies, both of which were unsuccessful because of the so-called sterility of the country and the savage hostility of the natives, nothing was accomplished by that feeble pretense of obeying instructions. Further action was delayed following the death of the Spanish king in 1598, but when Philip III got the wheels of government well greased, he sent direct orders to the viceroy to get off the seat of his pants and to pursue the survey on up the coast of North America, posthaste.

It was again to Viscaino that the responsibility fell. The voyage of exploration involved two small caravels and an even smaller "fragata." Viscaino assumed control of the fleet, sailing on the caravel *Captaina*, which carried an assortment of men, including pilots, draftsmen and priests so that all discoveries would be properly ascribed in record and with navigation charts.

Setting sail from Acapulco on May 5, 1602 to explore the southern extremity of the peninsula of California they were plagued by driving, persistent Northwest winds which, according to the journal writer were, "by the fore of the human race, in order to prevent the advance of the ships and to delay the discovery of those countries, and the conversion of their inhabitants to the Catholic faith."

The tedious voyage continued for weeks and it was a wretched band of seafarers that at last gained the portals of San Quentin, San Diego and Monterey. Sixteen had died of scurvy and numerous others were too ill to function. One of the vessels, skippered by Toribio Gomez de Corvan, was sent back to Acapulco with the disabled men, but by the time she arrived, the greater number of her people had perished.

On Jan. 3, 1603, the other two vessels, the *San Diego* and the smaller *Tres Reyes* continued northward. They were separated by a gale and the larger of the two vessels entered a great Bay for refuge which may have been a section of San Francisco Harbor but more probably Drakes Bay where they searched for the remains of the Spanish galleon *San Agustin,* wrecked there in 1595.

(The *San Agustin*, commanded by Captain Sebastian Cermenon had been given orders to "chart all harbors homeward." After a demanding passage across the Pacific, Cermenon brought the galleon to an anchorage near Point Reyes from where he planned to survey the coast. A sou'wester altered his plans, driving the vessel aground, a total loss along with her cargo of beeswax, porcelain and silks. The survivors sailed south in an open boat, after naming the place, La Punta de los Reyes.)

Viscaino resumed his voyage northward until Jan. 20, gaining a point on the southern Oregon coast, a prominent white bluff in Lat. 42 degrees, to which he applied the name Cape Sebastian. His crew was suffering terribly from scurvey and with the weather threatening, the ship returned to Mexico.

In the approaching gale, the *Tres Reyes* had taken refuge in the lee of Cape Mendocino, having become separated from the *Captaina.* When the winds subsided, under pilot Antonio Flores, the vessel sailed northward gaining the 43rd parallel, reaching a great headland to which was applied the name Cape Blanco, a landmark which may or may not have been sighted by Ferrelo. Flores had officially discovered what would someday be known as the most westerly point of continental United States. At the time, Flores believed that California was an island.

Viscaino presented a good argument for establishing supply stations at San Diego and Monterey but despite the hardships endured in the expedition, his words fell on indifferent ears, Spain being convinced that little pressing need existed to colonize the unpromising lands to the north or to push on toward a "northwest passage" near the place where Juan de Fuca had claimed his strait to be located.

Yet, though no official record of de Fuca's discovery was recorded by Spain or Mexico, the approximate location appeared on all navigation charts for the next two centuries. The old Greek's account which appeared in *Purchas, his Pilgrimes,* published in England in 1625, was generally accepted throughout the world.

Disgusted with an indifferent viceroy, Viscaino returned to Spain seeking a royal mandate to establish Monterey as a supply station for ships returning from India and the Philippines. While there, he became seriously ill and passed on in 1606, his ambitious plans going by the wayside. In fact, there were no more "official voyages" by Spanish ships in the Viscaino cause for 160 years, the annual galleons making their landfalls north or south of Cape Mendocino, the headlands of Oregon becoming familiar to many of those old Spanish shipmasters, but for no other reason than to alert them to set a course southward to Acapulco and San Blas.

Despite the prevailing tales of the mythical strait, and of a city of gold called Quivira with untold riches, the Spanish remembered the stories of hardship and death in the earlier exploits and lost their desire to go north, satisfied with the riches pouring in from the Orient. Bog-

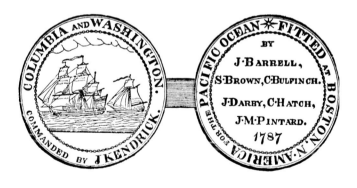

The Columbia Medal showing obverse and reverse sides. They were used like coins by Gray and Kendrick for trading with the Northwest Indians. Lower, Captain Gray's sea chest carried by him in his circumnavigation of the world. The chest is owned by the Oregon Historical Society.

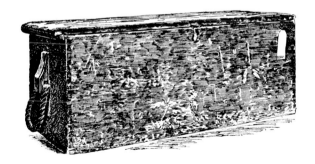

ged down by internal affairs, costly wars and repression, Mexico was neglected by the mother country, the galleons often becoming prey for the pirates and privateers that made the Pacific their hunting grounds. Spain's attempts to protect her treasure ships became more feeble.

In the interim, religious strife broke out in Mexico. On April 2, 1767, charged with conspiring local government overthrow at the expense of the king, the Society of Jesus in the Spanish dominions was arrested and thrown into prison upon order of Charles III. About 6,000 persons were involved, and it fell to the gruff Gaspar de Portola, an officer in the Catalan Dragoons, to enforce the indictment which meant the banishment from the land of those people who had done so much for the culture of New Spain. They built the first vessel ever launched from California soil — *The Triumph of the Cross*, and introduced grape culture, to name a few.

Upon the brotherhood of St. Francis, the king bestowed the missions. Accumulating the wealth of the Jesuits in California, they took total possession, though later the Dominicans laid claim to a portion.

By the middle of the 18th century, shocking news of foreign intervention into the neglected lands to the north suddenly made Alta California of great importance to Spain. The Russians had entrenched themselves in Alaska and had, according to rumor, planned to seek real estate to the south. Threatened by possible intervention and the constant harassment of English privateers plundering the treasure-laden galleons, Carlos III grew determined to build a new stronghold in the Western

world to thwart any defying the supremacy of Spain.

By the end of 1768 and early 1769, three ships were launched at the new naval port of San Blas, and again we find a possible link with shipwreck on the Oregon coast. Father Francis Junipero Serra, of the Franciscan order, enthusiastic in deportment, headed an expedition in 1769 in California "to establish the Catholic religion among a numerous heathen people, submerged in the obscure darkness of paganism; to extend the dominion of the King, our Lord; and to protect the peninsula from ambitious rulers of foreign nations."

To be done by the Franciscans at their own expense, the benefits were to accrue chiefly to the crown of Spain.

At the same time, Gaspar de Portola, newly commissioned governor of California, personally led a large group of dragoons 500 miles northward through rugged virgin territory to further the boundaries of the mother country.

But our story returns to the trio of ships built at San Blas. The vessels were to carry the sea portion of the expedition and were to rendezvous with the overlanders at various settlements along the California coast. On Jan. 9, 1769, the *San Carlos* sailed from La Paz, followed on Feb. 15 by the *San Antonio*. The last to depart was the *San Jose* on June 16. All took on cargoes of seeds, grain, farm implements, household utensils, church ornaments and vestments, furniture and beeswax. Initial destination was to be San Diego.

After losing eight of her crew from scurvy, the *San Antonio* arrived first, on April 11. Twenty days later, the *San Carlos* limped through the Silver Gate under a few shreds of sail, with only her master, cook and one seaman functioning. The others had fallen victim to scurvy. The third vessel, the *San Jose*, never arrived and was listed as missing with all hands. Though generally accepted that she was wrecked somewhere off the Mexican coast, it is quite probable that this vessel was driven northward by a series of gales, becoming the second Spanish ship lost in the Nehalem sector of Oregon.

This theory was strongly advanced by historian Silas B. Smith whose mother was Celiast, daughter of Indian Chief Kobaiway of the Clatsops, and whose father was Solomon H. Smith who came with Nathaniel J. Wyeth to Oregon territory in 1832.

Smith believed that the wreck of the *San Jose* represented the second appearance of white man in the area, the other involving the so-called treasure ship of which we will deal later.

According to the account as revealed to him by the local Nehalems, handed down by their progenitors, a ship carrying men with white skin was driven ashore and wrecked on Nehalem Spit. The crew survived and gaining the shore, lived for some time with the natives. A large part of the vessel's cargo was beeswax and the finding of such an abundance of the substance through

Carver's map of 1778, showing "the River of the West" falling into the Strait of Anian; also the four great rivers which take their rise within a few leagues of each other.

Start of the shipbuilding industry in the Pacific Northwest. The first vessel built on the North Pacific coast was the *Northwest America* instigated by Capt. John Meares at Nootka Sound in 1788. From a sketch published in London in 1790.

the years verified the wreck site. In the course of several months, according to the narrative, the castaways became obnoxious through violation of the traditional marital rights observed by the Nehalems. A battle ensued in which the strangers were forced to defend themselves with sling shots, indicating they had lost their arms in the wreck. Smith's account alleges that the intruders all eventually met death leaving as a memorial only the great amounts of beeswax.

Other stories of the account vary in detail but the wax was and still is undeniable proof of at least one shipwreck and probably more. Many of the cakes, sized for shipment were ten pounds or more. Some were inscribed with monograms and numerals, one of which bore the letters I.H.S. (the first three letters of the name Jesus, in Greek and symbolic of the Roman Catholic faith).

Despite later attempts by mineralogists to pronounce the substance as a paraffin (ozokerite) produced in nature, it has now been proven beyond a doubt that it is indeed beeswax, and of the Ghedda variety.

Smith was certain that the wreck was the missing *San Jose* which was never again reported after sailing from La Paz on June 16, 1769.

Another persistent story left in the wake of the above incident involved the survival of some of the castaways, who intermarried and dwelled among the local Indians. One of their number was a blue-eyed, golden-haired man who became the husband of a Nehalem woman, and the father or grandfather of a blue-eyed freckle-faced boy with Indian features. Becoming highly respected, he was part of an Indian family to which belonged a noted chief who resided on the shores of a lake. The chief's name was Cullaby, and the lake bears his name to this day.

Edward Cullaby, son of the old chief, told the following story to John Minto in 1845, an account handed down by his father who in turn had learned it from his grandmother when she was old. It told of a supposedly Spanish ship en route from the California missions. Blown off course and wrecked, there remained but one survivor found by the Indians seriously injured with a timber across his back.

A young girl named Ona took pity on the castaway and she and her father looked after him while he slowly recovered from his injuries. The two charitable natives set up shelter near the place where the shipwrecked man had been found because it was a considerable time before he was free enough of pain to accompany them to the tribe's village.

The rescuers were kept in touch with the main camp however, and thus Ona learned that the brother of the chief was very angry because the paleface had been saved and that he intended to kill him when the opportunity arose.

When the castaway recovered, the chief's brother was very jealous. Ona, on the other hand, had become very fond of him. A skilled and a brave man, he often showed up the local Indians in hunting, fishing and in other feats, which only tended to bring more anger against him.

Once, a sudden storm hit an Indian fishing party and

This photo, which appeared in the April 26, 1931 edition of the *Oregon Journal* offered mute evidence of an early day sailing ship coming ashore near Three Rocks and the Salmon River, long before white men officially came to the Oregon coast. The evidence was skeletal remains exhumed from a shallow grave including those of an eight foot giant black man and his Caucasian companions. They were believed to have met with foul play at the hands of the local natives. An underwater obstruction (still present) at the river entrance is believed to be the remains of an ancient shipwreck. A bone spearhead was found lodged in one of the skulls and a whalebone war club was lying nearby.

destroyed their canoes. All made it to shore but the chief's brother and one other. The castaway managed to rescue them both. Through that act, the chief came to admire him greatly, but the jealous brother despite the fact his life had been saved, still wanted to kill the ''white eyes'', and in turn soured other tribal members against the man.

Becoming close to the chief, the castaway taught him how to use firearms, having salvaged some guns and ammunition from the wreck. According to the account, the wreck occurred in the land of the Tillamooks and it was among the Tillamook people the white man lived.

On finding that his daughter was in love with the paleface, and that great animosity was growing among his people, the chief said, "I do not know my own people. We will go to live among the Clatsops. My sister is the wife of their chief."

The lovers were married and the three journeyed north pursued by the jealous chief's son and some of his henchmen. In a showdown, the white man shot his pursuer.

As the story continues, it tells of the castaway and his wife being accepted into the Clatsop tribe and living near a small clay butte on Lake Cullaby, with summer dwellings at Neacoxie and Quatat. He instructed the Indians in the use of weapons and became a gunsmith for the tribe.

Then in the late 1700's just before the turn of the century, after the white man had lived many years among the Clatsops, a ship like the one on which he had been wrecked came near the shore. The crew landed in a small boat but later returned to their ship leaving two of their number behind. Those two soon died of a strange disease which spread among the Tillamooks. Sweeping through the tribe with dire results, the sickness soon reached the Clatsops, hundreds dying.

The white man isolated his family and then went to the village of Quatat to give what aid he could. Both his father-in-law and the chief's son died, and finally the castaway himself.

His and Ona's son, years later, married the daughter of the chief's son. Their offspring was Cullaby or Quaicullaby, for whom the lake is named.

Being an illiterate people, the Indians handed their legends and accounts down by word from one generation to the next. Had only they been able to preserve it in writing, the pages of history would be filled with astounding and dramatic stories. Little doubt remains, however, that early unrecorded shipwrecks, before white man's history was written, occurred on Oregon's beaches, several perhaps, especially between the mouth of the Columbia River and Tillamook Bay.

A blond Indian is also mentioned by Lewis & Clark, but on their arrival in 1805, sufficient intercourse with whites had been established to account for such an oc- currence without recourse to the vent of the year 1769 — if the wreck earlier mentioned was that of the *San Jose.*

In fact, when Lewis & Clark reached the mouth of the Columbia, the Clatsops presented them as gifts, large chunks of beeswax. They of course, did not immediately realize its source.

A blond Indian is also mentioned by Lewis and Clark, but on their arrival in 1805, sufficient intercourse with whites had been established to account for such an occurrence without recourse to the event of the year 1769 —if the wreck earlier mentioned was that of the *San Jose.*

In fact, when Lewis and Clark reached the mouth of the Columbia, the Clatsops presented them as gifts, large chunks of beeswax. They of course, did not immediately realize its source.

Captain William Clark wrote in his journal on Dec. 31, 1805:

"With the party of Clatsops who visited us last was a man of much lighter colour than the natives are generally. He was freckled with long dusky red hair, about 25 years of age, and certainly must be half white, at least. This man appeared to understand more of the English language than the others of his party but did not speak a work of English. He possesses all the habits of the Indians."

Soto, of whom Gabriel Franchere spoke, was a halfbreed (probably part Indian, part Spanish) found at an Indian village near the Cascade foothills. The nearly blind old man spoke through an interpreter, claiming to be the son of a Spaniard who had been wrecked near the Columbia River. Franchere arrived in Oregon territory in 1811 aboard the ill-fated *Tonquin.* Soto told him:

"I was the son of a Spaniard who had been wrecked at the mouth of the river; that a part of the crew on this occasion had got safely ashore, but were all massacred by the Clatsops with the exception of four, who were spared and who married native women; that these four Spaniards of whom his father was one, disgusted with native life, attempted to reach a settlement of their own nation toward the south, but had never been heard from since, and that when his father with his companions, left the country, he himself was quite young."

Further proving the presence of Caucasians among the Indians of Oregon long before recorded discoveries, Alexander Henry of the Northwest Company at Astoria noted in his journal Dec. 8, 1813:

"The old Clatsop chief arrived with some excellent salmon and the meat of a large biche. There came with him a man about 30 years of age who had extraordinary dark red hair, and is the supposed offspring of a ship that was wrecked within a few miles of the entrance of this river many years ago. Great quantities of beeswax continue to be dug out of the sand near this spit, and Indians bring it to trade with us.''

Again, on Feb. 28, 1814, the entry in Henry's journal read:

''They bring us frequently lumps of beeswax fresh out of the sand which they collect on the coast to the south where the Spanish ship was cast away some years ago and the crew was all murdered by the Indians.''

Fur trader Ross Cox, while at Astoria in 1814, noted that an Indian belonging to a small tribe on the coast, south of the Clatsop country, was fair, his face partly freckled and his hair red. Slender, and about 5 feet 10 inches tall, Cox described him as of splended physique, going by the name of Jack Ramsay, a tattoo of sorts on his left arm attesting to that fact. He had not undergone the traditional head flattening practiced by the Oregon coastal Indians, but was reputedly the son of an English seafarer who deserted from a trading vessel and took up life among the Indians, taking to himself a squaw as his wife. The elder Englishman had supposedly died in the 1790's. Though he had other children by his Indian wife, only Jack had red hair and virtually none of the Indian features derived from maternal ancestors. To have been

A light Oregon mist hangs over the coast, looking southward from the steep slopes of Cape Perpetua.

survived by a son of Jack's age, the deserter would had to have jumped ship about 1781, and during that period only Cook had visited the Oregon coast and he reported no deserters, which leaves a mute question. From what English ship could the man in question have come? Was he a pirate? Was he sailing on a vessel other than British?

The intriguing tales of wrecked ships along Oregon's coast in pre-history times continue to mystify.

Missionaries Daniel Lee and Joseph H. Frost, in their book, *Ten Years in Oregon,* (1844) wrote, "about 30 or 40 miles to the south of the Columbia are the remains of a vessel which was sunk in the sand near shore, probably from the coast of Asia, laden at least in part with bees-wax."

Sol Smith and John Hobson on their 1848 trip along the Oregon Coast between the south entrance of the Columbia and Nehalem Bay, reported seeing "several pieces of a junk between Clatsop and Nehalem", which Hobson believed to be Chinese. When S.A. Clark, historian, arrived at the scene in the 1870's, he reiterated that there were two wrecks to be seen at the mouth of the Nehalem.

In 1898, when treasure hunter Pat Smith, one of hundreds who searched for Spanish treasure alleged to be buried on the lower slopes of Mt. Neah-kah-nie or on Nehalem Beach, came upon the remains of a vessel that had been uncovered by shifting sands, he removed several pieces of teak. Efforts by him to get a salvage endeavor underway were thwarted due to lack of funds.

British vice consul E. M. Cherry, when stationed at Astoria, had for many years been intrigued by the promise of Nehalem treasure. He planned a salvage effort to exhume the controversial wreck in 1929, but with the depression, and the $30,000 needed for a cofferdam, he could find no investors. Thus the ancient ribs rose and fell with the shifting sands, fluctuating tides and swirling currents.

Though beeswax is still occasionally found along the Nehalem beaches, the treasure has alluded the most dedicated hunters.

Probably no historian of his time researched the maritime mysteries of Nehalem as much as Sol Smith. He relates details of yet another alleged appearance of white men among the Nehalem Indians, which, if true, might have been the first time Caucasians were seen by the Oregon Indians. The legend was told to him from descendants of the local tribe.

"Survivors of a shipwreck were seen on an afternoon in strawberry time. The astounded natives watched with fear and trepidation thinking that perhaps their legendary god Tallapus had returned. The ship had been driven on the sands during the night, the first to see the castaways being an Indian woman from the ocean side of Clatsop Plains. She had wandered down to Clatsop Beach in the early morning and was startled by the appearance of the

two strangers with white skin and long flowing beards down to their chests. The wreck from which they had come was lying in the breakers. Just above the driftwood line the survivors had a fire going over which they were cooking some food and popping corn. They made signs to the squaw for water. She in turn, both frightened and excited, ran to the village as fast as her legs would carry her, 'I have found people who are men, and who yet are bears,' she shouted in the midst of the slabboard dwellings.

"Leading the tribesmen to the scene, the tribal chief was not fully satisfied that they were really men until he had carefully examined their hands and found they agreed perfectly with his own. They were further amazed by the popping corn, something they had not before seen."

The northern Oregon coastal Indians thereafter referred to all white skinned persons as Tlo-hon-nipts, which translated means, "of those who drift ashore," in other words, castaways. Apparently those were the first Tlo-hon-nipts ever seen by the Indians of northern Oregon, and for decades thereafter they believed that all such people were brought in from the sea.

The two survivors were soon claimed as slaves. Meanwhile, on learning the value of metal, the Indians recovered all such material from the wreck whenever tide and surf permitted.

When it was discovered that one of the castaways was adept at making knives and tools from iron, the remains of the wreck were burned to obtain every last spike. The Indians named the iron worker, Konapee, and though he and his companion were at first made to labor incessantly, in the course of time they were held in high favor and granted the rights of Indian nobility.

Konapee selected a site for his dwelling on the lee side of the Columbia's south entrance, somewhere near present day Hammond. The natives then and long after his death referred to the place only as Konapee. Among the articles this historic figure had when he was shipwrecked were numerous Chinese coins which were retained and highly cherished by the Clatsop people and always referred to as "Konapee's money."

It has often been suggested that the vessel on which Konapee and his companion came was a Japanese or Chinese junk, which had drifted across the Pacific with the prevailing current system, after becoming disabled at sea. Others claim it to have been a Spanish vessel inasmuch as it was carrying India corn, and Chinese cash, plus, the survivors were evidently Caucasians. This, of course, does not rule out the fact that several prehistoric junks were wrecked on Pacific Northwest shores, a known fact that will be pursued farther on in the chapter.

It is within the realm of possibility that the old Indian to whom Franchere referred as Soto, was the son or grandson of Konapee. Clatsop Indians long claimed that Konapee in later years "reached the land of the sunrise," going from his Clatsop home to the Cascades, where he married an Indian woman. Historians have speculated that Konapee may have been shipwrecked in Oregon about 1725, a century after the pilgrims landed at Plymouth Rock.

If only Konapee could have kept a diary or made contact with the civilized world of his time, he indeed would have held a premier place in the history of the Pacific Northwest. Little is known of him except that he was obviously resourceful and intelligent, living long among those primitive people, gaining both their respect and admiration. Through him, the Clatsop people, and subsequently other tribes, learned about the value of iron for making fishhooks, tools and weapons. In fact, Konapee's knowledge acquired by the Clatsops afforded them prestige and power over rival tribes. Kobaiway who was chief at the arrival of Lewis and Clark, had acquired all of this knowledge and was considered one of the great chiefs in coast country, possessing sufficient wealth to support 20 wives and to thus form alliances with other tribes. Many slaves were at his beck and call to take care of the personal wants and the needs of his huge household. Much of his wealth accrued from skills left by Konapee which afforded valuable items for inter-tribal bartering.

Another highly respected Indian leader was one-eyed Chinook Chief Concomly (sometimes called Comcomly) who resided in a village on the north side of the river entrance near the present town of Chinook.

It is interesting to note that the first white men to visit the Columbia River area, prior to Lewis and Clark, were astounded that the Indians knew the value of iron and that some had metal arrowheads, hatchets and other implements. Cook noted the use of iron among the Northwest Indians in 1778 and was of the opinion that it was so widespread that it could not have been introduced by the Spaniards on their voyages of 1774 and 1775. The English explorer further found among the natives considerable copper and brass, "and it is almost a certainty that these come by way of the sea and not by land," so observed Cook.

It is also of interest that the first Shoshone Indians confronted by Lewis and Clark after they crossed the western mountains spoke of the Great River (Columbia) which led to the ocean where white men lived.

One might ask where all the metal came from that was in the possession of the Indians? The obvious answer is that it came from shipwrecks, most likely Spanish, English or Oriental. The Russians, though occupying parts of Alaska in early times, initially had vessels that for the most part were lashed together with leathern thongs. The people of Japan, long a hermit nation, could only have made contact with the Indians through castaway junks whose metal supply would at best have been minimal.

What about possible piratical action? The courses and acts of the buccaneers of old were seldom chronicled, and though far more is known of their treachery in the Caribbean and Atlantic, there was action in the Pacific. John Oxenham, or perhaps the Dutchman Pichilinguies, reaped havoc in the Pacific and though they were not known to have been in Pacific Northwest waters, it is not impossible. Sailing countless sea miles, keeping no journals or logs, it is quite possible that pirates landed in Oregon, buried their treasure and traded metal objects to the Indians for staples, and water replenishment. It is further possible that hostile action against Spanish ships could have resulted off Oregon, one old legend telling of ships firing at each other off Mt. Neah-kah-nie, which leads us to the Treasure Ship story that has become a hallmark of maritime intrigue.

Silas B. Smith whose mother was Celiast, daughter of the Indian chief Kobaiway of the Clatsops, and whose father was Sol Smith tells of the time-honored legend of a ship "appearing in the offing at that place (Neah-kah-nie) and coming to, dropped a boat which was rowed ashore. A box, or chest was carried by the men who made a landing and ascended the mountain-side. A hole was then dug, into which was lowered a chest, a black man then being killed, both of which were covered with earth." The killing of the man is controversial inasmuch as the Indian word for a dead person is similar to that meaning a crucifix. It is also speculation that the chest contained treasure though such tradition has persisted from the outset. As earlier mentioned, thousands have dug and some have lost their lives in their determined search for the elusive treasure.

It is a further conjecture that the man killed and buried with the treasure chest was a slave, the pirates aware of the fact that Indians never rifled a grave for fear of spirit retaliation, thus preserving the safety of the chest. Spanish ships frequently took on African slaves available at Manila to any paying the right price. It is also possible that it was a cross placed over the chest after it was lowered into the ground. The legend went on to tell of strange figures being cut into several large rocks, supposedly to help find the treasure at a later date or to mislead any stranger who might try to find its location.

From the coming of the early white settlers, those moss-covered rocks were found with the many strange figures and numerals just as the legend had told, and of course those rocks more than anything else intensified the search.

The legend further alleged that the party that came ashore to bury the treasure chest departed in their ship, the incident being separate from the vessels wrecked in the area. The reputed location of the chest is on the southwest slope of Neah-kah-nie where through the years the land area became pock-marked with holes dug by seekers. Air holes, ancient drain tiles and hollow spots brought quickened heartbeats, but as yet there has been no public claim to a single gold doubloon, piece of eight or precious gem. The beaches, on the other hand, have yielded only beeswax.

From time to time an occasional artifact of gold, either of Spanish or Oriental origin was found at various places along the Oregon coast, from Cape Perpetua to the Columbia River, indicating that such items fell into Indian hands after the plundering of early wrecks.

It is also possible that the Neah-kah-nie treasure chest, due to the constant erosion, earthquake or seismic activity might have been washed into the sea. Every indication points to the fact that such an incident actually did occur, but the chest may forever remain out of human grasp, unless long ago and far away some clever soul found a way to purloin it from its well hidden lair.

Both Hudson's Bay and Astor employees were accused at one time or another of secretly removing the treasure for personal gain, but such accusations bore little credence. According to one account, an empty pack train started south from the Astoria trading post in the early 1800's. It went down into Nehalem country and returned with all the packs bulging and each member of the party secretive about the exploit. Rumor persisted the pack train was loaded with loot removed from a place on Neah-kah-nie, and, that was how John Jacob Astor (though not present) got started on the road to becoming a millionaire.

And now as to the story of the missing galleon *San Francisco Xavier,* reputedly the first vessel wrecked on the Nehalem shores. Built at Cavite in the Philippines in 1691, she measured 175 feet in length with a 50 foot beam, carrying 80 cannon and 1,500 tons of cargo. Constructed like other Manila galleons, her frames were of teak and other durable hardwoods, such as lanang and molave. Diocesan records attest to the fact that on one voyage she departed Acapulco with 2,070,000 pesos for trading purposes in the Orient.

The *Xavier* was one of the transpacific galleons that was reported missing at sea, (in 1705), and it has long been conjectured that she is the ship that crashed ashore on Nehalem Beach, from which the greater amounts of beeswax in the area have been extracted. There is considerable evidence to allow for the claim, much of which has already been presented in the Indian legends of shipwreck and of the traces of white blood found among the early Indians. It is also quite possible that in addition to her beeswax cargo, the galleon carried treasure, inasmuch as she went missing while returning to the West Coast from the Indies.

Adding to the complexities of the tangled riddles of shipwreck in early Oregon, is another intriguing incident that centers around Three Rocks, near the mouth of the Salmon River, 23 miles north of Yaquina Head. Lying about 800 yards offshore, the three grayish outcrops have become symbolic with an ancient shipwreck which reputedly occurred between there and the river mouth. Referred to as Three Rocks wreck, the persistent legend somewhat parallels those of Mt. Neah-kah-nie and the Nehalem beaches.

In the bygones, Indians told the first white settlers in the Cascade Head area (the Salmon River empties into the ocean at the southern extremity of Cascade Head) of a white-winged ship that long years before had been wrecked at the mouth of the Salmon River. Strange men came ashore and buried a treasure chest.

The story was received somewhat with tongue-in-cheek until years later when pieces of wreckage were found on the beach. Fishermen further complained of snagging their nets on some underwater obstruction off the river entrance. Then in 1931, while clearing a summer camping site for tourists, E. G. Calkins, owner of the land (a former county commissioner) at Three Rocks Beach, came upon a mysterious find. The area habited by Indians for hundreds of years before white men came, was full of shell mounds and middens. While leveling a mound with his plowshare, Calkins came across some Indian relics. Interested friends came with rakes and hoes to carefully search, finding such items as whalebone war clubs, stone pestles and a broken iron kettle, not unusual instruments for old Indian camp sites. Nearby, however, was unearthed an oversized human thigh bone which aroused considerable interest. Further probing of the soil produced the entire skeletal remains of a giant, its skull two-thirds of an inch thick with broad cheekbones and forehead, and a perfect set of large teeth. Nearby, a normal sized skeleton was uncovered. The "superman" was the center of attention.

Dr. F. M. Carter, physician, and Oregon historian Dr. John Horner were called in to give their expert opinions of the find. Carter, after his examination, was astounded to discover what had once been an eight foot giant of the negroid race. Some of his huge bones were cracked or broken suggesting he might have been tortured before death came. The skull of the smaller skeleton, reputedly Caucasian, appeared to have been pierced by an arrow or struck by some weighty instrument.

Calkins and his neighbors reasoned the find to be evidence of ancient pirate activity and began to look for clues to the treasure so long rumored to have been buried in the area, and, as a direct link, turned their attention toward the ancient wreck said to be lying off the Salmon River. Those who had encountered the obstruction claimed it was perhaps 100 to 150 feet in length. Calkins and others before him had occasionally recovered pieces of hardwood ribs with copper bolts.

Long before the skeletal finds, Dr. Carter was familiar with the long standing legend of the Three Rocks wreck, and a persistent tale of 20 men who reputedly buried a chest, leaving two of their number to guard the spot, while they travelled on. One was said to have been a large black man who later quarreled with and struck dead his companion, a white man. The Negro then incurred the wrath of the local Indians, was turned upon and killed.

As early as 1603, Morga, a governor of the Philippines, visited Mexico and told of his islands supplying New Spain (Mexico) with gold, cotton, cloth, mendrinaque and cakes of white and yellow wax. The year of Morga's visit was the same year that an earlier-mentioned galleon went missing with all hands, probably somewhere along the West Coast, and if not in California waters, perhaps in Oregon.

In the summer of 1974, Edward Calkins, son of the late Elmer G. Calkins, on whose land the skeletal remains were discovered in 1931, applied to the Army Corps of Engineers for a permit to dredge in a tide flat at the entrance to the Salmon River to exhume the ancient remains of what has been referred to as the Three Rocks wreck. He wanted to dredge an area 30 feet wide, 70 feet long and ten feet deep, using a land-based crane with a clamshell and dragline bucket. An exploratory hole was to be dug first to ascertain that the obstruction was actually a wreck. Hoping to find items of great value within, and to link the wreck with the skeletal remains found nearby years earlier, Calkins pursued his desire with the encouragement of many interested parties.

The story related to him by his father was virtually the same as the aforementioned, both originating from Indian legend:

A monstrous canoe with wings was blown into the mouth of the Salmon River and wrecked. This version, however, mentions three men instead of two, a giant black and two Caucasian companions having been left to guard something of value recovered from the wreck, supposedly a chest or box containing treasure. Twenty others left the scene to make their way south to New Spain, but were never heard from again.

The three who remained lived among the local Indians for a considerable time, the black man, because of his great stature and strength being worshipped as a god. When his mortality was proven, the Indians became angered with the strangers and in a skirmish, all three were murdered.

But alas, Calkins had his request for dredging revoked by both the Army Engineers and the State of Oregon because of possible damage to estuary life. The 60 year old Lake Oswego man was further informed that there was "insufficient evidence of shipwreck in or near the Salmon River area."

He presented several reasons for believing the wreck to be in the Salmon River estuary, displaying some long misplaced news photos taken in 1931 of the burial site where the skeletal remains were uncovered by his father while he was leveling ground for a campsite at the Three Rocks resort community on the north bank of the river. The ancient Indian midden gave mute evidence of the three strangers sharing a violent death, one of the leg bones shown to have been shattered, a two-inch bone spearhead lodged at the base of one skull, and a large stone imbedded in another. It appeared as though the trio had been set upon with a vengeance, by a large number of natives. Perhaps the sanctity of the Indian marital rites, customs or traditions had been violated causing determined retaliation, some have conjectured, but whatever, something of a major consequence occurred to trigger the tragic demise of the castaways.

The late professor Dr. John B. Horner, earlier mentioned as having been called in to express his views on the skeletal find in 1931, was an historian at Oregon State College (now University) and an expert on Indian lore. It was he who gathered up all the contents of the shell mound and midden, taking them back to Corvallis for a museum which was then in the planning stages. His studies showed the skeletal remains to be from 260 to 300 years old, which would have dated the incident prior to the mid 1600's. His estimates were partially made from the size of the spruce trees that Calkins cleared from atop the burial site. Witnesses claimed the diameter of the trees to be as "large as table tops."

It was not till 1973 that the latter Calkins revived his interest in the Three Rocks wreck, attempting to prove his father's theory of a link between the wreck and the gravesite. The plot thickened. Going to Oregon State University to research the items removed from the gravesite, he found nothing, no bones, no skulls, no artifacts, in fact, even the 3,000 word essay Horner had written on the historical find was missing. Nobody at the school could shed any light on the subject.

Perhaps it was the story that appeared in The Oregon Journal, April 26, 1931, that prompted many amateur and professional treasure seekers to search the Salmon River area. The theft of the material may have been the target of some misguided latter day pirate seeking to get the inside track.

Skeptics who did see the artifacts removed from the site claimed them not to be Indian in nature, that the so-labeled war club was actually the remains of a belaying pin—the stone pestle, a ballast rock, and a teapot or kettle originating from a foreign country—rejecting the theory of violence. One way or the other, the strangers in the grave were other than Indian and they had been there long before the recorded coming of the white man to the Oregon coast.

Dooming Calkins' recovery of the wreck was legislation enacted in 1975 proclaiming 9,670 acres of land surrounding Cascade Head to be a federally protected scenic and scientific research area, including the Salmon River estuary, claimed as the "smallest and most pristine on the Oregon Coast."

Nevertheless, the State Land Board was impressed with his request and did not rule out the possibility of some future scientific follow up.

During the hearing on the question, Dr. Stephen Dow Backam, Linfield College professor and authority on coastal Indians, testified that in his research into Oregon coast shipping disasters of past centuries, he found no documented evidence that a ship was ever wrecked in or near the Salmon River. Still he conceded "We cannot always know the truth . . . If there is indeed a ship or its remains in the Salmon River estuary, I would think it would be of special historical and archeological interest."

Objecting to Calkins' proposed method for salvaging the wreck, the professor said:

"I think the only permissible way to excavate such a vessel or artifact would be through rigorous archeological techniques and there are well established techniques for the excavation of ships."

Backham concluded, "I would encourage further efforts if any of five shellmounds located within a half mile of the skeletal remains had shown evidence of shipwreck." He did cite excavations such as the Mewok Indian village site north of San Francisco Bay in the early 1930's, where porcelains and spikes gave evidence of a wreck of one of the Manila galleons.

Calkins recalled that his father had told him of gillnetting at the mouth of the Salmon River as early as 1913. On several occasions his nets had become tangled on an obstruction seven or eight feet below the surface, within 300 yards of the place where the skeletons were unearthed 18 years later. Twice when his nets were pulled free, bits of wreckage, including a curved piece of wood resembling the rib of a ship, were attached. Among the wreckage were copper nails, heavily corroded.

Other gillnetters also complained of the obstruction, which at that time was considered some worthless hulk. Calkins now believes that this same hulk may be the legendary treasure ship of ancient times.

A metal detector has been used in the area and has shown definite activity in one particular spot, near where the wreck is alleged to be. A 14 foot steel probe has outlined a submerged wooden object at about the nine foot depth.

Two woodworking experts have suggested half-inch core samples taken from the sunken object show a vari-

ety of ironwood found only in the Southern Hemisphere.

With all the intrigue involved concerning possible recovery of the mysterious ship, the State is standing fast on its conclusions:

"On one hand we see a potential opportunity to add to the historical background of our coast area and on the other hand we see the proposed disturbance of a fragile estuarine area of great value. . . . The division is charged to protect the aquatic resources of the waters of this state. However, everyone benefits from new information on historical events. We are not prepared to close the door on a possible historical or treasure trove find . . . The Division of State Lands would consider a subsequent application in this matter, provided that additional substantiative evidence of the ship is obtained by non-destructive testing and submitted to the division."

Will the real answer ever be known? Only time will tell.

Another intriguing find of ancient vintage on the Oregon coast was a 20-foot copper-sheathed beam discovered at Del Rey Beach, north of Gearhart by Clatsop County commissioner Dave Megrath in the winter of 1973. The nails holding the copper to the wood were all stamped with the traditional "broad arrow" insignia used by the British Admiralty since 1661, to mark naval stores. The beam now at the Columbia River Maritime Museum in Astoria could have come from the HMS *Sulphur*, wrecked in 1839 on Clatsop Spit off the Columbia River bar, or from some unrecorded wreck of an earlier British ship or privateer.

Michael Naab, curator at the museum, said records show copper sheathing was not introduced on Admiralty ships until 1771. The broad arrow insignia was also found stamped in double rows on the drift pins protruding from the sides of the beam.

Indian legend told of another ancient vessel being wrecked near the mouth of Elk Creek near Cannon Beach. Some of the remains were later seen by the pioneers. Part of the wreckage of the USS *Shark*, wrecked on Clatsop Spit in 1846, also drifted ashore south of Cannon Beach, the cannon affixed to the piece of decking being responsible for the naming of the town. The rusted old weapon and the ship's capstan are still displayed alongside the highway.

The late Senator Richard Neuberger of Oregon, an historian in his own right, believed the giant black unearthed near Salmon River was interrelated with the incident at Nehalem. According to his speculative conclusions, the Negro was the slave of his Caucasian companions. They were survivors of the wreck and were responsible for the removal and burying of the fabled chest. It was a known fact that blacks from East Africa, as earlier mentioned, were commonly used as slaves in former times. They were publicly sold in places like Manila and it was common practice on the galleons to allow passen-

gers to bring their slaves as attendants on Pacific cros-
gers to bring their slaves as attendants on Pacific crossings. Neuberger's theory was that the men buried the
chest well above the tideline below Mt. Neah-kah-nie,
then, being castaways from the nearby wreck, began
Spain. On reaching the Salmon River they encountered
hostile Indians, were set upon and murdered.

If the wreck, or one of the wrecks of ancient vintage
lying off Nehalem beaches is the *San Francisco Xavier,*
there could be a fortune in gold, silver or gems awaiting
the finder. And, if one of the wrecks in the Columbia
River, Nehalem or Salmon River areas is the *San Antonio,* rumored to have been wrecked near San Miguel
Island, the treasure could be even more alluring. As she
was about to sail from Manila in 1603, the Chinese and
Filipinos were engaged in a massive revolt. With her
destination as Acapulco, the ship became the sanctuary
of several wealthy families of influential Spanish officials who sought safety and protection in New Spain.
With them went fabulous amounts of personal treasure
— millions of dollars in uncut stones, jewelry, cash, gold
and silver bullion and the general cargo carried by every
galleon. It is claimed that the vessel departed Manila
with more riches than any other galleon in the two and a
half centuries of Pacific trade. It is not impossible that
the ship, which went missing without trace, lies molder-
ing off the Oregon coast and not in California waters as
some have suspected. The truth may never be known.

Diving is extremely hazardous near San Miguel and
in all of the Channel Islands as well. The barrier in
Oregon is the constantly shifting sands, that cover the
traces and usually make salvage impossible or not finan-
cially feasible. There are also the tidal fluctuations, currents and surf to be reckoned with.

Other Spanish vessels of old, wrecked along the
Pacific Coast include the *San Sebastian,* believed to have
been lost somewhere near Santa Barbara or in the Channel Islands; the *Santa Rosa,* claimed on the outcrops of
Bishop Rock, south southeast of Cortes Bank, California, reputedly with $700,000 in bullion and specie. Al-
ready mentioned, the *San Agustin* ran aground in Drakes
Bay in 1594. These and the other early Spanish wrecks
which occurred along the Oregon and Washington coasts
in the 17th and 18th centuries indicate far more early
activity by Caucasian mariners in Pacific Northwest waters than history has recorded.

Some historians have speculated that Spanish explorers of old visited and examined what we know today as
the Curry coast of Oregon, then sailed northward, entered the Umpqua and there refitted. This conjecture has
no official source.

Toward the end of the 18th century, Spain dispatched
the *San Carlos* from Mexico to find out whether San
Francisco Bay could be entered from the ocean side. In

June 1775, the small caravel passed safely through the
Golden Gate and dropped her hook. This action caused
more uneasiness on the part of England, what with her
arch enemy's influence and her empire growing in North
America. New agitation and threats of war were rampant. Spanish ships next sailed as far north as British
Columbia, gaining a firm foothold at Nootka Sound and
endeavoring to set up a fortress at Neah Bay inside the
entrance to the Strait of Juan de Fuca. Sub Lieutenant
Manuel Quimper brought the *Princesa Real* to the latter
destination in 1791, but the little brick fortress was unsuccessful and soon fell into decay.

Three years earlier, Estevan Martinez, ex-pilot of
Juan Perez, commanding the *Princesa,* and Lieutenant
Gonzalo Haro in the *San Carlos* explored many of the
islands, inlets and straits on the lee side of Vancouver
Island.

Retaliation from England almost touched off a major
war between the two maritime nations.

When Captain Robert Gray sailed along the Oregon
coast and officially discovered Tillamook Bay in 1788,
the question remained as to whether he was actually the
first Caucasian seen by the Tillamook Indians or the first
white explorer to land in Oregon. Items his men found in
the possession of the Indians gave every indication of
early contact with castaways, or perhaps pirates.

Along the shores of Yaquina Bay, skeletal remains of
Caucasians were discovered many years ago and nearby
were found several copper coins bearing the inscription,
"English Trade Tokens, 1788." There was also a brass
handled ship's cutlass.

Bancroft, in his *History of the Northwest Coast,*
says, "In 1700-50, the Philippine treasure ships continued to cross the Pacific by the northern route without
touching on the California coast and a French vessel
under Fondac took the same course."

The sea-roving adventurers of other centuries who
came from the old world, pitting their frail ships against
the unknown tempest, may well have dropped anchor at
one or more of the indentations along the Oregon coast
for refuge from storms or replenishment of water.

Perhaps the discovery of Oregon belongs to the
Spanish navigator Bartolme Ferrelo who, sailing north of
California as earlier told, entered the latitude of Oregon
in 1543. As will be recalled, he served as Cabrillo's pilot
in 1542-43, but when the latter died his final instructions to his counterpart were to sail northward. He reputedly reached Cape Blanco when forced to retreat before
adverse weather, sickness and because rations had been
reduced to a few biscuits.

It would be this humble writer's guess that the
shores of Oregon were known to many foreigners long
before recorded discoveries, and that some of the strangers were Orientals.

Try this one on for size. It is alleged and preserved through Indian legend that about 500 years ago, just before Columbus discovered America, an old Chinaman survived the wreck of his junk on the shores of Oregon. Turning pirate, he enlisted a host of blood-thirsty savages, (bad Indians) who, using war canoes, ranged between the Columbia River and Coos Bay, even as far south as the Coquille, pillaging and plundering one native village after another. The fierce Oriental taught his redskin buccaneers how to make and wield weapons of metal which were used with frightening results on their victims.

Such a legend is by no means preposterous, for it is a known fact that more than 60 Oriental junks were found wrecked or adrift in the Pacific up till 1875. And before such information was available, hundreds, maybe thousands of junks were blown away from the forbidden land of the rising sun, by stress of weather or breakdowns, drifting with the prevailing currents toward the North American continent. Others from China and Formosa met similar fates. In the year 1874 alone, some 22,000 junks were registered in Japan and many were found derelict or wrecked from Alaska to Mexico, in the Hawaiian Islands and throughout the South Seas. One is known to have been wrecked on Clatsop Beach, just south of the Columbia River in 1820, and five years before that another came ashore near Point Conception, California. Still another was cast ashore near Cape Flattery, Washington in 1833. A junk is believed to have been wrecked on the island of Maui in Hawaii as early as the 13th century. Nobody knows how many of these ancient craft were rudely deposited on Northwest shores before recorded history.

Japan was an empire as early as 660 B.C., under Emperor Jimmu, proverbial descendant of the sun goddess. Even if one measures that nation by the foundation of the Japanese state, laid in the 5th century by the Yamato clan, whose chief priest assumed the role of emperor, it is ancient. Japan borrowed heavily on Chinese culture in the 6th and 8th centuries and its modes of water transport, exclusively by junk, modified from the Chinese version, varied little through the years. It is only natural to assume that scores of these craft were swept away from the home shores. Japan was a closed nation, by strict edict, its people forbidden from departing in vessels, on warning of death. Strangers were likewise forbidden to enter Japan, lest they face execution or life imprisonment.

China's history even antedates that of Japan. Hsia is traditionally the first dynasty, but Shang (1523-1027 B.C.) is the first in documented history. Chinese junks, for centuries the most seaworthy vessels afloat, were unexcelled in junkdom and far better designed and constructed than their Japanese and Formosan counterparts.

Not only capable of crossing the Pacific under sail, they could further remain seaworthy in any ocean and against the most storm-tossed seas. However, the early Chinese showed little inclination toward eastward crossings of the Pacific, preferring the better known trade routes along the Asian and African continents.

Marco Polo once recited the wonders of the junk, claiming it to be the finest craft afloat. First to have watertight compartments, balanced rudders and battened sails, such vessels were honored for lengthy voyages in ancient times. Still on the scene in China in the nuclear age, junks were perhaps the finest deep-water vessels until the advent of modern shipbuilding technology. Registered up to 400 tons, some junks carried 200 to 300 persons. Fashioned with two or more layers of planks and three to five masts, they had as many as 50 separate cabins for merchants, passengers and crew.

It has been stated the junk may have had its origin in China more than 4800 years ago, developing gradually into a highly seaworthy, and somewhat complex vessel, despite its rather unorthodox exterior appearance.

With such efficient ships, the Chinese mastered the rudiments of fishing and trading along the country's vast coastline. They also became a great naval power in the 1500's under the Ming dynasty, boasting 3,100 war junks, 400 transports, and 250 multi-masted treasure ships, claimed to have been up to 300 feet in length with beams of 150 feet. The latter vessels, built more like scows, were unwieldy, designed to carry heavy cargoes and treasure from East Indies ports back to the homeland after delivering Chinese goods to supply ports in Asia and Africa. Such specialty junks were protected by the highly maneuverable war junks which threw fear into potential enemies and were likewise able to squelch the sneaky Chinese pirates in their nefarious forays.

Chinese tradition tells of a junk that set out from China in 219 B.C., its destination, the "Isle of the Blest." That destination may be what we know today as Japan, but unfortunately the junk was driven eastward for months by a series of terrible gales to a mysterious foreign land called Fu-sang, possibly the Oregon or California coast.

There was a similarity with some Oriental words among the early dialects of Northwest Indians, and the fusion of Oriental characteristics in physical features indicated intercourse between the two races. It is a near certainty that Japanese or Chinese people viewed the shore of Oregon long, long before sightings by Spanish eyes or those of other foreigners. They, however, probably came not by choice but by accident, being driven from their Oriental habitats by the undeniable forces of nature, many never again to return from whence they had come.

Stories of Spanish treasure and shipwreck have crept into every area along the Oregon coast, but perhaps the center of the most lore and intrigue continues to center around Mt. Neah-kah-nie, and the Nehalem beaches. Joseph H. Front's diary of 1841 said this about the prominent headland:

"This mountain is called 'Ne-a-karny' after one of the deities of these natives, who, it is said by them, a long time since, while sitting on this mountain turned into a stone, which stone, it is said, presents a colossal figure of Ne-a-karny to this day. And in our passage over the mountains, which is a prairie on the side next to the ocean, we discovered a stone which presented a figure of this kind."

Silas Smith said that "Mt. Ne-kah-ni" meant the precipice overlooking the ocean, the abode of Ekahni, the supreme god.

Lee Frost, gives the Clatsop word "Arcarna", meaning chief deity, while Mrs. Ed Gervais, a Nehalem Indian, claimed the word originated from the survivors of a Spanish wreck who saw elk on the side of the mountain and exclaimed, "Carne!" meaning meat.

Inasmuch as the authorities disagree on the origin of the name, it is of little wonder that none of the ancient tales, legends and stories surrounding the headland agree. Enough proof remains, however, to give every indication that many mystifying maritime events did occur. Nobody can deny the Ghedda beeswax, the ancient remains of ships, the trinkets, implements, artifacts and skeletal remains which never belonged to the Indian culture.

At Treasure Cove, on the northern base of Neah-kah-nie is a cave just above the tideline, the name having derived from tales of pirate treasure legends told by the Indians. According to the legend, three strange vessels engaged in a battle offshore in ancient times.

North of Treasure Cove is Smugglers Cove, with piratical overtones. These two places have also beckoned many adventurous treasure seekers.

Commercial fishermen from Garibaldi long claimed that a vessel had been sighted in the depths near Neah-kah-nie's Short Sands Beach and was believed to be of Spanish origin.

Pirate treasure has long been rumored near the Rogue River entrance in southern Oregon and along places like Starr Creek in southern Lincoln County, where buccaneers are alleged to have carved directions to the location of the trove in the trunks of large trees. Though there are numerous places along the coast where tales of pirate activities run rampant, some may be true but most are just fantasy.

Scourge of the sea, those salty rogues of the days of piracy, who loved to prey on Spanish ships were a contingent of French, Dutch and English adventurers. Later, joined by fugitives from the law, deserters of ships and runaway slaves, they made their own code of lawlessness, pillaging towns and commandeering ships. With-

out pity for their victims and placing little value on their own lives, they went far beyond the original intention of revenge against powerful and ruthless Spain. Starting in the Caribbean and the Atlantic they roamed as far as the Pacific. Blood flowed like wine in the savage battles they waged, and Spanish ship commanders cowered at the sight of the skull and crossbones flag being raised. Though history's pages reveal little concerning pirate activity in Oregon waters, it is a gold brick cinch that they were there, cutlass, pike and pistol, gold doubloons, pieces of eight and jewels. Wherever the galleons operated the pirates stalked, be they illegitimate, or carrying the noble name of privateer with the backing of a belligerent nation.

Gold bullion has been reported found by divers off the entrance to the Columbia River, reputedly from the bowels of an ancient ship, and other little treasures have been uncovered along the coast through the years. The finders usually keep their troves a secret, for fear of others invading the site and of Uncle Sam slapping a healthy tax on said property.

It would be safe to say that both Orientals and Caucasians dwelled among the coastal Indians for centuries, but the mists of time have secreted their activities forever. Still more evidence remains to be found, and who knows, maybe some day a lucky finder will unearth a vast treasure.

From the sands at Monzanita, looking north towards historic Mt. Neah-kah-nie.

CHAPTER TWO
INDIAN SKIRMISHES

Fact: America once belonged to the Indian. Fact: white man purloined it from him. Illiterate, satisfied and shunning progress, the red man was ripe for exploitation, and, the cruel process nearly led to his extermination. Those who fought back were considered savages of the most despicable kind. Often mistreated and detested, their acts of reprisal, though sometimes bloodthirsty, were the only way the defiant ones knew to seek their revenge. Any white who sympathized or took the side of the Indian was frequently ridiculed. Few were the friends of the exploited, possible exceptions being the clergy and Indian agents who often fought a losing battle in gaining justified rights for the conquered.

Despite the attitude toward the "true" Americans, many befriended the white settler, offering invaluable assistance in time of need, sometimes without thanks or compensation.

Though many skirmishes erupted between the hostile Indians and the early white settlers in the southern half of Oregon territory, northerly tribes along the coast were a peaceful people generally speaking, affording little resistance to the white juggernaut which eventually spelled their demise and relegated them to the reservations.

The Rogue River War of 1855-56 was the most significant Indian uprising in Oregon. The most important of the many forts constructed to throttle the Indian belligerents was Fort Lane, named for the first governor of the territory.

Just how long the Indians had resided on the Oregon coast before the coming of the white man is an unsolved question. Ethnologist John P. Harrington once stated: "Indian ownership of the coast reached back doubtless for a hundred generations, and a map in 500 A.D. probably would have shown the same ownership as that made by Lewis and Clark 1300 years later."

Many historians believe that these people originally migrated across the top of the world where Asia (Siberia) and Alaska almost touch. Nor is it impossible that Indians may have settled in Oregon territory a thousand years before the advent of Christ's walk on earth. This compares with the white man's fraction of ownership of less than two centuries. Though the coastal Indians left no monuments, no buildings and only a simple culture, they used the land with the wisest of conservation methods and did little to mark it with ruin. In fact, in all of the hundreds of years the Indians owned Oregon, it remained for the most part just the way God had made it. Yet in less than two centuries, our present civilization, with its so-called progress has destroyed much of its natural beauty and is now in a desperate battle to save what remains.

Tears must indeed flow from Indian eyes when they remember the tales of their forbears of the many rivers and streams once teeming with fish, an abundance of game and an uncluttered countryside, with tall stands of timber, isolated beaches and acres of land for everybody. Those tears flow heavier at the sight of garbage along the wayside, endless asphalt ribbons of black, crowded haunts, depleted forests, endangered species, polluted ocean waters, and stagnant ''pulp mill'' air.

Though the Oregon coast is still beautiful, some of its original charm has faded like the last rose of summer.

When Lewis and Clark came west they found the sizes of the Oregon coast tribes varied greatly in number. They estimated the Coos Indian population at 1,500. Some of the tribes were even larger. By the middle 1850's, some had almost been diminished, the Port Orfords the smallest, with only 27 total—nine men, nine women and nine children. The chief's name was as big as his tribe—Chat-al-hak-e-ah.

The Port Orford area, an ancient coastal Indian stamping ground was the scene of an historic struggle between local Indians and would-be settlers. The year was 1851.

Captain William Tichenor, one of the earliest to navigate the Pacific Coast by steam powered vessel, played a major role in the incident. That experienced mariner, after several earlier commands, became skipper-owner of the steamer *Sea Gull* in which he voyaged from the Golden Gate to the Columbia River with an eye toward settlement of some prosperous appearing location from where trade could be carried on by sea. Intrigued by the Port Orford area he visualized a desirable portal for serving the newly developed mines in the Oregon hinterland, making shipments in both directions. Accordingly, Tichenor took his steamer to the then pioneer town of Portland, and there talked up the merits of his findings. The captain's enthusiasm found attentive ears and soon a party of nine eager participants were loading their gear aboard the *Sea Gull*. Cargo consisted of provisions, firearms, a 5 pound cannon and tools to found a new colony.

Sailing southward, the steamer reached Port Orford on June 9, 1851, dropped her hook and lightered her freight to the beach. The colonizers were W. H. Kirkpatrick, J. H. Egan, Joseph Hussey, Cyrus Hedden, R. E. ''Jake'' Summers, P. D. Palmer and Messrs. McCune, Rideout and Slater, all rugged adventurers who had hope for the future.

While the initial efforts were underway, Captain Tichenor joined the landing party long enough to help survey the area, and then bidding the men farewell departed for San Francisco to purchase additional supplies for the newly formed colony.

All the while the local Indians looked on with curiosity and animosity, strangers coming to their traditional lands, taking over without concern or remuneration. At first, they appeared friendly and prone to trade, but after the steamer was well out to sea their attitude changed abruptly. As they became troublesome and abusive, the settlers found themselves in dire straits. Fearing for their

lives they watched for the opportunity to move their little encampment to a prominent bastion abutting the beach, a place that was to become known as Battle Rock. With herculean effort, the nine moved their provisions, set up the 5-pounder and prepared to defend themselves. They didn't have to wait long. The very next day the Indians returned, 40 strong, armed with bows and arrows. Hovering about in the near radius, they shouted obscenities at their adversaries. As night came on, large bonfires crackled along the beach, the natives shouting and whooping it up with strange war dances. Other Indians came to join them until the ranks swelled to 60.

Shortly after dawn, the attack began, the colonizers retreating to the summit of their stronghold. One of the more aggressive chiefs made a wild charge toward the outer sentry and in the ensuing struggle seized his musket. Coming to his aid, one of the nine clubbed the Indian attacker and drove him back. Then followed a hail of arrows whirring into the encampment. The battle was on.

With vastly superior numbers the redmen moved up the hill. The leader of the white brigade, Kirkpatrick, in desperation grabbed the firebrand and sent a volley from the cannon, throwing the attackers into confusion. This was followed up by a round of fire from the rifles, some of the retreating Indians falling in their tracks.

Three counter-attacking natives managed to break into the camp but were promptly knocked down with gun butts. For 15 minutes musket fire and arrows passed each other in flight, but the superior firepower, finally forced the Indians to break ranks and retreat. Thirteen of their number had fallen. Fleeing to the nearby rocks and hills they continued a shower of arrows, most falling well short of the intended mark.

The settlers knew it was but a matter of time until the Indians would resume the battle, and if not annihilated the settlers would be starved out. Further, their supply of ammunition was fast dwindling.

Another attack was made that afternoon but the Indians were not anxious to get close for fear of the deadly firepower. The frustrated chief finally appeared on the nearby beach, threw down his arms and made peace signs. Allowed to enter the stronghold he asked permission to carry away his fallen warriors. Permission was granted. During the discussions, Kirkpatrick told the chief that his men would be gone in 14 days, hoping in the interim that the *Sea Gull* would return with reinforcements.

After clearing the battlefield, the Indians sent in another round of arrows which fell short of their target, but then, respecting Kirkpatrick's promise to be gone in two weeks, they retired the side. On the 15th day, however, the battle was resumed. The angered chief commanded his warriors to charge the fortress, but fearing the fate of their comrades they refused, desiring instead

Indian village, after a print in "A Voyage of Discovery to the North Pacific Ocean 1790-1795, by Capt. George Vancouver."

to keep up a steady hail of arrows from about 300 yards distance, most of which did little damage.

With but eight rounds left, the pitiful party faced a crisis. The Indian grapevine wireless summoned other warriors to get in on the final kill. Soon they numbered 150 strong, but for some providential reason they underestimated the simplicity of ultimate victory, temporarily withdrawing their forces to a small creek to prematurely celebrate, despite the fact that 20 of them had fallen in battle as opposed to four injured white men. The Indians left only a few of their number to keep an eye on the movements of the enemy.

Pretending to strengthen their stronghold, Kirkpatrick held a parley with his men and it was decided they had no choice but to escape from Battle Rock under the guise of night. As soon as their movements were unobservable, they silently gathered what supplies they could carry, sneaked down from their perch and slipped into a nearby forest. Tired and bedraggled, the men groped onward for five miles through the thicket and then did a switchback toward the ocean hoping to throw off any pursuers.

No sooner had they reached the ocean beach then they were spotted by 30 armed Indians who immediately gave chase. Back into the tall timber they went, and though nearly played out, travelled almost continuously for two days and nights, alternating between the forest and the beach until finally reaching a big river, which was probably the Coquille. There, to their dismay and discouragement, they sighted two Indian villages, containing perhaps 200 persons. Too weary to proceed, they set up a temporary camp on a nearby ridge, kindling a bonfire to ward off the night's cold.

On the following day, the local Indians, aware of the hostilities that had occurred at Battle Rock, advanced on the strangers forcing them to again take to the woods for protection. This time the little party went eight miles up river and then crossed on a log raft. Subsisting on salmon, berries and roots, they made their way back to the coast and added to their menu with a feast of mussels. So passed the fourth day following their escape.

Almost on the verge of exhaustion, they finally reached the Cowans (Coos) River, and there found some peaceful Indians who were adept at bartering. To get the natives to ferry them across the river they had to trade the clothes off their backs. Moving northward toward the Umpqua where they knew a white settlement was located, they mistakenly went up the wrong creek and had to retrace their steps. Finally, on the 8th day they reached their destination where the Umpqua settlers took them in. Warm clothes and hot food awaited the weary travellers at the tiny settlements of Umpqua City and Gardiner.

Ironically, Captain Tichenor had brought the *Sea Gull* back to Port Orford the day after the party escaped. Traces of violence and bloodshed caused the good captain to fear his newly founded colony had been wiped out. Fearing further violence, the skipper weighed anchor and steamed out for San Francisco to enlist assistance.

His pleadings attracted a band of men who had struck out in the California gold fields, and who were both ready to do battle and to help colonize the Port Orford area. Their leader was James Gamble, and to back up his new recruits, Tichenor loaded a half dozen field pieces, including a six pounder and an assortment of small arms.

A few days later the new party landed and set up a fortress near the former battle scene, complete with two blockhouses and an encompassing picket fence. The Indians held their peace, but the restless colonists began fighting among themselves. When the *Sea Gull* returned, Gamble insisted Tichenor take some of his insubordinate settlers back to San Francisco.

Meanwhile, the uneasy peace existed, the Indians often casting an evil eye in the direction of the newcomers, but always fearful of the adverse results of an attack. The *Sea Gull* made her periodic visits to the settlement, making two voyages a month between San Francisco and the Columbia River with calls at Port Orford, Trinidad and Humboldt Bay. In February 1852, the *Sea Gull* ran aground on the hostile outcrops of northern California. Though her stout hull received serious damage, Tichenor got her afloat and inside Humboldt Bay, but with water rising fast in the holds the ship had to be beached to prevent her from sinking. Examination of the hull showed that the vessel was a constructive total loss. Fate had been kind in sparing the crew.

Several years later, Tichenor distinguished himself (1869) by taking the first shipload of lumber across the tricky Coquille bar for the account of Grube, Pohl & Rink who had established a sawmill on the north side of the river, above Parkersburg.

Several other incursions by hostile Indians erupted on Oregon's southern coast where the coming of the white man was firmly protested.

After Captain Levi Scott laid plans for the town of Scottsburg on the Umpqua, in 1850, Winchester, Payne & Co. dispatched the schooner *Samuel Roberts* (Captain Coffin) up the coast from California with supplies, but en route, two other rivers were mistaken for the Umpqua. The schooner first tried to enter the Klamath River and found it unnavigable. Next, the Rogue River was tested, where two of the company's crew rowed ashore. Immediately they were surrounded by a band of abusive Indians. Poking at and taunting the intruders, the Rogue tribesmen ripped the buttons from their clothing. Tempers began to flare, the entrapped men retaliated by shoving the Indians away with their gun butts, not daring to fire for fear of their lives.

Captain Coffin, observing their predicament, worked the schooner close to shore where he fired a cannon charge of nails and grapeshot which landed in the trees over the heads of the Indians. Terrified, they fled into the forest. Quickly seizing their chance of escape, the two whites launched their skiff and made a hasty retreat to the schooner.

The northerly voyage continued until the Umpqua was reached, (on the central Oregon coast) and then satisfying himself that the bar had sufficient depth, Captain Coffin made his epic entry, the *Samuel Roberts,* perhaps being the first commercial deepsea vessel to enter that river.

Word quickly spread concerning the potential of the Umpqua area with its tall stands of timber and adequate bar entrance, plus the fact that the Indians were not troublesome such as in the southern coast areas. Winchester, Payne & Co. fitted out the schooner *Kate Heath* which came north from the Golden Gate with 100 men, including A. C. Gibbs, who later was to become governor of the state.

As the *Heath* entered the river on Oct. 10, 1850, a wrecked ship was seen hard on the shoals at the entrance, which greatly surprised the pioneer party. She was the *Bostonian* which had been dispatched around the Horn from Boston under Captain Woods for the account of a merchant named Gardiner. While attempting to cross the bar, the vessel had missed stays, drifted out of the main channel and became firmly implanted on the sands. Every effort was made to get her afloat but to no avail, the supercargo, George Snelling, Gardiner's nephew, directing the unloading of the cargo, most of which was saved and lightered up river a few miles and sheltered beneath a canvas covering of salvaged sails. The place was named Gardiner and is so known to this day.

In the interim, the Winchester, Payne group had settled near the river entrance, naming their settlement Umpqua City.

The only early Indian flareup in the Umpqua region occurred just after the establishment of Scottsburg. Captain Rufus Butler was assaulted by a local chief, but in the melee managed to fracture his attacker's skull by gun butt. Infuriated by this act, a small Indian band retaliated by laying seige to Butler's house. Fighting a one-man war by firing through the cabin windows, his death would have eventually been a certainty had not some nearby settlers been made aware of his situation. Armed, they came to the scene and routed the Indians.

When the *Samuel Roberts* sailed up the Umpqua for a survey of suitable areas, she ran hard aground on a small island two miles below Scottsburg. Undoubtedly spirits had been used unsparingly before the grounding as all hands decided to leave their stranded vessel until the incoming tidal flow raised the lower river. Retiring to the beach, they popped the bung from a barrel of brandy and toasted their predicament. Hangovers and a wrecked ship brought about a rude awakening for the imbibers. The shoal still bears the name of the schooner to this day.

The Umpqua bar was destined to achieve a sinister reputation. Though pioneer shipmaster Captain J. B. Leeds rendered an opinion that it was the least dangerous on the Oregon coast, the facts did not bear out his conclusions. The larger percentage of the initial ocean going vessels to cross the bar came to grief. Beginning with the *Bostonian,* the following met with disaster: *Caleb Curtis* in 1851; *Almira, Nassau* and *Roanoke* in 1852; *Oregon* in 1854 and the *Loo Choo* in 1855, none of which were due to Indian hostility.

Three Indian tribes, the Tillamooks, (Killimucks) Nehalems, (Naalems) and Nestuccas, (Nea-Stocka) which lived in what we know today as Tillamook County, were of the Salishan linguistic group. Not a war-like people like their counterparts in southern Oregon, they were generally peaceful and faithful to tradition and ritual. They registered little protest over the coming of the white settlers nor over the loss of their lands.

Noted for practising head-flattening, that mode of disfigurement was considered a sign of distinction. To the freeborn child, it was his birthright, and occasionally the first child of a favorite slave wife was so honored. Intermarriage between flatheads and non-flatheads was uncommon, the men of important families usually seeking wives from some other flathead tribe than their own. It is also of interest to note that though the flatheads sometimes waged bitter war against each other, they never captured one another for the purpose of enslavement.

Coast Indians known as "canoe Indians" were squat in stature with short bowed legs, caused from long hours at the paddles. On the other hand, they had unusually good muscular development in their arms and shoulders. Their canoes were fashioned well, and accommodated from one to 40 paddlers. Hollowed out from cedar logs, the finishing touches were done by burning. Some of their craft measured 60 feet in length, were well designed and highly seaworthy. With a skill akin to that of the Polynesians in canoe building, the coast Indians were not adept at navigation. They did not depend on sail, and were perfectly content to remain within sight of land, their navigation aids being the bold headlands created by the hand of the Great Spirit. Some Indians remained strictly within the bounds of rivers and lakes. With an overabundant bonanza of fish and game in their happy hunting and fishing grounds they had no desire to stray westward into the vastness of the ocean. "Land of many waters" is the meaning of the Indian name, Tillamook.

Disregard for the gentle qualities of these people was indicative of the careless actions of some of the early white settlers. There was a traditional tribal burial ground in the lower Kilchis Valley in the mid 1800's. Youthful pioneer John Hathaway and his friends were in need of a boat and thoughtlessly went to the burial grounds to fulfill that need. Indians generally placed their deceased inside their canoes which served as a casket. With the body were placed the dead person's personal belongings. Then the craft was raised upon blocks or poles and covered by a light wooden overlay or another canoe.

Hathaway, fully aware that he was on sacred ground, purloined a death canoe and with the help of his cohorts emptied its contents on the beach, washed out the craft and carried it away. When news of the atrocity reached the tribal settlement the Indians were infuriated and the vandals were fortunate to escape with their scalps.

Such unholy acts became commonplace, yet seldom were the culprits ever punished or reprimanded. Had an Indian ever rifled the grave of a white man he would have been lucky to escape with his life. Not only did the early settlers take the redman's land without compensation, but further felt no remorse even in desecrating a gravesite.

Old town Waldport is actually built over an Indian burial ground. When the town was platted, the remains of scores of dead and their decaying canoes were piled together and burned without the slightest thought of re-burial. Anything of value was removed from the canoe caskets and kept for personal gain.

So often the white man labeled the Indian as a savage, a vermin of sorts that needed to be stamped out. Those American natives were considered a thorn in the side if they stood in the way of progress.

In 1806, Lewis and Clark estimated the Tillamook Indians numbered about 1,000. By 1871, 65 years later, figures had been reduced to only 28 Nehalems, 83 Tillamooks and 55 Nestuccas still dwelling on their original tribal lands. The Clatsops at the mouth of the Columbia River, once a flourishing band, had been cut to only 56. And, sad to say, the astounding reduction was due almost entirely to the "curse" placed by the white man on his red brother, mainly in the form of disease, liquor, exploitation and abuse.

Frances Fuller Victor records the details of an epidemic that was passed onto the Clatsop Indians after an early Yankee ship visited the area. The sickness spread down the coast from one tribe to the next taking the lives of an estimated 30,000 Indians. And that of course was only one of several such incidences. Many other natives were victims of "firewater," becoming hopeless alcoholics. Then there was the tragic spread of venereal disease transmitted from the Caucasian. Often times entire tribes were found infected, even to the new born children.

Gravesite of Chief Comcomly at Astoria. He was leader of the Chinooks and a firm friend of the early fur traders.

David Doughas, noted botanist, on visiting Clatsop country, recorded in his journal on October 11, 1830:

"A dreadfully fatal intermittent fever broke out in the lower parts of this river (Columbia) about eleven weeks ago, which had depopulated the country. Villages which had afforded from one to two hundred effective warriors are totally gone; not a soul remains. The houses are empty and flocks of famished dogs are howling about, while dead bodies lie strewn in every direction on the sand of the river."

Chief Kilchis, one of the finest and most respected of the Tillamook tribe, a man who often befriended the white settlers, was a typical victim of outright disrespect. It was he who showed the first white settler to come to his land, Joe Champion, in 1851 where he could find shelter and a temporary home in the massive stump of a hollow spruce tree. He told his people, "I do not like to see the white man come to Tillamook because wherever he goes he takes all the land, but there is nothing we can do about it, so, it is best not to hurt his feelings."

His wise and prudent manner came to the fore in the Clarke murder incident at Grand Ronde. A Tillamook Indian came to the Clarke cabin, to rob it of a keg which he believed contained liquor. He was apparently unaware that the Reverend Clarke was a teetotaler, and away at the time. Instead, the misguided Indian encountered the preacher's wife who firmly resisted his demands. Enraged, the Indian stabbed both the woman and her young daughter to death, burned the house down and escaped. The double murder created a panic.

Down from Yamhill to the tribal settlement of Kilchis Point came an angry well-armed army of settlers. The chief met them with a warm welcome, but in their wrathful mood they shoved him aside refusing to shake his hand. Instead, they picked out the Indian who was as-

sumed to be the culprit, and without aforethought or trial, turned into a lynch mob. Chief Kilchis attempted to intercede, insisting they had the wrong man. He offered to help find the murderer if only they would be patient. But patient they would not be, and shortly had a rope strung over a tree limb with a hangman's knot at the bitter end. Within minutes the poor victim swung, a lifeless corpse.

Restraint on behalf of the chief was almost unbelievable. Though seething inside he remained passive. Following their dastardly act, the unruly mob attempted to befriend Kilchis. Now it was his turn to refuse to shake their hands, boldly proclaiming that the "blood was on their hands." And, indeed he was right for they had hung an innocent man.

Chief Kilchis displayed greater wisdom and justice than any of his white counterparts, for despite all that had happened he eventually apprehended the guilty individual and sent him to Yamhill for trial, in custody of the local sheriff.

In the aftermath of that unfortunate incident rumors of an Indian uprising ran rampant. The white settlers built a breastwork and armed themselves against possible attack. Kilchis' people were sullen and restless, but apparently were no more anxious to make war than the pioneers. The incident was closed.

After the death of the wise old chief, the settlers were quick to grab the traditional tribal lands of the Tillamooks, Nehalems and Nestuccas. The depopulated tribes were helpless to resist. Though the Indians had lived on their lands in relative peace for generations, within a few decades, they were robbed of virtually everything that rightfully belonged to them in accordance with worthless treaties which they did not fully understand. In return, they were to suffer disease, poverty and heartache.

Compensation you say? Well . . . one of the last members of the Tillamook tribe, an Indian woman, by an act of Congress received the amount of $112 for tribal lands, and that is probably one of the few personal payments made following the unratified treaty of Aug. 7, 1851.

Perhaps by modern standards the coastal Indians would have appeared ignorant and primitive, but as was earlier mentioned they were far more adept to the natural ways of conservation than the white people will ever be. And as for communication they far excelled the pioneers of their time. The local Indians on the coast knew of the success of the Sioux in their battle against General George Custer in 1876 long before the white settlers. Their mysterious method of passing news from one tribe to another was remarkable, sort of a open air party line that bridged forest, hill, mountain and river. The Custer defeat was one of the few great victories in the West for those oppressed people.

Fighting blood was far more apparent in the Indians of southern Oregon and the difficulties with the Coquille and Rogue River Indians in the 1850's increased almost daily. Making no attempt to hide their objections to the white invasion they were ready and willing to resist the trespass upon their lands. But their best efforts were little more than a holding action against superior forces. Lt. Col. Silas Casey was sent from San Francisco under orders from General Hitchcock with an army of 90 soldiers to set up a fort at Port Orford, the express purpose, to punish the Coquilles for any hostile acts. A brigade under Lt. Stoneman later reported: "A large number of them were killed and the moral effect of the operation was very great."

That delayed action was reputedly an effort to punish the local Indians for their earlier actions against the nine white men defending themselves at Battle Rock.

Fort Orford was built and garrisoned till 1856, when after the shaky treaty was signed, the post was abandoned.

The Rogues, Chetcos and other southerly tribes were successful in some reprisal acts against the white settlers. It is alleged that a conspiracy came about when Indian Chetco Jenny became the wife of special agent Ben Wright. She conspired with Enos, a local member of her tribe, to murder her husband. The grisly climax found the two Indians roasting the agent's heart and making a meal of it.

By 1852, prospectors had moved into many parts of southwest Oregon which rallied the Indians to commit acts of hostility. The pioneers were always quick to respond, usually with greater violence. Following is an account kept in the journal of Joel Palmer, concerning the burning of an entire Indian village in Curry County in 1854:

"About three miles north of our boundary line, a stream empties into the ocean, known by the Indian name as Chetco. Here are many indications of having once resided a numerous people. In the fall of 1853, one Miller and several associates located land claims in this vicinity. They first built their houses about a quarter of a mile from the river to which the Indians made no objections. Subsequently, knowing that the newly discovered mines would attract an influx of people, the whites projected a town speculation, formed an association and selected a site at the mouth of the Chetco River. The face of the country is such that the crossing must be at the mouth of the river by ferry. Here were two Indian villages on opposite sides of the stream, of 20 lodges each.

"This ferry was of considerable importance. The new townsite included one of the villages, and when preparations were made to erect a house within its limits, the Indians strongly protested; but at last acquiesced; the cabin was built and occupied by Miller. Hitherto the Indians had enjoyed the benefit of the ferry; but now Miller informed them that they must no longer ferry white people. The Indians, however, sometimes did so and were threatened with the destruction of their lodges if they did not desist.

"The misunderstanding became so acute, that several men who had been fighting Indians on the Smith River in California, were called in by Miller and quartered in his house for nearly two weeks. Becoming unwilling to remain longer, they were about to return to their homes. Miller objected to their leaving until they had accomplished something for his relief, as on their departure he would be subject to the same annoyance as before. The next morning at daylight, the party consisting of eight or nine well armed men, attacked the village and as the Indians came from their lodges, 12 were shot dead. The women and children were allowed to escape. Three Indians remained in the lodges and returned the fire with bows and arrows. Being unable to get a sight of those Indians, they ordered two squaws, pets in the family of Miller, to set fire to the lodges. Two Indians were consumed in the conflagration. The third, while raising his head through the flames and smoke for breath was shot dead. What added to the atrocity of the deed is, that shortly before the massacre, the Indians were induced to sell the whites their guns, under the pretext that friendly relations were firmly established. In the next two days all the lodges in the village were burned, except two, belonging to the friends of an Indian who acted with Miller and his party. This horrid tragedy was enacted Feb. 15, 1854. . . . In all, 23 Indians and several squaws were killed.

"The other settlers condemned his atrocity and told Miller he would have to face the consequences alone. Miller was subsequently arrested and placed in the custody of the military at Fort Orford; but upon examination before a justice of the peace, was set at large, 'on the ground of justification, and want of evidence to commit.' "

An atrocity you say? Yes it was, one of many suffered by the natives of western Oregon, victims of a greedy new generation of intruders.

Consider the following incident as reported in the journal of Special Agent Smith on Feb. 5, 1854:

"A most horrid massacre, or rather an out-and-out barbarous mass murder, was perpetrated upon a portion of the Nah-so-mah band residing at the mouth of the Coquille River on the morning of Jan. 28, (1854) by a party of 40 miners. The reason assigned by the miners by their own statements, seem trivial. However, on the afternoon preceding the murders, the miners requested the chief to come in for a talk. This he refused to do. Thereupon the whites at and near the ferry-house assembled and deliberated upon the necessity of an immediate attack upon the Indians. A courier was sent to the upper mines, (Randolph) some seven miles to the north, for assistance. Twenty men responded, arriving at the ferry-house in the evening preceding the morning massacre.

"At dawn on the following day, led by one Abbott, the ferry party and the 20 miners, about 40 in all, formed three detachments, marched upon the Indian ranches and 'consumated a most inhuman slaughter, which the attackers termed a fight. The Indians were aroused from sleep to meet their deaths with but a feeble show of resistance; shot down as they were attempting to escape from their houses. Fifteen men and one squaw were killed, two squaws badly wounded. On the part of the white men, not even the slightest wound was received. The houses of the Indians, with but one exception, were fired and entirely destroyed. Thus was committed a massacre too inhuman to be readily believed.''

Many Indians joined outlaw bands in hit-and-run sneak attacks which generally proved more effective than head-on battles. Many of the Indians of the southern Oregon coastlands had grown ruthless and bitter. There was a showdown battle at Pistol River in 1855, when Captain Abbott moved against the Chetcos. Simultaneous with that battle, Yankee troops attacked an Indian settlement ten miles up the Rogue River. Driving the spike even deeper, a few weeks later, Army detachments with superior weapons and manpower subdued hostile Indian bands headed by Chief John and Indian Limpy at the mouth of the Illinois. It wasn't that the Indians were inferior warriors, far from it, but outnumbered and outgunned they nearly always ended up with their feathers pinned back.

The redmen struck back in isolated incidences but every time they gained an upper hand heavily armed militiamen moved in to back up the hard pressed resisters. Usually the white settlers had sufficient strength to fight their own battles such as an attack made on an Indian village at the mouth of the Coquille resulting in the deaths of ten Indians, the wounding of 11 and the capturing of 40 squaws and children. At virtually the same time, a group of volunteers attacked, without warning, a party of Indians in canoes who had their hands busy maneuvering through swift rapids of the Rogue River near Lobster Creek. Firing from the river banks, the attackers slaughtered all but one Indian brave and two squaws.

The Indian "telegraph" was busy. Rightfully agitated by such acts, red warriors made a sneak attack on 60 Army regulars escorting a pack train. Woefully outgunned, the Indians lost six of their own, many others sustaining injuries. Before the rifles ceased firing and the arrows stopped whirring, three troopers had fallen. The Indians fled to the hills.

Returning to Joel Palmer's journal of March 8, 1856

we find another account of turmoil between the two factors.

"A party of volunteers encamped for some time at the Big Bend of Rogue River, above Agness, returned, and a part of them encamped near the To-to-tin village, three miles above the coast; the remaining portion having passed on to the mining village at the mouth of the river. On the morning of Feb. 22, at daylight, the camp near the Indian village was attacked by a party of Indians supposed to number about 300, and all but two (of the whites) it was supposed, were put to death, one man making his way to Port Orford, the other to the village at the mouth of the Rogue River. With one exception, all the dwellings from the mouth of Rogue River to Port Orford have been burned and the inmates supposed to be murdered. Five persons, however, had made their appearance, who at first were supposed to have been killed. Benjamin Wright, the Special Agent for the district, is supposed to be among the killed...

"The extraordinary success of the hostile bands and the ease with which the Indians had invariably gained a victory, inspired a belief that they were abundantly able to maintain their position, and rid themselves of the white population. In every instance where a conflict had ensued between volunteers and hostile Indians in Southern Oregon, the latter had gained what they regarded a victory.

"The avowed determination of the people to exterminate the Indian race, regardless of whether they are innocent or guilty, and the general disregard for the rights of those acting as friends and aiding in the subjugation of our real and avowed enemies, has had a powerful influence in inducing these tribes to join the warlike bands.

"It is astonishing to know the rapidity with which intelligence is carried from one extreme of the country to the other, and the commission of outrages, of which there have been many by our people against the Indians is heralded forth by the hostile parties, augmented and used as evidence for the necessity for all to unite in war against us."

At midnight on Feb. 22, 1856, the Indian tribes in the Rogue River area embarked on a revengeful stampede. Practically every home inhabited by white settlers in Curry County was burned to the ground and many were killed. Pent-up frustrations by the Indians had reached the breaking point and in a last ditch act of desperation they went on the warpath.

It was to be their last act of organized reprisal. With their manpower reduced to a fraction of their former numbers, due much to the earlier spread of influenza, measles and smallpox, their offensive was met head on by powerful reinforced Yankee military forces. The Indians were brought to their knees at every turn and before the rifles had cooled, the settlers were already making plans to take over tribal lands. The natives had met their Waterloo.

One of the last gallant leaders, Chief John, surrendered at Big Bend in late May of 1856. As the curtain came down, the militia marched a bedraggled band of defeated warriors to the tribunal, where the treaty, unjustified and unfair, eventually placed the conquered, broken in pride and spirit, on restricted reservations.

The treaty was a farce, a virtual disgrace to the United States government. The faces of those involved should have been as red as the stripes in our national flag. In fact, Congress never did ratify the document. It was tantamount to a massive rip-off against the true natives of America. Efforts at seeking a peaceful and legal means of settlement that would have granted just pay for lands taken, and a right to maintain their traditional way of life came to naught. Worthless documents were filed in an obscure corner of the nation's archives to gather layers of dust.

Agent B. R. Riddle made the following report in 1862:

"Ever since I have been in charge of this agency, constant complaint has been made to me...that the government has acted in bad faith with them (the Indians). They say they made a treaty with the government, abandoned their country, and in consequence with the stipulations of the treaty they removed to this reservation where they have continued to live and in doing so have fulfilled their part of the agreement, but not so the government. On the contrary, it never has ratified the treaty and has done nothing but pay them in promises...They have waited patiently for the "Great White Father" (in Washington D.C.) to fulfill his promises. It does seem to me that the government is very tardy in the matter of ratifying these treaties."

Then came the final straw. Indians were granted the right to sue the U.S. government. Ridiculously, they had first to prove they were the original owners of the land; then the actual worth of said land had to be determined. Enveloped in red tape, efforts to do so were halfheartedly pursued and came to naught. It was also the intent that the Indians should receive interest on their lands from the time of the signing of the treaties. Nearly a century and a quarter has since faded into history, the old Indians have passed on, others succeeded them, Indian lands have become white man's parks, resorts, towns and cities. Still, those ancient claims, for the most part, remain forgotten and probably will until our country crumbles into dust. The rape of the American Indian has gone down as a colossal atrocity ranking on a par with the slave trade in blacks.

The ideal life of the coastal Indians in the green years, with their potlatches and feasts, may have had some shortcomings but it also had highlights. The Indian

Indian nobility. "Stum-ma-nu, a Flathead boy." Indian baby boys of the higher ranks went through the head-flattening process, which was common among the Indians along the northern Oregon coast. Oregon Historical Society collection.

men spent much of their time fishing, using traps and weirs, mostly to catch their favorite dish, salmon. This prized gift from the sea was often dried for winter usage or pounded into a flour to mix with dried camas root (skunk cabbage) or dried berries. They would also catch smelt by using dip nets, a custom of the central Oregon coast Indians. The V-shaped frame device was called a squaw net. The men caught the fish but the preparation was mostly handled by the women. Experts at stream, river, shore and offshore fishing, the men also made good use of harpoons with razor sharp bone or horn spearheads and spruce shafts to catch the whale. They were brave enough in their dugouts to come almost up to the side of the leviathan before driving the lance home.

The northern Oregon coast Indians when first seen by white men in the 1840's were found to be, for the most part, peaceful, resourceful and uninhibited. Little did they realize that on the first day they saw the great white wings of Spanish ships it was the harbinger of their eventual demise.

When the pioneers first settled the Alsea River country there were 17 Indian villages at the most advantageous fishing and hunting locations. Originally it was estimated that perhaps as many as 350 Indians occupied every 100 square miles, this of course, before their rapid decline.

There was an Indian sub-agency located at Yachats till 1875, where most of the "Yahutes" based their operations after the treaty was signed. Today, a white man's cemetery is located where the station once stood and the Indians no longer roam their favorite stamping grounds at the mouth of the Yachats River. They once referred to it as the "little river with the big mouth at the foot of the mountain."

The late Nona Strake told of her recollections of early day Waldport in a Lincoln County Times newspaper interview in 1960:

"My folks came to the Alsea Bay in 1883. I was a small child, but I can distinctly remember the Indians' skulls and bones that we saw most everywhere we went in what is now Waldport. There were just four houses of sorts, one of these a log cabin, here at that time and they were mostly quite near what we now call old town waterfront. My mother had to hang her first washing out on the salal bushes to dry and she got quite a shock when she saw a human skull grinning up at her from the ground under a bush. We soon got used to sights like that. Near Rocky Point where Highway 101 leaves town to the south, an old skull had sat up on a limb of a big spruce so long it had grown a thick coat of green moss.

"Another skull lay on the ground near the path to our first old school house. It had lain there almost unnoticed for no one knew how many years. Then one day one of the small boys, on his way to school, ran out and gave it a boost with his bare foot...kids all went bare footed in those days. Something in that old skull jingled! He took out several silver half dollars.

"The Indians had always buried a man's silver coins in his mouth. His paper currency was usually placed under his shoulders. This was proved in the case of old Chief Yaquina John's son. The Indian leader lived upon the point which still bears his name, south of the Alsea. When his only son died he had him entombed in a small building just large enough to hold his body and a few of his possessions, in what is now near the middle of Waldport. Around this he built a small picket fence all of which he whitewashed. Then he, the chief, had a wide swath cut through the big old growth spruce and all underbrush cut out so he could see the white tomb from his cabin on the point. And what about the chief's son's tomb itself? Someone had torn off some of the fence pickets and part of one wall and we could see plainly inside.

"From a snarl of rotted blankets, spruce root basket weave and long black hair, a dried and shrunken arm was upthrust—stark and accusing! From one crooked finger still hung a silver ring. The beast, in human form, who had boasted that he had taken $25 out from under those dead shoulders, had evidently not had enough nerve to cut off the gnarled finger to get the ring."

Robbing Indian graves was a pastime of many early settlers. Even in death the Indians could not rest in peace.

Chief Joseph of the Nez Perce left some words that long haunted the conscience of his oppressors.

"Say to us if you can say it," he repined, "that you were sent by the Creative Power to talk to us. Perhaps you think the Creator sent you here to dispose of us as you see fit. If I thought you were sent by the Creator I might be induced to think you had a right to dispose of me. Do not misunderstand me, but understand me fully with reference to my affection for the land. I never said the land was mine to do with it as I chose. The one who has the right to dispose of it is the one who has created it. I claim a right to live on my land, and accord you the privilege to live on yours."

The wise old chief went on to say:

"All men were made by the same Great Spirit Chief. They are all brothers. The earth is the mother of all people, and all people should have equal rights upon it. You might as well expect the rivers to run backward as that any man who was born a free man should be contented penned up and denied liberty to go where he pleases."

Lottie, late daughter of Chief Jackson, last of the once flourishing bands of Coos full-blood Indians.

When the last of the hostile Indians had surrendered in southern Oregon in 1856, they were gathered 1,300 strong at a temporary reservation at Port Orford. It was like the last act of a morbid drama as the surviving members of the warring tribes milled forlornly about among the armed guards. It was the doom of a race of free men who had roamed the beaches, coastal plains and foothills of Oregon country for countless generations. All the chiefs of note were present and not less than 300 warriors known for bravery, perseverance and fighting ability. That was just one of many such treaty gatherings in the Pacific Northwest to spell the end of hostilities between the white man and the Indian.

One central Oregon coast reservation was fixed as the future abode of 2,700 red men, from Cape Perpetua to Cape Lookout, and from the Pacific Ocean to the watershed of the Willamette. It all sounded pretty good in words but was tantamount to a fantastic deception, for much of the assigned area was soon to be gobbled up by the settlers, until only a few scattered reservations remained.

Chief John, already mentioned, and Chief Sam of the Table Rock tribe were rightfully skeptical of the hollow promises. Many other Indians as well totally opposed the treaty but due to overwhelming forces that held all trump cards they sullenly agreed to the signing. But, it was too much for some to bear. Chief Enos grew restless and eventually broke the treaty while Chief Yaquina John attempted to instigate a revolt. He made a bold attempt to seize Army guns, overpower the military guards and return to his traditional fishing and hunting grounds. The vise, however, was clamped tight. Yaquina John and his son Adam were quickly apprehended and placed in irons. A few years later they were removed from the stockade and marched aboard the steamer *Columbia* for transport to San Francisco and confinement at the dreaded Alcatraz prison. Mavericks that they were, no way would they give up. En route south from Portland on the steamer, the rebels managed to break free, overpower their guards and make a bold attempt to seize the ship. A wild melee erupted and before peace could be restored Adam's leg had been so mangled from the blows of a meat cleaver that it had to be amputated.

When the *Columbia* berthed at San Francisco, the heavily guarded renegades were turned over to the authorities at Fort Flint. The story of their plight fell on some sympathetic ears and after several court hearings it was finally decided to pardon those last holdouts, the pitiful remnants of a once flourishing tribe.

The last days of Yaquina John were quiet ones, but his one-legged son Adam ended up in Klamath country as a chief in the image of his father, but one whose influence never got beyond the borders of the reservation.

Monument to the ingenuity of man. The mighty Trans-Columbia River Bridge spanning the mouth of the Columbia and connecting the states of Oregon and Washington. Circling over the city of Astoria at its southern terminus it is one of America's longest continuous bridges measuring 4.3 miles, the greatest clearance above the river being 205 feet, the highest point of the giant steel superstructure 301 feet above the water.

Foundation pilings penetrate as far as 230 feet below sea level, pier bases weighing up to 830 tons. Opened in 1966, it took three years to build using a construction crew of 325 men. Left center, is the remnants of Desdemona Sands. This great link in Highway 101 replaced a fleet of state-operated ferryboats. From State of Oregon photo.

Looking northward from the famous Sea Lion Caves toward Heceta Head, one of the most scenic attractions on the entire Oregon coast.

CHAPTER THREE
THE DECEPTIVE RIVER

Roll on you mighty river, from your source in the melting snows of the rugged Canadian Rockies to your confrontation with the Pacific Ocean. As your volume begins to grow, you roll onward fed by the Okanogan, Kootenay, Snake, Yakima, Deschutes, Willamette and many others. You form the boundary lines of Washington and Oregon, cutting through the Cascade and Coast ranges on your 1,243 mile trek. Second greatest of all continental American rivers, vessels navigate your waters from the Pacific to deep into the hinterland. Cities, towns, villages, dot your shores, and deepsea ships from the farthest portals of the world fill their holds at your bustling ports. You command a vast drainage basin, some 285,000 square miles encompassing parts of seven western states.

From your discovery by the intrepid Captain Robert Gray in 1792, you have continued to grow and prosper, while for countless generations before the white settler came, you catered to every need of a once vast Indian population. You witnessed the epic arrival of Lewis and Clark who reached your mouth in 1805, and you knew the determined efforts of David Thompson two years later in finding your source and exploring your entire course. You witnessed the American settlement and the creation of Oregon territory. Timber abounded along your upper tracts and salmon filled your depths; you provided necessary irrigation water in arid lands, and in modern times the great dams within your waters, the Grand Coulee and Bonneville, provided the electrical power for the livelihood of hundreds of thousands of citizens.

Spewing out into the Pacific some 262,000 cubic feet of water per second, only your great counterpart, Ol'Miss, can make a greater boast. Indeed you are the queen of rivers, O mighty Columbia.

Historically and commercially the Columbia was once referred to as the mighty "River of the West." Its existence long unknown to Caucasian eyes was the object of persistent rumors that linked it with the fabled "Northwest Passage," that was to have afforded a direct route to the Indies from Europe.

So hidden was the Columbia's deceptive entrance that early explorers passed within a few leagues and were unaware of any opening. The Spanish, Portuguese, British, French, Dutch and Russian mariners of old all passed nearby and were oblivious of an entrance. The bold navigator, Bartolme Ferrelo had long heard rumors of such a river when he reached Oregon's southern limits in 1543, and the great navigator Sir Francis Drake reached Cape Arago, Oregon, in 1579, but did not find the Columbia. Certainly, 13 years later Juan de Fuca (Apostolos Valerianos) must have passed by it on his way to discovering the strait that bears his name. Martin d'Aguilar and Sebastian Viscaino had the river in mind when they sailed up the coast. It eluded Juan Perez in the ship *Santiago* in the summer of 1774. Logging the geographical features of the area, he had no stomach for searching out an entrance amid white-lipped breakers along an inhospitable shoreline. Francis Drake reached Cape Arago, Oregon in 1579, but did not find the Columbia. Certainly, 13 years later Juan de Fuca, (Apostolos Valerianos) must have passed by it on his way to discovering the strait that bears his name. Martin d'Aguilar and Sebastian Viscaino had the river in mind when they sailed up the coast. It eluded Juan Perez in the ship *Santiago* in the summer of 1774. Logging the geographical features of the area, he had no stomach for searching out an entrance amid white-lipped breakers along an inhospitable shoreline.

Spanish authorities were none too pleased with Perez's decision, and kept his findings a secret from foreign navigators until an organized expedition could be summoned the following year. Heading the effort was Lt. Bruno Heceta, Perez reduced to second in command. The schooner *Sonora*, trailing in the wake of the *Santiago*, was in command of Lt. Juan Francisco de Bodega y Quadra. The two vessels passed close to both the Columbia and Grays Harbor without entering. Several miles north of the latter, a boatload of men was sent ashore for fresh water and wood. Whether or not they provoked the natives is not known, but the party was attacked and every man killed. Fired with revenge, Quadra wanted to take 30 of his best men and declare war on the Indians. The other officers, however, interceded, and under a The other officers, however, interceded, and under a cloud of gloom the two vessels sailed away.

Shortly afterward, the two Spanish ships were actually off the Columbia River bar, Heceta placing in his journal an excellent account of the geographical surroundings but recording no acceptable opening. The entrance was a cauldron of silver breakers from (Cape Disappointment to Point Adams) end to end. Virtually refused an invitation to enter, though certain that the river existed at the locale, he marked it on his charts and continued the miserable voyage southward.

On return to New Spain, the leader of the expedition afforded his superiors the details of the estuary and of a mysterious river which they failed to enter, but which they named Ensenada de Heceta, or Rio de San Roque. And there the Spanish hopes of discovery ended.

Enter one Captain James Cook, most renowned of English navigators and explorers, who had already made two epic voyages of discovery in the Pacific. It is he, (Cook) reasoned Lord Sandwich, the best in His Majesty's service "that I shall dispatch to the Northwest Coast to find the fabled Northwest Passage," which would allegedly afford a sea link between England and the Orient. Cook, eagerly accepting the challenge arrived off the Oregon coast in March of 1778, but strange as it may seem, this man with possibly more natural abilities than any of his counterparts, was frustrated in finding either the entrance to the Columbia or the Strait of Juan de Fuca. Instead, he made a beachhead at Nootka Sound on Vancouver Island where he repaired his ships. A short time later, Cook was to meet a violent death at the hands of angry Hawaiians on the Kona coast of Hawaii.

With Spain's influence beginning to wane, word leaked out of a fabulous market for Northwest furs in the Orient. Suddenly, ships of a dozen maritime nations appeared. Northwest Indians had furs in abundance and were willing and anxious to trade.

Out of this new trade America's foremost contribution to the ranks of great explorers came on the scene. Though Captain Robert Gray's express purpose was to find a bounty in furs, he was destined to become one of the all-time historical greats.

Capt. Meriwether Lewis, commander of the Lewis and Clark expedition, 1804-1806. Born in Virginia Aug. 18, 1774, he was a captain in the regular army 1795; private secretary to President Jefferson 1801, and was governor of the territory of Missouri in 1807. He died Oct. 8, 1809, one of the great figures in American history.

Though not in charge of the original Northwest expedition, he commanded the secondary vessel, the little sloop *Lady Washington,* consort to the ship *Columbia Rediviva,* an ex-privateer. Master of the lead vessel was the capable Captain John Kendrick. The vessels departed Boston on Sept. 30, 1778, laden with such trading items as knives, hatchets, blankets, axes, iron bars and trinkets. Not a trade of conquest, the backers of the fur seeking adventure cautioned commander-in-chief Kendrick not to infringe on any Spanish dominion and not to offend any subjects of his "Catholic Majesty," that they were to treat the Indians with courtesy and to purchase from them any land which they might acquire.

The respective vessels got separated in the "roaring forties" on rounding Cape Horn, but plans had already been made to rendezvous at Nootka in such an eventuality.

The *Columbia* was so seriously damaged by heavy seas that she had to put into Spanish-controlled Juan Fernandez Island where the commandant treated Kendrick and his crew kindly, allowing them to make repairs on their ship.

William Clark, of the famous exploration team of Lewis and Clark died at St. Louis Sept. 1, 1838. He was born in Virginia in 1770. Serving as a lieutenant in the infantry before his famous trek west, he later became a brigadier general and was governor of Missouri Territory from 1813 to 1821. Later still, he became superintendent of Indian affairs at St. Louis, a post he held till his death.

Captain Gray reached the West Coast first and en route up the coast put into Tillamook Bay, becoming the accepted discoverer of that body of water. His little sloop crossed the bar on August 14, 1788. Only a few weeks earlier, Captain John Meares, a Britisher, had passed the same location and pronounced it an impassable entrance, choked with shoals.

Gray was greeted by Indians in dugouts bringing berries and boiled crab, apparently as a welcome gesture. The gifts were gratefully received, the scurvy victims being the first to get their badly needed vitamins. Such a reception was totally unexpected, but though the initial experience was profitable and mutually cordial, it didn't remain that way.

First mate Haswell wrote in the *Lady Washington's* log:*

"On the 16th we had pleasant weather with a moderate breeze to the eastward at this time an amazing number of the natives were along side with boiled and roasted crabbe for sale which our people purchased for buttons etc., they had also dryed salmon and berries in abundance.

"At noon we weighed and came to sail with a very moderte breze which died away to a purfect calm and the flud tide still setting strong swept us on a reef of rocks, the water was smooth as glass and the tide still flowing the vessell could receive no material Damage we run out our Kedge with a small worp and hauled off, the sea breze cuming in prevented our getting out we veared a scope and moared with two bowers.

"About this time the old chief who came onboard of us on the lee about 6 Leagues to the Northward he had a great number of the natives with him all armed and they had no skins with them tho' they were well convinced it was them alone we wanted and he had promised to supply us with some however tho' he had not fulfilled his engagement he mett with a very polight reseption . . .

"Having nothing else to do but wate for the next days tide to depart, Early in the Afternoon I accompaneyed Mr. Coolidge onshore in the long Boat to amuse ourselves in taking a walk while our boat was loaded with grass and shrubs for our stock we took all the people in the Boat who were affected by the scurvy our number in all amounted to seven the disposition of the people seemed so friendly we went worse armed than ordinary we had two Muskets and three or four Cutlasses we boath took our swoards and each of us a pistol on our first landing we visated there Houses and such vietles as they eate themselves they offered to us but they are so intolerably filthy there is nothing we could stumac except frute.

"They then amused us showing there dexterity with there arrows and spears they began a war dance it was long and hedious accompaneyed with frightfull howlings indeed there was something more horrid in there songs and jestures which accompanied it than I am capable of describing it chilled ye blud in my veins. The dance over we left the natives to themselves and walked along the beach to the boat where the people were cutting grass and only one or two of the Natives with them we went past ye boat a little way but within call to a small sand flatt in hopes to find some clams while we were digging for these shell fish a young Black man Markus Lopeus, a native of the Cape de Verd Islands and who has shipped Captain Grays servant at St. Jago's being employed careing grass down to the boat, had carelessely stuck his cutlass in the sand one of the natives seeing this took a favorable opportunity to snatch it at first unobserved and run off with it one of the people observing him before he was quite out of sight called vehemently threatening to shoot him in hope he would abandon the stoln goods and make his escape but had given posative orders to our people not to fier but in case of the most absolute im-

*Haswell's limited education allowed him a bit of liberty with the king's English.

mergence when for self defence it might be necessary.

" 'Twas the hollowing of our people that first roused our attention and we immediately flew to know the cause, we were informed of the sercumstances adding that the Black Boy had followed him in spite of everything they could say to the contrary.

"I was struck by the daingerous situation the ladd was in and feared its concequences doubtings of there being a posability of saving him free from the impending danger but resolving no project shoud go untried without hesitation ordering the boat to keep abreast of us we ran toward the village we mett several chiefs persons whose friendship we had taken every opportunity to obtain by kinde youseage and liberal preasants, In deed it seemed before this period we had fully effected it, to these people Mr. Coolidge offered several articles to them of great value to bring back the man unhurt, this they refused intimating there wish for us to seek him ourselves, I now remarked to Mr. Coolidge that all the natives we saw were unusually well armed having with them there bows arrows & spears however we proceeded still further and turning a clump of trees that obstructed our prospect the first thing which presented itself to our view was a very large group of natives among the midst of which was the poor black with the thief, when we were observed by the main boddy of the Natives to hastily approach them they instantly drenced there knives and spears with savage fury in to the body of the unfortunate youth. He quited his hold and stumbled but rose again and stagered towards us but having a flight of arrows thrown into his back and he fell within fifteen yards of me and instantly expired while they mangled his lifeless corpse.

"We were now by our passing a number whom as I remembered before we supposed to be our friends situated between two formidable parties those we had passed being reinforsed by a great number from the woods they gave us the first salutation by a shower of arrows. Our only method was to go get to the boat as fast as possible for this purpus we turned leaving the dead body for it would have been the highth of imprudence as our Number was so small to have attempted its rescue we made the best of our way for the Boat assaulted on all sides by showers of arrows and spears and at length it became absolutely necesery to shoot there most dairing ringleaders which I did with my pistol Mr. Coolidge and one man who was with us followed my example and Mr. Coolidge ordered those who were in the boat to fier and cover us as we waided off for the boat could not come within a considerable dis't of the shore. But undaunted by the fate of there Companions, they followed us up to the middle in the water and slightly wounded both Mr. Coolidge and myself in the hand and totaley disabled the person who was with us onshore who fainting with the loss of blud lay lifeless for several hours and continued to bleed a torrant till the barb of the arrow was extracted, we jumped into the boat and pushed off and were soon out of arrow shot when we found this they launched there Canoes intending to cut us off indeed they were well situated for it but some werre timid some were bold and not half paddled but keeping a constant fier from the boat they came bairly within arrow shot at them and in a few moments not one Canoe was to be seen all having fledd, duering the whole of the night it was dismal to hear the hoops and houlings of the natives they had fiers on the beach near the spot where the ladd was killed and we could see great numbers of them passing to and fro before the blaze.

"I must confess I should not have lett them enjoy there festervile so peaseabley had I been Cap Gray but his humanity was commendable.

"Murderers Harbour, for so it was named, is I suppose the enterence of the river of the West it is by no means a safe place for aney but a very small vessell to enter the shoal at its enterence being so aucwardly situated the passage so narrow and the tide so rapid that it is scarce posable to avoid the dangers. It is probably whenever a vessell goes there they may procure twenty or thurty good sea otter skins. We know but little of the manours and customs of these people our stay among them was cut short, the men ware no cloathing but the skins of animals well dressed, the women wore nothing but a petticoat of straw about as long as a highlanders kilt, there hutts were very small made of boards and a matt on the flore they appeared to be very indolent and were intolerably filthey there canoes were very well shaped for paddling and every housefull purpus there language we attained no knowledge of and I am of opinion it was very Hard to lern.

"I am posative it was a planed affair, which first gave rise to our quarrel seeing how fue we were they had hopes of overpowering us and making themselves masters of our cloths and arms and had we been taken it would have been no difficult jobb three people left onboard. It was folley for us to go onshore so ill armed but it proved a sufficient warning to us to allways be well armed ever afterwards.

"Indeed I think it prudent no boat should land among the midst of such numerous tribes without another well armed boat to protect her landing."

From the preceding account, of much historical value, we learn, first that Haswell believed that Tillamook or Murderers Harbor was the fabled River of the West; that the actions of the Indians gave evidence of contact with white man long before Gray's "official" discovery, and that the Indians were familiar with the value of metal implements.

Before entering Tillamook Bay, Gray had raised Cape Mendocino on the northern California coast (August 2, 1788) where he was greeted by friendly Indians in deerskins who paddled out in a canoe to greet the 90 ton sloop. An uneasy anchorage, however, prompted an early departure. Another indenture in the Oregon coastline which the log recorded in latitude 44 degrees, the ''entrance to a large river,'' may have been Coos Bay or Siuslaw River.

Though there remained yet four years before Gray would discover both Grays Harbor and the deceptive Columbia River, his unfortunate experience on Tillamook Bay kept him from making any outward mention of that historical Oregon visit, for undoubtedly he, unlike his first officer Haswell, was not totally convinced that it was indeed the fabled River of the West, nor did he believe it to be of any great value as a trading mecca.

Flag at half-mast, *Lady Washington* sailed away from Murderers Harbor, her crew saddened by the three day experience. Intent on finding new bar entrances from which to seek additional pelts, they hugged the coastline, sailing northward past the latitude of the elusive Columbia.

Gray, a native of Rhode Island, was a descendant of Plymouth colonists and had served in the Revolution. Not until after leaving the Northwest Coast did he take to himself a wife. After his long adventure, he perhaps repined of bachelor life, his wife bearing him five children.

There was a reunion at last as the *Columbia* and *Lady Washington* fell in company with each other, the former having just departed Nootka Sound bound for China. In the interim, Gray had explored the entire east coast of the Queen Charlotte Islands, (June 1789) visiting places where the natives had never before seen Caucasians. For some reason, which the history books have never explained, Gray and Kendrick, after their rendezvous, decided that they would change commands, Gray taking the larger 230 ton *Columbia* with its valuable cargo of furs to the Orient while Kendrick, in the *Lady Washington,* remained on the Northwest Coast seeking more pelts.

Gray took his new command to Canton, sold the cargo on a slightly overstocked market and in turn loaded tea for Boston. Sailing via Cape of Good Hope, he was to become the first American navigator to circumnavigate the globe. His accomplishment was heralded on his return to Bean Town, thousands swarming the waterfront to welcome the Yankee maritime hero. With him, Gray brought from the Sandwich Islands a young Hawaiian chief named Attoo, who got as much attention as the captain, inasmuch as Bostonians had never before seen a man of his race.

John Kendrick was also an outstanding seafarer and navigator, but unlike his counterpart, was never in the right place at the right time to gain international recognition for his accomplishments. When he was given command of the 1788 expedition he was considered the best

qualified man. At 45, he was married with a family including six children. During the Revolution he commanded a privateer with great success.

Though the initial fur trading enterprise had not lived up to expectations from the monetary standpoint, and though some of its promoters wanted to withdraw on the return of Kendrick, it was finally decided to send the *Columbia* out on another fur trading voyage in conjunction with a fleet of smaller vessels.

Departing Boston ahead of the *Columbia* was the brig *Hope,* commanded by Joseph Ingraham. Almost simultaneously, the brigs *Hancock* and *Jefferson* sailed from Boston for the Northwest Coast as did the *Margaret* from New York. En route, Ingraham, former officer on the *Columbia,* discovered a myriad of small islands just north of the Marquesas group, which he fittingly named Washington, Adams, Franklin, Knox and Lincoln.

Gray followed after the fur trading vessels on what was to become the most celebrated voyage of discovery in American maritime annals. Departing Boston on Sept. 28, 1790, he reached Clayoquot Sound on June 5 of the following year. For the remainder of the season the ship hugged the Northwest shores darting in and out of inlets and islets in search of furs. Entering an inlet and sailing more than 100 miles within, from latitude 54° 30′ to latitude 56°, Gray did not find its termination. For a time he reasoned it to be the River of the Kings, told of in Fonte's narrative. Running into trouble with hostile natives who attacked his landing party killing one of his officers and wounding two seamen, he returned to the ocean and fell in with the *Hope,* which had already acquired a cargo of furs and was Canton-bound.

Gray then returned to Clayoquot Harbor for the winter, his crew building a little post which was named Fort Defiance. There, they were kept busy building a small schooner named *Adventure.* Designed for coastal trading, she was truly a Northwest project with all materials coming from local sources. The blacksmith made sharp little instruments from scraps of iron as trading articles to barter with the natives for their best pelts.

Gray, a mild-mannered, modest man of great character, was a descendant of the Pilgrims. He never neglected his missionary duties and each Sabbath held services, usually aboard ship, to which the local Indians were invited and encouraged to attend. He treated their sick from the ship's medicine chest and shared eatables.

The natives, however, did not reciprocate in kind, a conspiracy being uncovered in which the fort was to be captured and all killed within. It was reputedly the warriors of that same tribe that two decades later were to annihilate the entire company of Astor's ship *Tonquin.*

To gain their goal of conquering Fort Defiance, the chiefs had attempted to bribe the Sandwich Islander, Attoo, into betraying Captain Gray, offering in turn to make him an Indian chief. Had the Hawaiian accepted, he might have been the only man in history to have served as a dual chief among both Hawaiians and Indians. His assignment was to wet the priming mechanisms on the fort's guns so they could not be fired when the attack was made. At first, Attoo was tempted, but then repented, confessing all to Gray. Without his assistance, the natives lost their ace-in-the-hole, and junked their nefarious plot.

Gray and Kendrick were never to meet again after switching commands. The *Lady Washington,* converted to a brig, sought in the Pacific Isles a cargo of sandalwood after rounding Vancouver Island without gaining many furs. Before leaving the Northwest coast, Kendrick had legally purchased tracts of land from tribal chiefs at Nootka which he hoped to sell in Europe. After a voyage to the Orient, he met an untimely death in 1793 at Karakakooa (Kealekekua) Bay, Hawaii when grapeshot fired from a saluting British vessel accidently struck and killed him.

Almost 300 years had passed since Columbus discovered the Western continent and then in the year 1792 a great event took place with the discovery of the Columbia River. The mystery that had kept early explorers from finding the legendary River of the West for two centuries after Juan de Fuca's discovery was almost unbelievable.

Captain Robert Gray, commanding the *Columbia Rediviva* had his mind more on securing beaver skins than discovering great rivers and harbors, but his uncanny sixth sense led him to discoveries that made the probing explorers blush with envy. Always on the lookout for safe anchorages and good trading areas, he was to discover Grays Harbor and the Columbia River within a few days of each other.

On the morning of May 7, the harbor now bearing his name was sighted from a distance of six miles, and, according to the journal, did not have an inviting appearance. Drawing closer, "the jolly boat was lowered away and sent off to look for an anchorage, the ship standing to and fro, with a very strong weather current."

Though the boat was gone for several hours she was unable to locate a safe place to drop anchor. But Gray, never deterred by negative findings, was determined.

Returning to the ship's journal:

"Sail was made and the ship stood boldly in for the shore. We saw from our masthead a passage in northeast by east having from four to eight fathoms, sandy bottom, and as we drew in nearer between the bars, had from ten to 13 fathoms, having a very strong tide of ebb to stem. Many canoes alongside. At 5 p.m. came to in water sheltered from the sea by long sand bars and spits. Our latitude observed this day was 46° 58′ north."

For three days the ship remained at anchor, and trading with the Indians was rewarding. Many canoes continued to come alongside and though pelts always held priority, something drove Gray on to find the great River of the West, which he was certain existed not far south of his position. Leaving behind many valuable furs, he again assumed the role of explorer and in his own words sought "our desired port." Already Gray had made maritime history, but what was about to happen would soon eclipse all of his other accomplishments.

On the morning of May 11, 1792, at the break of dawn, an extensive discoloration was noted in the ocean, suggesting the outflow from some mighty river. There was excitement aboard, all hands eagerly scanning the shoreline. Shortly after, according to the journal, "we saw the entrance of our desired port, bearing east southeast, distance six leagues."

It was no mirage, no illusion, not this time. The same shrouded opening that had eluded the eye of Heceta on August 15, 1775, the attention of Captain John Meares July 5, 1788, the crafty abilities of Captain George Vancouver, just two weeks earlier, was now in telescope view. Gray had done it again, and was favored by no better weather conditions than experienced by the many explorers before him. The wind was veering between west and northwest, and the breakers were relentless white fury.

Gray had a profound trust in God, and this coupled with daring, zeal and just plain intestinal fortitude rendered him a leader without rival. He was not to be denied. Standing into potential danger he faced the possible loss of his ship, a fate that was to befall many vessels negotiating the Columbia River bar after his time.

As recorded in the ship's journal: "At 8 a.m. being a little windward of the entrance of the harbor, bore away, and ran in east northeast, between the breakers, having from five to seven fathoms of water. When we were over the bar we found this to be a large river of fresh water, up which we steered. Many canoes came alongside. At 1 p.m. came to with the small bower, in two fathoms, black and white sand. The entrance between the bars bore west-southwest, distant ten miles. The north side of the river a half mile distance; a village on the north side of the river west by north, distant three quarters of a mile. Vast numbers of natives came alongside. People employed in pumping the salt water out of our water casks, in order to fill with fresh, while the ship floated in. So ends."

That brief entry told little of the anticipation and the thrill of crossing the bar. Nor did it tell of the fears of possible stranding or of falling into the hands of hostile natives bent on plunder.

The journal's final entry for that momentous day, "So ends," seems trivial, but not so. Gray and his crew of "Bostons" had accepted the challenge and had won the sweet fruits by seeking and finding. The Columbia River had at last been discovered and unlike his Grays Harbor find, Captain Gray was in no hurry to leave. This was that "desired port," of which he had spoken. The first two days were spent hosting and trading with excited Indians who by the score surrounded the tall ship.

On the 14th day of May, adverse weather, blowing a fresh gale, prompted Gray to up anchor and put on canvas, "stand up the river northeast" where the channel proved narrow. By "4 p.m.," according to the ship's journal, "we sailed upwards of 12 or 15 miles when the channel was so very narrow that it was almost impossible to keep in it, having from three to eighteen fathoms of water, sandy bottom. At half past 4 the ship went aground, but did not stay long and was easily got off. We backed off, stern foremost, into three fathoms, and let go the small bower, and moored ship with kedge and hawser."

The jolly boat was then sent out to sound the channel, with negative results, it being reasoned they had taken the wrong passage. Had they gone up the other side of the river, the channel would have been adequate for further penetration but instead it was decided to go back downstream where good anchorage was available.

On May 16, the crew laboring at the oars of the ship's boat pulled the *Columbia* further downstream where soundings were taken. That afternoon "being very squally we came about two miles from the village Chinouk (Chinook) with many natives alongside," stated the vessel's log.

The next days were spent painting the ship, caulking the pinnace and making other repairs; all the while trading with the Indians continued. Later, Gray officially named the river for both his ship and the nation; the two prominent features at the river entrance were labeled Point Adams and Cape Hancock, the latter for the old Boston governor who accorded him a boisterous welcome when he completed his circumnavigation of the globe. Cape Hancock, in later years was renamed Cape Disappointment to denote the frustrating experiences of the earlier Spaniards, who sighted the headland but failed to see the entrance to the river.

On May 20, after ten days in the estuary, the weather was pleasant and light spring breezes afforded desirable conditions for putting back to sea. On the full tide at 1 p.m., anchor was weighed and sail set. Within an hour, as the vessel negotiated the tricky bar, the wind suddenly died. Grave danger faced the crew as the *Columbia* drifted into the breakers toward menacing shoals.

The log entry showed the first officer's concern:

"Without a breeze to shoot her across the tide, we were obliged to bring up in three and one-half fathoms of water, the tide running five knots."

Again within the hour, good fortune smiled on Captain Gray for before the grasping spit snared the ship, a fresh breeze sprang up, sail was made and the vessel crossed over the bar.

"At 5 p.m.," continued the log, "we were out, clear of all bars, and in twenty fathoms of water. A breeze came from the southward; we bore away to the northward, set all sail to the best advantage. At 8, Cape Hancock bore southeast, distant three leagues; the north extremity of the land bore north by west."

Just how long the Columbia River would have remained closed to commerce had not Gray made his discovery will be left to speculation, but the fact that one of the most exact of explorers, Captain George Vancouver, had made an open statement that no opening, harbor or place of refuge for vessels, was to be found between Cape Mendocino and the Strait of Juan de Fuca, and that the coast, "formed one compact, solid and nearly straight barrier against the sea," may have long thwarted others in the search.

Before leaving the coast, Gray told Vancouver of having lain in what appeared the mouth of a great river in latitude 46° 10′, but the Britisher was at first skeptical of the claim. The subsequent survey of the river made by the English, though accurate, was partially an attempt to water down the accomplishments of Gray. But try as they did, it was the Yankee who was the man of the hour.

Some weeks after the great discovery, Gray's ship struck a rock on the east coast of the Queen Charlotte Islands, narrowly escaping foundering before Nootka could be reached for repairs. Again, Gray's good fortune had surfaced. On departing the latter portal for Canton, he was never again to return to the scene of his greatest triumph. Passing away at Charleston, S.C. in 1806, he left a wife Martha and four daughters nearly destitute, his Boston estate valued at a mere $214.13.

Before departing the Northwest coast, Gray had conveyed to Captain Ingraham of the *Hope*, and to Quadra, the Spanish commandant, details of his discovery of the Columbia River and its bar. He also gave the Spaniard charts and descriptions, of Grays Harbor, (which he had named Bulfinch Harbor) and of the mouth of the Columbia. This was fortunate, for it was through those men that the world first came to know of Gray's accomplishment. He himself, made no general announcement of his discoveries. Always in the modest role, he tended to underestimate the value of his findings.

At the time, Spain and England were on the verge of war, but during negotiations in the Northwest for a peaceful settlement, Quadra showed Vancouver the charts and details of Gray's discovery. When Vancouver sailed south to Monterey he left Lt. William Robert Broughton, master of the HMS *Chatham*, to make an active survey of the Columbia River for 100 miles upsteam. The highly qualified chart maker found the Columbia River, near the sea, to be about seven miles in width with a depth varying from two to eight fathoms, crossed by shoals which made navigation difficult. He chose to call that arm of the sea inside the river, Gray's Bay, and then moving several miles upsteam gave the

British a piece of the glory by insisting it to be the official mouth of the river, actually 25 miles from the ocean, where the width was hardly 1,000 feet.

England hardly manifested itself in the eyes of the world when Broughton formally took possession of the river and the surrounding area in the name of His Britannic Majesty—seemingly an unjust claim in the light of Gray's discovery and of his willingness to share his good fortune with others. The British were probably more concerned about flexing muscle in their differences with Spain, and it must be further born in mind that relations between the United States and England were still strained in the wake of the Revolution.

On entering the Columbia River, Gray had carried a letter signed by the President of the United States, George Washington. It read:

"To all Emperors, Kings, Sovereign Princes, State and Regents and to Their Respective Officers, Civil and Military, and to all Others Whom It May Concern:

"I George Washington, President of the United States of America, do make known that Robert Gray, Captain of a ship called the *Columbia,* of the burden of about 230 tons, is a citizen of the United States, and as I wish that the said Robert Gray may prosper in his lawful affairs, I do request all the before mentioned, and of each of them separately, when the said Robert Gray shall arrive with his vessel and cargo, that they will be pleased to receive him with kindness and treat him in a becoming manner, etc., and thereby I shall consider myself obliged.

"September 16, 1790, New York City.
George Washington
President
Thomas Jefferson, Secretary of State..."

There was a strange reception for the *Columbia* on her epic arrival inside the Columbia River, if one could term it as such. The appearance of the ship was greeted with fear and trembling on behalf of many of the Indians who had never seen such a great "winged canoe." A well-manned boat was sent ashore to a nearby village and all of its inhabitants fled in panic, except the aged and infirm. The kindly treatment by the strangers and the presents given the aged induced the others to return.

Many of the superstitious Indians reasoned the *Columbia* to be a great floating island, and the landing party cannibals sent by the Great Spirit to ravage the land. Word of the event spread by "moccasin telegraph" to the surrounding tribes, the excitement reaching a fever

pitch. Perhaps the most eager to trade was the popular Clatsop Chief Comcomly residing on the south side of the river's mouth.

Never again would the place be the same, and little did the natives know that their traditional life style would soon change. In quick succession came the British vessel *Jenny* of Bristol (1792) followed two and a half years later by the ship *Ruby* in command of Captain Charles Bishop, who wintered on the river. Then came scores of vessels of many flags opening up a flourishing new era of maritime commerce and settlement in the far west.

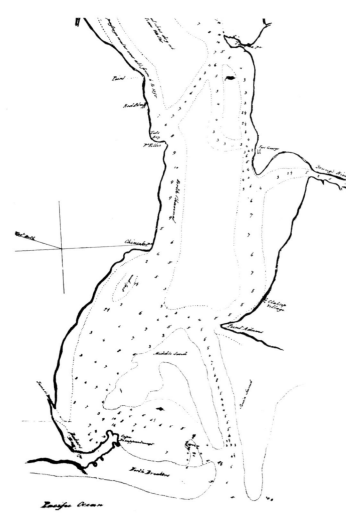

Warre and Vavasour chart of the entrance to the Columbia River. Details were made up from a private Hudson's Bay Co. chart used by masters of ships frequenting the bar in the 1830's and 1840's. Courtesy Public Records Office, London.

CHAPTER FOUR
EARLY ASTORIA AND ENVIRONS

It stands to reason the first settlement on the Oregon Coast, other than Indian, should have been at the mouth of the Columbia River.* Oregon's initial colony was Astoria, pawn of John Jacob Astor, a New York industrialist who sent out an adventurous party by sea and another by land to locate a place suitable for a fur trading post. The ambitious mission was accomplished in 1811.

There had been a few trappers ahead of Astor's expedition collecting pelts at scattered Northwest sites, but it took a sufficient financial outlay to establish a trading post.

Another promising expedition, just ahead of Astor's men, met with ill-fortune. The ship, *Albatross,* commanded by Captain Nathan Winship, set out from Boston in the summer of 1809, and with his brothers Abiel and Jonathan, he also planned to set up a colony on the Columbia River for fur trading purposes. With a crew of 21 men, the vessel arrived off the Columbia May 26, 1810. After successfully crossing the bar, the party sailed 40 miles upriver to a place they named Oak Point. Desiring good relations with the Indians, the Winship brothers legally purchased a parcel of land and began building a post and cultivating ground. Come late spring, however, the river ran wild, overflowing its banks and inundating their lands. Except for that act of nature, the Winship settlement could well have diminished the importance of Astoria.

Dismantling their post, the Winship party moved downriver to a more desirable location, which infuriated the Indians. To avoid a confrontation, the *Albatross* sailed for California to let the situation cool before trying again the following year. On their return, they were both surprised and disappointed to find Astor's Pacific Fur Co. contingent well entrenched at Astoria.

Astor, who had picked the brains of factors in the Hudson's Bay Co. while traveling by ship from his native Germany to New York, decided to launch out in the fur trading business while only 20 years of age. Establishing a flourishing business in eastern Canada by friendly relations with the Indians, he desired to test the riches of the far west. Accordingly, he dispatched the well-found 290-ton ship *Tonquin,* commanded by a rock-hard disciplinarian, Jonathan Thorn, to sail to the Northwest coast with a crew of 20. Departing New York in the fall of 1810, the vessel reached the latitude of the Columbia River March 22, 1811.

During the trying voyage, near mutiny was averted, the former naval skipper having driven his informal party of men—seamen, clerks, trappers and voyageurs—to borderline insubordination. There was hardly a man aboard who would not gladly have thrown him to the sharks. An excellent navigator and wise in the ways of the sea, Thorn lacked both tact and manners, holding to a "Bligh" image of driving men and taunting them till their blood grew hot for revenge.

Standing off the river entrance, under highly unfavorable conditions for bar crossing, Thorn issued an order which should have placed him before a board of inquiry for conduct unbecoming to a shipmaster. So

*Lewis and Clark constructed Fort Clatsop in 1805 but left it to the Indians on
their departure. A replica was constructed in 1955 near Lewis and Clark River.

John Jacob Astor, fur baron of New York, organized the Pacific Fur Co. in 1810, and sent one party by sea and another by land to the mouth of the Columbia River, where Astoria was founded in 1811.

anxious was he to gain his destination, that he sent his first officer Ebenezer D. Fox, seaman John Martin and some of the voyageurs out in the ship's boat to seek a channel deep enough for the *Tonquin's* crossing. When Fox made strong protests the captain defiantly warned him of insubordination and the loss of his papers. Into the seething billows the whaleboat was cast off.

When dawn arrived the next day, the boat was nowhere in sight, so Thorn, true to form, ordered a second boat out manned by Alexander McKay and David Stuart. It returned several hours later with nothing to report.

Showing little remorse for his hasty actions, the shipmaster then ordered second officer John Mumford and a handful of others out to sound the channel, this too proving useless. The first boat never did return, its seven occupants swallowed up by the bar breakers. Then the pinnace was manned, it too narrowly escaping foundering in rough seas. Before it could get back to the *Tonquin,* another life had been claimed. Outdoing the cruelty of Bligh, the infamous Captain Thorn now had the blood of eight needlessly sacrificed men on his hands.

Despite the tragic loss of life, that determined tyrant proved his navigation prowess, for without chart or pilot he got his command across the bar under the most unfavorable conditions. Though happy to be in sheltered waters, the crew had hatred seething in their hearts bemoaning the loss of their shipmates.

Anchoring between Tongue Point and Point George,

the party landed and settled on a spot at the south side of the river mouth which was to become the Astoria settlement. In the interim, a wide search was made for the bodies of the missing, but to no avail.

Aboard the *Tonquin* was a variety of cargo including the frame for a 30-ton schooner which was to be the means of water transport for the colony. The vessel was assembled on the beach and was christened *Dolly,* to honor Astor's wife.

Tall timber was felled, land cleared, a stockade erected encompassing a storehouse, barracks and other structures. With the fury of activities, curious, but friendly Indians milled about, eager to trade. All the while, Thorn's infernal impatience persisted, he being anxious to get all the cargo offloaded, the official details concluded and the anchor weighed for a trading junket to Vancouver Island for beaver and sea otter skins. "Impatience dries the blood sooner than age or sorrow," Chapin once wrote. And certainly his words of wisdom proved true in the case of Captain Thorn. On the subsequent voyage to the west coast of Vancouver Island his impatience and poor judgement led to the demise of his ship and all hands, with the exception of one Indian interpreter who had been taken aboard when the vessel was delayed by headwinds in Baker's Bay.

While the *Tonquin* was trading with the natives, in Clayoquot Sound, Thorn exerted undue authority treating them in an obnoxious manner even to the point of having a chief thrown overboard. The Indians, seething at such treatment, returned disguised as peaceful traders though heavily armed beneath their tunics. Once aboard ship, a bloody assault erupted resulting in the massacre of all but five of the ship's company of 23, including Thorn. Four tried to escape in the ship's boat but were overtaken by the war canoes and promptly murdered. One badly wounded crew member remained on the ship until the savages returned for plunder. As they swarmed aboard he touched off the powder magazine blowing the *Tonquin* sky high, taking his own life and the lives of at least 100 natives.

Only Lamazee, the Indian interpreter, who because of his race had been allowed to escape during the initial attack, was left to reveal the grisly details after making his way back to the Astoria post.

At the time of the tragedy, another Astor supply ship had been dispatched from New York. The *Beaver,* commanded by Captain Sowles, arrived off the Columbia in May of 1812, but her skipper was not sure that he had the right location, firing several rounds from the signal cannon, off the bar, to arouse the attention of the colonists. This went on for two days, Duncan McDougall and Donald McLellan finally going via Indian canoe across the river to Cape Disappointment to hang rags on trees and kindle bonfires as navigation aids.

Clatsop Chief Comcomly and six of his braves went out to meet the *Beaver,* and Captain Sowles, encouraged by favorable bar conditions made sail and crossed safely, later coming to anchor off the little settlement. The arrival gave new hope and assurance to the hard-pressed post. post.

Later that year, fears of an invasion by the warlike northern Indians was voiced both by the local natives and the colonists. The Neweetee Indians of Vancouver Island, believed to be part of the tribe that massacred the *Tonquin's* crew, had sailed their great war canoes southward to seek salmon off the Columbia River. In prior years, such warriors had been the bane of the more peaceful Northwest tribes, striking like the Vikings, raiding, pillaging and carrying off slaves. Accordingly, the guard was doubled at the feeble little post in the eventuality that the savages might lay seige to the settlement. Uneasiness continued for a short period, but after the Neweetees caught their bonanza of fish and had refreshed themselves, they paddled back home with no effort toward conquest.

Astorians had not been apprised of the War of 1812, in fact, it was not till the arrival of Donald McKenzie, a Pacific Fur partner in January 1813 that they learned the news. He had heard of it through John G. McTavish, a North West Co. partner, at Spokane House, during his overland trek. McTavish had been sent as a representative of his outfit to present an offer for the purchase of the Astor colony. When he reached the fort in April, he carried a letter from his uncle, an agent for North West Co. at Montreal which revealed the ship *Isaac Todd,* out of England, accompanied by a frigate of war, would lay claim to everything under the American flag on the Northwest coast. McDougall, then in charge of the post was additionally disturbed because the *Beaver* had not yet returned to the fort from her trading voyage.

A parley was held between McDougall and McKenzie and it was decided that due to the war, and the fact that Astor would be unable to send more ships with supplies or to export pelts, the establishment should be abandoned and sold by early fall. The Pacific Fur partners accordingly made plans for their departure, and McTavish in turn legally purchased the holdings and merchandise connected with the colony.

All details having been attended to, it was a chagrined Captain W. Black, master of His Majesty's sloop of war *Raccoon* that arrived off the river in late November 1813. Unable to cross the bar until December 12, due to its irascible condition, his frustrations were to be further extended when he learned that he was to be denied a great naval victory by cannonading the Astoria fortress to the ground with his ship's guns. He was to learn to his bitter disappointment that the post had been sold to subjects of the Crown. Expecting a formidable fortress, Black, after eying the settlement exclaimed:

"What! Is this the fort I have heard so much of? Great God! I could batter it down with a four-pounder in two hours!"

And certainly his boast was no exaggeration for more likely its destruction might have been completed in half the time. Fortunately the unorthodox trading post and fortress never had to defend itself from either the hostility of the Indians or from British guns.

Using undue pomp and protocol, Black officiated at a ceremony utilizing a bottle of wine to christen the establishment and to raise the flag of England. His booming voice echoed across the lower Columbia as he officially announced it as a posession of His Britannic Majesty. The name was henceforth changed to Fort George, honoring King George III. McTavish became the new governor, and the North West Co. assumed full control.

Chief Comcomly who had observed the ceremonies, was totally confused. By his reasoning, the Astorians had become the slaves of the British overlords and the "war canoe" *Raccoon* would carry them off to a life of servitude. Quite the contrary. Most of the Americans remained behind and were placed in the employ of the new owners.

In the interim, a heated dispute erupted between Astoria factor William P. Hunt who had come to the post overland, and McDougall, who then under the North West Co. had become second in command at Fort George. Hunt was indignant over the sale of the post and its furs, claiming it to have been premature. He thus made an attempt to repurchase it, but his best efforts accomplished nothing. He finally collected the Pacific Fur papers and departed Astoria April 3, 1814 aboard the *Pedlar.*

Under the new ownership, the business did well, due much to the crafty trading abilities of Tom McKay, son of Alexander McKay, the latter a victim of the *Tonquin* tragedy. The Indians were so impressed by his charisma, humor and cunning that he in their eyes could do no wrong.

Though the post was under British control, a large share of its employees continued to be Americans. When the Treaty of Ghent was signed on December 24, 1814 providing that all territory and possessions taken by either England or America during the War of 1812 be returned, Astoria eventually came back under the Stars and Stripes. Following a ceremony at the post in 1818, in essence, Astor interests again became owner of the holdings. Not wishing to buck the powerful and successful North West Co., and due to earlier financial losses, the post was slowly phased out and eventually abandoned.

Then in 1821 the place took on a new significance. The Hudson's Bay Co. had combined with the North West Co., creating a trading dynasty. Company factor Dr. John McLoughlin arrived at Fort George in 1824, acquired rights to the post and set up a little kingdom

Astoria, an early drawing probably made soon after the post was established in 1811. Note little schooner *Dolly*, center right, assembled at the settlement after her components were brought by the ship *Tonquin* around the Horn.

over which he was a powerful influential baron. His major interest did not lie in the decaying remains of Astoria but 100 miles up the Columbia, where he established Fort Vancouver, a center that minimized the role of the post at the mouth of the river.

One of McLoughlin's men, James Birnie, was left to restore Fort George, which became a subsidiary to Fort Vancouver. As the activity and importance of the new post grew, the other served mostly as a lookout station and port of entry for incoming and outgoing ships.

Hudson's Bay Co., an enterprise which is still a factor in the economics of Canada and to some extent the world, fared far better in the Northwest fur trade than did its predecessors. Early Astoria continued to play second fiddle to Fort Vancouver, but remained alive as the terminus of all Hudson's Bay ships and other vessels coming to the Columbia.

Make no mistake about it, entering the Columbia River in those early times was no occupation for the novice. Many a brave mariner was to become victim of such dreaded marine graveyards as Clatsop Spit, Peacock Spit, Sand Island and Desdemona Sands.

Ironically, the Hudson's Bay Co. used no "official" pilots per se, and for the most part, no charts of the tricky entrance. Masters of company ships studied the north channel well and always used it when crossing in or out. However, there was one employee of the fur company, Alexander Lattie, who frequently acted as pilot for first-time arrival vessels.

In his *History of Oregon* (San Francisco 1886-88) Bancroft claims there was a company chart of the Columbia bar but that it was kept secret from others. British Army officers Henry J. Warre and Mervin Vavasour in 1845-46 used and credited it on their maps of the river, documents still in the public record office in London.

Lattie, a Scotsman, who joined Hudson's Bay as a seaman, arrived at Fort Vancouver in the summer of 1831 aboard the ship *Granymede*. During the next decade and

a half, despite his sometimes erratic behavior, he worked up to first officer and was considered the most knowledgeable pilot for the Columbia River bar in the 1830's and 1840's. In that era, Hudson's Bay expanded its coastal trading as far north as Russian Alaska and south to California and the Hawaiian Islands. Lattie was to see maverick Yankee fur trading ships reaping a bonanza in sea otter skins under the nose of the British. More Americans continued to pour in to the new frontier.

Lattie in 1845 became Hudson's Bay clerk at Fort George, but continued his piloting duties. Though never having been designated as an official bar pilot he was the closest thing to it, superior to Indian George, (a native pilot) till the Provisional Government's Board of Commissioners on Pilots and Pilotage selected Selah C. Reeve to act as "Bar Pilot" in the spring of 1847.

In the interim, the Columbia River bar established a fearful reputation. It was not a place for foolhardy navigation. Shifting sandbars were a constant concern, the channel depths often changing without notice.

Great concern was expressed in 1849, when a heavyweight of the U.S. Navy, a screw steamer arrived off the river. At that date she was the mightiest ship to attempt the bar crossing. The USS *Massachusetts* of 750 tons carried 161 officers and men of the 1st Artillery, one of the first contingents of American troops sent to Oregon. Coming from New York via Valparaiso and the Hawaiian Islands, her presence caused great excitement.

Astorians breathed a sign of relief as did the men on the *Massachusetts* when she was safe inside the river. While settlers lined the river banks to witness the advent of the smoke-puffing warship she got aground on a sandbar off Tongue Point and held fast. The Reverend Samuel C. Damon, (editor of the *Honolulu Friend*) a passenger aboard the ship, eulogized the pilot Lattie as "well acquainted with the navigation of the Columbia. His services were immediately secured for the *Massachusetts,* as otherwise we might have been detained for many days."

The warship was freed with the change of tide under Lattie's guidance and though she hit another sand obstruction, her revolutionary "Ericcson's propeller" provided the incentive to get her afloat and on her way to Fort Vancouver.

Just a few weeks after the *Massachusetts'* arrival, the second largest vessel to enter the Columbia, the 641 ton *Sylvie de Grasse,* became a calamity. In July of 1849 after taking on a cargo of lumber she stuck fast on a sandbar near the place the warship had stranded, hanging there like a barnacle. The cargo suddenly shifted causing a dangerous list. Despite frantic efforts to save the vessel she had to be left to die a slow, tormenting death, just east of present day Astoria.

There was another pioneer who claimed to be a Columbia River bar pilot. His name was James D. Sauls, a black man who had been a member of the crew of U.S. Navy's *Peacock* which was wrecked on the infamous Peacock Spit on July 18, 1841. According to Charles Wilkes' *Narrative of the United States Exploring Expedition,* James D. Sauls, ship's cook, had joined the vessel at Callao and deserted after arrival at Astoria. In 1844 he was charged with threatening to incite the Indians and was asked to leave Oregon City. He went to Clatsop County, and was hired by Wheeler and McDaniel to hold their Cape Disappointment claim. The *Oregon Spectator* of Dec. 24, 1846 told of his having been charged with causing the death of his Indian wife but that nothing had been done to punish him.

His erratic and limited role as a river bar pilot occurred in 1846:

Lt. Neil Howison, master* of the USS *Shark* told of three men in a boat coming to meet his vessel at the river entrance. Greeting the 198 ton war schooner were W. H. Gray, H. H. Spalding and A. L. Lovejoy. He learned from them that there were no regular bar pilots, "but that there was a black man on shore who had been living many years at the cape, was a sailor and said, if sent for he would come and pilot the *Shark* to Astoria."

Howison continued:

"He was accordingly brought on board, and spoke confidently of his knowledge of the channel; said he had followed the sea twenty years; and had been living here for the last six. He ordered the helm put up, head sheets aft, and yards braced. With an air that deceived me into the belief that he was fully competent...In 20 minutes he ran us hard ashore on Chinook shoal, where we remained several hours thumping severely. We got off about 10 p.m., without having suffered any material damage, and anchored in the channel. At daylight I was pleased to find Mr. Lattee, (Lattie) formerly mate of a ship belonging to the Hudson's Bay Co., and now in charge of the port of Astoria, on board.

"Upon the vessel's grounding, the gentlemen visitors, feeling themselves somewhat responsible for the employment of this pretended pilot, immediately put off to Astoria, a distance of ten miles, to procure the services of Lattee, who promptly complied with the request...."

Lattie got the *Shark* safely across the bar. When farther upriver, Howison employed Indian George to act

*Lt. Howison, aboard the *Shark*, was in charge of the U.S. Surveying expedition. The *Shark* was skippered by Captain Schenck.

Astoria about 1846. This is the way the trading post appeared near the close of the Hudson's Bay control.

as pilot.

Had Howison known that Sauls was a deserter from the USS *Peacock* he probably would have pitched him overboard on the spot.

Lattie's somewhat checkered career was perhaps due to a bad drinking problem. While serving as mate aboard Hudson's Bay ship *Columbia* he was discharged at Honolulu by the ship's captain in March of 1842 for "undesirable conduct while under the influence of liquor." On another occasion in 1845, Captain Humphreys, master of the steamer *Beaver* discharged him at Fort Simpson for "riotous and improper conduct."

Later he became first mate of the company vessel *Cadboro,* but because of his problem was never given a command of his own. His good deeds were often mixed with the bad. When Lattie sailed upriver on the HBC vessel *Harpooner* on July 5, 1849, he brought news of the arrival at Astoria of the Army storeship *Walpole* which had long been awaited at Fort Vancouver. The vessel had suffered serious keel damage in crossing the bar by striking a shoal. Lattie was not serving as her pilot. At almost the same time, the French ship *L'Etoile du Matin,* which had been unable to secure the services of Lattie had also struck on the bar suffering a badly damaged keel and the loss of her rudder. Fate intervened; the vessel drifted into Baker's Bay on July 11, where Lattie and a small band of Indians went out to offer assistance. A box rudder was installed and with the help from seamen of other vessels in the vicinity the waterlogged wreck was pumped dry and taken upriver to discharge her cargo at Portland.

Unfortunately, it was Lattie's weakness for liquor that was his undoing. Oregon moonshine, labeled "Blue Ruin," was present when Col. John McClure, stupid from its effects, thought he was at war and fired at Lattie thinking him the enemy. At first, Lattie thought the colonel's actions were in jest; that is until a charge nicked his arm and hip causing the blood to flow. Infuriated, he went after his attacker with a sword, striking him while the gun was being reloaded. Undoubtedly intoxicated himself, Lattie beat McClure insensible, knocking him down and pounding him till he was a bloody mess. The enraged pilot then dragged the prostrate colonel to a cliff and dumped him over onto the rocks below.

The lenient local court ruled Lattie's act as purely self defense. The Clatsop County court record of August 1846 stated that McClure, "feloniously, willfully and of his malice aforethought did make an assault with an intent to commit murder with a certain rifled gun made of iron and steel of the value of sixty dollars, charged with powder and leaden ball or balls which he the said John McClure in his hands then and there had and held him the said Latty (Lattie) in and upon the arm and the hip of him the said Latty then and there feloniously willfully and of his malice aforethought did shoot, discharge and pene-

trate giving unto the said Latty then and there with the rifled gun as aforesaid in and upon the arm and the hip of him the said Latty two wounds as aforesaid . . ."

The court made no mention of Lattie's disposal of the body over the cliff. No charges were brought against him and immediately he was back at work as marine agent and pilot in Astoria.

Liquor, the bane of many early Oregon maritime men played a part in Lattie's death. The Reverend G. H. Atkinson's diary of Sept. 10, 1849 revealed: "I heard yesterday of the death of Mr. Lattis, (Lattie) a pilot. He is said to have become intoxicated, was poling a canoe at Vancouver, suddenly came to deepwater, run his pole down & finding no bottom he pitched into the River (Columbia) & did not rise."

Lattie's wife's donation claim paper stated only that "Lattie drowned in the Columbia, near the mouth of the Willamette." The *Honolulu Friend* printed in its obituary column, "Drowned in the Columbia River, September 4, Mr. Lattie, Pilot."

More and more commerce was attracted to the Columbia River in the mid 1800's. A fair majority of the ships crossing the bar suffered bottom damage and it was

Stern and forceful, Dr. John McLoughlin studied medicine in England and then entered the service of the North West Co. at Fort William, and on the union of that company with the Hudson's Bay Co., was placed in control of the united companies on the Pacific Coast. He moved the headquarters from Astoria to Fort Vancouver, where he ruled with autocratic power for two decades. Leaving the company in 1846 he retired to his claim at Oregon City, applying for American citizenship. Born in the province of Quebec, Canada in 1784, he died in 1857.

always a celebrated occasion when one had safely negotiated the treacherous bar. Crossing in and out was an experience unlike today, what with lengthy rock jetties, controlled channels, sophisticated aids to navigation on ship and shore, annual dredging projects, qualified pilots etc. A 48 foot bar depth and accurate charts round out present safeguards. Not so a century ago when nature ran its course.

Among the earliest vessels crossing the bar that brushed the shoals was Captain Broughton's HMS *Chatham* in 1792. She was hung up on Peacock Spit for several hours but managed to work free. Though many of the ships that negotiated the bar in the early 1800's suffered damage, it was the first major shipwreck that gave the Columbia bar its sinister reputation.

In March of 1829, the Hudson's Bay bark *William & Ann* draped her shape over the shoals at the river entrance. The details of the tragedy were never fully revealed, for the ship's entire company of 29 perished. It was like the old hymn read: "unknown waves before me roll, hiding rocks and treacherous shoal." Though none were spared to tell the tale, it may well be imagined the frantic efforts made by those miserable souls trying to escape through a welter of rigging, planks splitting beneath their feet, and green and white water cascading into wild geysers. It was tantamount to a lion devouring a lamb.

The wreck was a heavy loss for the Hudson's Bay Co. for the ship carried a valuable cargo destined for Fort Vancouver. The *William & Ann* had been in close company with the schooner *Convoy* of Boston before her fatal crossing. Through the sea mist, those on the Yankee vessel could see grim reminders of what had happened to the larger vessel but were helpless to render aid, her crew having all they could do to keep their own vessel from the menacing manacles of sand. The skipper of the *Convoy* carried the first news of the disastrous loss to the settlement at Fort George.

Parties were organized to search for any possible survivors or bodies, while further plans were made to recover any goods washed ashore from the wreck. In both cases, the results were negative. The Clatsops were one step ahead reaping a bonanza in supplies which the high tide brought to their shores. According to Indian tradition anything the sea brought them was rightfully their personal property. This interpretation of the law was immediately contested by the Hudson's Bay factors. A party was sent to the Indian encampment near Point Adams to demand the return of the goods.

Stubbornly resisting, the Clatsops turned down their thumbs on the request. One young brave impudently took from the spoils a broom, handed it to the intruders and told them to take it to their leader (Dr. John McLoughlin) at Fort Vancouver, and to tell him that was all he would get.

Fort Vancouver, stronghold of Dr. John McLoughlin on the Columbia River. It was the headquarters of the Hudson's Bay Co. from 1824 to 1846.

Infuriated by the gesture but aware of their inferior numbers the whites did a turn about and begrudgingly retreated, bearing the telltale broom.

Though it was Indian land that had been invaded yet, no way would they allow these "stubborn savages" to keep the spoils from the wreck. In the fall, when a sufficiently large and well armed brigade was organized, HBC planned action against the Clatsops to force the return of the "stolen goods." From the time Dr. McLoughlin was handed the broom he had impatiently awaited the day when he could punish the Indians for what he termed "impudence."

In the interim, the Clatsops had recovered, near their camp, a boat from the wreck that had drifted ashore, oars still intact. When news of the recovery reached Fort George, and later Fort Vancouver, rumor was circulated that the Indians had long before seized the craft and murdered its occupants. On that unfounded evidence, war was virtually declared on the natives. Asserting its total authority, the HB Company, alleging murder and thievery, dispatched a small schooner downriver, armed like a battleship. At Fort George the brigade was organized, half of which would go by water on the schooner and the other half as foot soldiers.

The attack was made without warning. Cannon on the schooner fired broadsides at the village scattering the Indians, sending them running for the protection of the forest as rifles blasted away from land. Ironically, only one of their number was killed, but the encampment was totally abandoned, the attackers moving in at will. Most of the salvaged goods were recovered. Another unjustifiable act had been perpetrated upon the natives.

Hudson's Bay factors glibly explained their actions as necessary to serve notice on the local Indians that they could not steal Hudson's Bay property nor defy its authority.

That was but one incident when fur company personnel attacked native villages seeking to punish the occu-

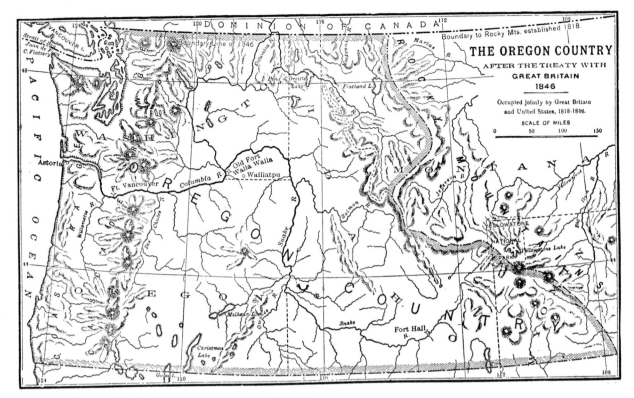

Map of Oregon Country in 1846. Up to the time this map was published most maps had shown but three settlements on the West Coast—one at Astoria, one at San Diego, and one at Monterey.

pants for hostile acts. Seldom were the tribes capable of combining forces for counter action against the superior firepower. The Pacific Northwest country which had been theirs for countless generations, was in essence, theirs no longer. Many Indians, resigned to their fate, felt the best option was to remain passive. Renegades who refused to yield often had their necks stretched. The traditional strain broken, Columbia River Indians became dependent on the Hudson's Bay Co., accepting the white man's ways and falling into a category of inferior third-class citizens. Some employees of the HB operation took to themselves Indian wives.

Another early shipwreck that had a profound affect on the early settlers at the river's mouth was that of the (Hudson's Bay) 209 ton British bark *Isabella*. She ran afoul of Sand Island, May 23, 1830, hardly a year after the fatal demise of the *William & Ann*. In that calamity, however, all of the ship's personnel escaped drowning.

After a lengthy voyage from London, under the command of Captain Thomas Ryan, the *Isabella* stood in for the bar. What appeared a routine crossing suddenly took a fatal twist, the breeze completely dying out. Drifting at the whims of the strong currents toward the encumbrance known as Sand Island, the anchors were dropped but the flukes would not hold and the vessel

continued her drift as if pulled by a magnet. Despite every effort, the canvas remained limp and the kedging process failed. Scraping over the outer tentacles of sand, the vessel lost headway and thumped down hard on the shoal. It was then that the angry breakers began their work of destruction, exploding like cannon fire against the ship's side.

With the recollections of the ill-fated *William & Ann* fresh in mind, the crew feared for their lives. Captain Ryan was forced to use stern authority to prevent any foolhardy acts. Anxieties intensified when a strong southwest wind suddenly erupted increasing the watery onslaught against the solitary hull, turning it wholly broadside for the final kill. The bilge pumps were no match for the inflow of brine and the men quit their places at the pump handles. The ship's carpenter reported holes below the waterline. Captain Ryan was faced with a serious decision. If there was a chance to save his cargo-laden ship he wanted to stay by his command, but in his hands lay the fate of the crew. With the timbers starting, the decision was made for him. He wanted to wait the turn of the tide to assess the damage but thought better of it. Boats were lowered away on the lee side and after a struggle with the elements managed to get free of the ship.

Fort George (Astoria) in 1845. But few changes were made at the post while the Hudson's Bay Co. was in control. For a considerable period, James Birnie, stationed there, had little to do but watch the coming and going of company ships. The engraving represents the place about the time Birnie retired from service.

With every intention of returning to the wreck, Ryan's heart sank the following morning when glancing seaward he saw a twisted mass of wreckage. The costly loss was to be felt again by the Hudson's Bay post, but then it could have been the *William & Ann* tragedy all over again. Captain Ryan's decision turned out to be the right one.

Though other wrecks were to occur within a few years of the Hudson's Bay disasters perhaps the one that had the greatest impact was the loss of 275 ton U.S. Naval brig *Peacock*. It occurred on the afternoon of Sunday, July 18, 1841.

Though the weather and sea conditions were not unfavorable, the ship's officers were totally unfamiliar with the Columbia River bar, and no pilot was immediately available. Shipmaster Captain William Hudson had been supplied with some course directions by Captain Josiah Spaulding, commander of the 500 ton ship *Lausanne,* which shortly before had visited the river.

A unit of Lt. Charles Wilkes' surveying expedition, which had been charting and sounding Pacific Northwest waters, the 18-gun sloop of war *Peacock* was on official business. Hudson, shouting orders from the poop, ordered Lieutenant Emmons aloft to the crosstrees to keep a weather eye out for the best channel. With her yards braced, the helmsman kept his eyes glued to the compass. Slowly responding, the vessel pursued her course. Emmons scanned the bar from his vantage point, searching for foul ground while the leadsman stood by. Taken by complete surprise, despite every precaution, a tentacle of sand appearing from the froth clutched the keel and brought the *Peacock* to a jarring halt. Pounding breakers carried her higher on the sands thumping her uncermoniously over the barrier. Boarding seas snatched the ship's cutter and twisted it like a pretzel. The decks became an obstacle course, the binnacle tore loose and one of the cannon broke free of its lashings and rolled from port to starboard like a bull on a rampage. Dodging the debris, the sailors tried frantically to lasso the heavy piece.

Darting around like a drunken man, Hudson was trying to shout orders over the deafening roar of the boarding seas. He ordered cannon, shot and all materials not bolted through the deck jettisoned in a last ditch effort to afford buoyancy.

Next, the rudder post cracked and the rudder was partially dislodged. By kedging, under the most difficult of conditions, the vessel's head was turned toward the sea, but not for long. Before 9 p.m. in the inky black-

Early sketch of Fort George, or Astoria, site of the Hudson's Bay Co. establishment.

ness, the anchor cables parted; the *Peacock* was driven broadside as the seas pounded into her with a vengeance. The sailors were wet, cold and miserable, for by midnight, water ran knee-deep on the gun deck. Working ceaselessly till dawn, the wretched souls had grown dog-tired and chilled to the marrow. Theirs was a futile effort against the forces of nature.

By 6 a.m., a large Indian canoe, bearing a "pilot" was standing off the wreck, but his services were useless. Evacuation of the survivors took priority over all else. As the canoe stoodby, the useable boats on the *Peacock,* with great difficulty, were gotten afloat, but on a second trip one was flipped end for end, throwing its occupants into the vortex. Miraculously none were drowned but all were well spent before the other boats could move in for the rescue. Mission completed, there was a grateful crew of sailors that toasted both their bad and their good fortune. All were accounted for. The *Peacock* was a total loss, but the scientific data, ship's papers and navigation equipment were recovered.

By the following morning the beaches were strewn with a hodgepodge of wreckage. Closer examination of the wreck site showed virtually nothing except the ship's bowsprit protruding upwards from the spit, like a grim tombstone. Thereafter, the barrier was known as Peacock Spit, and in the years that followed became an infamous graveyard of many ships and the final resting place of numerous brave seafarers.

Several weeks after the wreck, Wilkes arrived on the river aboard the USS *Porpoise* to find a replacement vessel for the ill-fated *Peacock*. The expedition commander managed to acquire the services of the brig

Thomas Perkins lying in Baker's Bay, a vessel that had been under charter to the Hudson's Bay Co. After reassigning the wreck survivors, Wilkes personally aided in the survey and charting of the Columbia River before sailing south to rendezvous with the USS *Vincennes* at San Francisco.

Unable to carry the *Peacock's* launch, the commander in a humanitarian gesture left her at the old Astor settlement to act as both a rescue and pilot craft to help prevent future tragedies such as befell the *Peacock.*

James Birnie who was in charge of Fort George was without authority to accept responsibility for the launch, so Dr. McLoughlin at Fort Vancouver, accepted the gift with gratitude, but kept it at Fort George in charge of the Hudson's Bay Co., until a provisional government was formed and the boat delivered to Governor Abernethy.

Astoria (Fort George) though having declined in importance after 1825, continued to play the port of entry role. Its only competition on the lower Columbia was the village of Chinook on the north side of the river, which from the outset was only a fishing village. Though traditionally an Indian center, early white settlers gradually moved in and changed its face.

It is of interest that one of the first regular river boats to operate out of Astoria to the upriver village of Cathlamet was started by the same James D. Sauls, the black man who ran the *Shark* aground on her initial visit to the Columbia River, and who was a deserter from the *Peacock*. Though his subsequent career was checkered, he, beginning in 1842, had had some success operating a small schooner on the river. Passengers, livestock, and general cargo were hauled depending on the whims of

the wind.

Navigation on the Columbia, under sail, was sometimes frustrating. In 1848 an ocean-going brig named *Sequim*, with good sailing qualities, required 54 hours to sail from Astoria to Portland, but often times during windless periods vessels would require as much as a week to cover the same distance.

Another pioneer navigator on the lower Columbia was Capt. Brazil Grounds who is credited with bringing the first cattle to Astoria in 1844 aboard his peculiar scow schooner *Calapooia*. The livestock was consigned to a gentleman farmer named John Hobson.

In 1846-47, when the river was solidly frozen over, the *Calapooia* was but one of several craft locked in the ice. Some 300 California-bound ship passengers were stranded on Sauvie Island near Portland for four weeks.

Pilotage of the bar and river continued synonymous with Astoria. The year the *Shark* was wrecked in 1846, the first state pilotage law was authorized, the governor appointed commissioners to examine and license pilots for the bar and river. The maverick pilots were finished. As of April 1847, S. C. Reeves was appointed as the first official pilot for the Columbia bar. A month earlier he had arrived from his native Newburyport aboard the brig *Henry*. Though he studied the bar conditions from every angle and acquainted himself with the vagaries of the river entrance, and though he had a year of successful piloting chores, his reputation was tarnished with the loss of the 400 ton British bark *Vancouver* May 8, 1848.

Perhaps it was overconfidence that prompted him to prematurely cross the bar against the protests of the *Vancouver's* master, Capt. Wm. H. Mouatt. Adverse winds and heavy river freshets prevailed. Still, Reeves was confident of a safe crossing. The forces of nature however, had other ideas. The *Vancouver* was carried out of the main channel onto the Middle Sands and was to become a total loss along with her valuable cargo of machinery and stores for Fort Vancouver. There were no casualties.

Captain Mouatt brought charges of negligence against the pilot amid persistent but false rumors that Reeves was involved in a conspiracy against the consignees. The charges were not upheld and the case was dismissed, but that same year, Reeves, acting as pilot, was again blamed, this time for the wreck of the 294 ton whaleship *Maine*, which was pummelled to pieces on Clatsop Spit August 25, 1848 after all hands escaped in boats.

Perhaps disillusioned by the adverse publicity, Captain Reeves sailed for San Francisco to get in on the gold excitement, but later while he was sailing his small sloop *Flora* in San Francisco Bay, it capsized in a squall (1849) drowning the erstwhile pilot.

Gold fever not only took much of the pioneer population from the Columbia River area but also many of its utilitarian work craft, one of which was the *Peacock's* launch. It had served well as a pilot boat and had excellent sailing qualities. Eight years after the wreck of the *Peacock*, we find the launch operated by George Gear and Robert Alexander, who logged a voyage of only 18 hours between Astoria and Portland. A group of gold seekers fresh with the news from California sailed in the

Largest sailing ship to enter the Columbia River, the five-masted auxiliary sailing bark *R. C. Rickmers*, stands off Astoria. The steam-powered vessel flying the German flag, carried 50,000 feet of canvas, her triple expansion engine producing 1,200 horsepower. She was owned by Rickmers & Co. and made her maiden voyage to the west coast in 1908.

launch to San Francisco from Astoria and took off for the diggings. Just one of a variety of vessels from all over the world to converge on San Francisco Bay, the launch joined the greatest fleet of ships ever to congregate in one harbor. Gold fever caused some of the little settlements along the banks of the Columbia to become ghost towns overnight.

Some of the more level-headed mariners continued to operate their vessels between the Columbia River and San Francisco, such as the schooners *Sabina* and *Eveline* which turned a handsome profit what with the skyrocketing freight rates.

The first official pilot vessel arrived at Astoria in December 1849. She was the fleet schooner *Mary Taylor* which came north from San Francisco under pilots J. G. Hustler and Cornelius White. They along with Job Hatfield performed the bar piloting duties for several years thereafter.

In 1850, Capt. George Flavel arrived at the Astoria port aboard the *Goldhunter*. Later he received the first branch license ever issued to a Columbia River pilot. Eventually he became baron of the river pilots, gaining a virtual monopoly.

It was another quarter of a century before Astoria was considered a world port of major significance, always in serious contention with mushrooming Portland. In the 1870's, during a three month period, some 25 deep laden square-riggers cleared the Port of Astoria with cargoes for Europe, not to mention the many domestic coasters.

For many years Astoria was the largest city on the Oregon coast, but the growing movement of forest products and by-products from the Coos Bay-North Bend area has prompted a renewed growth in recent years that

has outstripped Astoria in commerce and population. Sir Francis Drake's "Bad Bay" turned out to be a profitable region after all, and the nation's greatest soft wood export center.

For unique setting, history, flavor and vistas, however, no city in Oregon state quite compares with Astoria, the port through which virtually all commerce, small or large, commercial or otherwise passes when entering the Columbia River from the Pacific Ocean. It's a place truly born of the sea and dripping with salt.

Not only is Astoria the site of the first permanent settlement in Oregon country but it was on the strength of the little post that the United States was able to solidify its claim to lands in the Pacific Northwest.

Past masters of the area, the Chinookan-speaking Indians who held sway on both sides of the river entrance prior to the coming of the white man were not only master traders but, from their one woman shovel-nosed craft to their high prowed whaling and war canoes carrying 50 men, they controlled the land in peace. Lewis and Clark had a high respect for the natives. The Indians told the pioneer party that their best chance of survival was on the south side of the river, and passing the future site of Astoria they constructed Fort Clatsop, the first buildings erected by white men in Oregon and the first military post. Oregon's coast was the end of the trail west.

It's just history now and as great a hero as John Jacob Astor has become for his daring enterprise, it is estimated he lost $400,000 on the Astoria venture. In March 1847, the Astoria post office opened, first west of the Rockies. Becoming a trading center three years later, the village numbered 250 persons. The federal customs office opened in 1852 and the first salmon cannery was constructed in 1866. At the time of the great fire in 1883 which started at a sawmill and virtually wiped out downtown Astoria, the population had swelled to nearly 3,000.

By 1920, Astoria had risen to the place of Oregon's second largest city, boasting 14,027 citizens, but two years later was swept by another conflagration, far greater than the first. When the ashes had finally cooled, 32 city blocks had been obliterated including the entire business district and just about everything flammable. The Astoria spirit rose to the fore and the city was rebuilt again, this time with a generous proportion of concrete and bricks.

The waterfront was virtually renewed. Through both World Wars I and II Astoria played a vital role. Today, its population has sagged to about 10,500, about number 15 in the state, but in no way has the city lost its position as Oregon's first and most honored metropolis. It stands linked with the state of Washington by the fantastic Columbia River interstate bridge built in 1966, one of the largest of its kind in the nation, spanning the entire river mouth.

CHAPTER FIVE
THE HEROES AND THE COWARDS

THREE QUARTERS OF A CENTURY ago when a ship was aground on the Oregon coast, oar-propelled surfboats were the principal tool in rescue operations. Often pulled by teams of steaming horses to the wreck location, they were either manned by volunteer crews, or the trained personnel of the old U.S. Lifesaving Service. These remarkable boats were responsible for saving scores of lives.

Precursor to the present day Coast Guard search and rescue operations, the Lifesaving Service was founded in 1871 to protect the lives of those in peril on the sea or along its frontiers. The stations polka-dotting the American shoreline were each composed of eight surfmen under the supervision of a keeper, the station's officer-in-charge. The West Coast stations were initially under jurisdiction of the 13th Lifesaving District superintendent, located at San Francisco.

Stations were equipped with a surfboat and a lifeboat, sometimes only the former, a Lyle (line throwing) gun, a breeches buoy, a beach cart, faking box, life preservers, medical kits, Coston flares, axes, shovels, lanterns, picks and a slop chest full of clothes for survivors. Surfmen worked a six day week on a rotation basis, six having to be present at all times, as that was the number, plus the steersman (usually the keeper) it took to man the pulling craft. The stations that had volunteer crews usually employed only the keeper, and it was his responsibility to round up the volunteers whenever a ship was in distress.

At some stations, personnel patrolled the beaches, carrying by night a lantern and Coston flares, the latter used for signaling the station should a ship in trouble be sighted.

Not until 1908 were gasoline-powered rescue craft introduced to West Coast stations.

Often times surfmen were called on to launch their boats into the seething breakers swollen by driving southerly gales. Suicidal efforts were called for to save terror-stricken mariners or passengers trapped on ships being torn to pieces by the elements.

With none of the sophisticated lifesaving equipment of our day, it was strictly a case of men against the sea. Bleached ribs of many ships lie half buried in the Oregon beach sands while at the bases of the rocky monoliths, torn and mangled hulks rest in the silent depths. Occasionally from the beaches the remains of forgotten wrecks will reappear like ghosts, and again, in a short time vanish under the shifting sands.

True grit was the stuff of which many of the oldtime surfmen were made. One of the bravest working the coastal waters of the Oregon coast was Capt. John Bergman, a man of amazing endurance, courage and leadership. Born in Germany in 1847, he had been a seafarer from the age of 15. Take for instance the bleak winter of January 1883 and we will set up the drama that was to include Captain Bergman as the man of the hour.

Steaming southward on the second leg of her maiden voyage, the half-million dollar steam collier

Tacoma, out of Puget Sound, rode low in the water with more than 3,500 tons of Carbonado coal destined for San Francisco. Master of the steamer was Capt. George D. Kortz; the first officer, L. L. Simmons; second officer, C. Rodman; third officer, R. H. Willoughby and chief engineer, H. Wilson. There was apprehension aboard over the sour complexion of the weather. All Oregon coast landmarks had been obliterated.

Pitching and rolling under her heavy burden, the *Tacoma* strained in her every joint. Captain Kortz had confidence in his new steed, fresh out of the builder's yard in Philadelphia, for due to her excellent turn of speed and maneuverability, the shipmaster believed she could literally walk on water. But this was a most unusual night, the dull throb of the engines totally drowned out by the howling winds and crashing seas as the vessel passed through the darkness like a mysterious shadow.

Toward 9 p.m. in the dim light of the wheelhouse, the officers discussed the ship's position with the quartermaster. All agreed with the skipper that they were a comfortable distance offshore and in no danger. Full speed was maintained. But unfortunately, their collected intelligence was inadequate. Within a few minutes there was a grinding crash, the steamer vibrating from stem to stern, reeling like one inebriated. The sickening grating of steel against rock left little question about the seriousness of the encounter. The vessel had gone from full ahead to a dead stop, everything not bolted down having gone askew. Most of the crew were knocked flat on the

Captain John Bergman displaying his gold lifesaving medal in his sunset years, at Florence. Becoming somewhat of a legend for his heroic feats in the saving of lives, he was responsible for rescuing several persons from the ill-fated SS *Tacoma*, north of the Umpqua, in 1883. He later became keeper-in-charge of the Umpqua River Lifesaving Station.

deck or hurled from their bunks. The deep abyss of night made it all seem like a terrifying dream. As if a beehive had been disturbed, every man was scurrying about, the skipper shouting into the speaking tube for the engineer to give the engine full thrust astern.

No one aboard the *Tacoma* was at first sure what the ship had struck nor would they know till the break of dawn. In truth, the steamer had collided with a reef close to shore, four miles north of the Umpqua River.

Despite the full power of the engine, the steamer remained in a vice and the crew, some in near panic and many half clothed went about unorganized. The whistle blasted its mournful sound over the shrouded ocean. Walls of saltwater boarded running like mighty rivers down the slanting decks and out the scuppers. Flames in kerosene lamps flickered and died. Breaks in the steel plates grew larger, the hull strained, pipes broke and steam hissed forth.

Kortz tried to keep some kind of order until the damage could be surveyed by daylight, but as water crept up around the boilers, the fires went out and massive billows of white steam came up from below. Night seemed an eternity, nobody ate or slept.

Came dawn at last; the situation was worse than the captain had dared imagine. Battered below the waterline, coal spewing out of the flooded holds, engine room inundated and the main deck as if hit by a hurricane. All but one of the lifeboats had been either stove or carried overboard, clean of the davits. With no aid in sight, action had to be immediate.

Under extreme difficulty, Captain Kortz and six of his men managed to get the usable boat lowered over the lee side. Contrary to the usual custom of the sea, the shipmaster decided to try for shore to get assistance for his vessel rather than to remain till the bitter end. Narrowly missing being smashed like an eggshell, the boat managed to get free of the wreck, and then with backs and arms straining to the uttermost the oarsmen challenged the mountainous breakers. With Kortz at the steering sweep, the craft made a phenomenal run in closing the 400 yards between the wreck and the beach. Almost broaching to, the lifeboat was carried high up on the sands, the occupants stumbling out drenched to the skin. Almost immediately, a giant curling sea snatched the craft away and smashed it to kindling on the nearby rocks. The last link with those on the *Tacoma* had been broken. Would it be their crypt?

After a long walk through the driving rain and wind, the shipmaster and his men finally made contact with the little lumber town of Gardiner, a few miles up the Umpqua River, a settlement that had a kinship with the sea and a people who were familiar with the urgency of men facing peril. Whenever a ship was in trouble, everybody dropped everything and headed for the rescue scene. Gardiner which in those years loaded some 50 windjammers with lumber per annum was well acquainted with shipwreck in and around its bar.

In 1883, the government had not yet established an official life-saving station on the Umpqua. Certainly it was urgently needed. Everything was voluntary. With food, spirits, blankets and medicines, the citizens of the town hurried to the place opposite the wreck. Driftwood fires were kindled, a dory was hauled to the beach by a mule team in the hope it could be launched into the breakers. All of this was done without regard for the chilling wind and rain that continued unabated.

With the start of another day, those keeping the vigil could see that the steamer had broken in half. The survivors had taken refuge in the messhall but when the bulkheads parted they were forced out on the open deck to hang doggedly on to anything solid enough to resist the relentless seas that pummelled the ship. Death stared them in the face. The thermometer kept going down, and the leaden canopy above was dropping a freezing sleet that drove in almost horizontally. Ice formed on the twisted rigging and visibility was barely a quarter mile. The surf was in such condition that it would have taken a miracle to reach the wreck. It was sheer agony for those who waited.

Though the tug *Sol Thomas* was bar-bound inside the river, her skipper, Captain Lawson, was urged to put to sea and get a line to the wreck. Risking both his vessel and crew, he agreed to try. Though successful in surmounting the wrath of the river entrance there was no way he could get close enough to the wreck with a lifeline. Plunging and rolling like a cork, the *Sol Thomas* could do nothing but stand helplessly by.

In the interim, some of the local citizens walked southward several miles along the beach to Coos Bay where there was a lifesaving station situated in the lee of an islet on which stood Cape Arago lighthouse. The post of keeper, (a government employee) was held by Capt. James Desmond. A recently established facility, funds had not allowed for a paid staff of lifesaving personnel; volunteers were used in each emergency. The Umpqua party requested the immediate services of the craft to rescue the wretched souls aboard the *Tacoma*. At the same time, the tug *Escort No. 2,* (Captain Magee) on Coos Bay, was enlisted to meet and tow the surfboat to the wreck scene. The two vessels were to rendezvous off Cape Arago.

Volunteers responding to the call to man the surfboat were C. E. Getty, Tom Hall, Joe Collumber, George Wilson, Andrew Jackson, George Morris, L. Geiger and C. B. Watson, in addition to Captain Desmond.

Two days had now passed since the advent of the wreck. The seas had battered the *Tacoma* into near submission, only the masts and stack still standing defiantly.

As the Arago lifeboat readied for her epic run, we turn to an eye witness account by the late Chandler B.

Watson, one of the volunteers. He wrote his account in his sunset years (1929) after a career as a lawyer and journalist, some of his recollections conflicting slightly with other facts in the case.

"Late one evening a man in oilskins and sou'wester appeared at the office and excitedly announced that the steamship *Tacoma* had gone ashore above the mouth of the Umpqua River and was being hammered to pieces on the sands. She had a crew of 50 men and a few passengers with no means of getting ashore except by making rafts of the deck wreckage, the boats having been stoved and broken. There was a fearful storm raging and the messenger had been sent down the beach to call out the lifeboat. It was my duty to organize the crew and send the lifeboat to the rescue. I at once set about to gather a volunteer crew. Several vessels lay in the harbor but the sailors were loath to leave snug berths for so strenuous a service.

"I succeeded in getting enough to promise to man the boat, but inasmuch as a tug would have to accompany it to the scene of the wreck, and that neither the tug nor lifeboat could be taken out until high tide which would not occur until four o'clock in the morning, it was proposed that I should take another crew to launch the lifeboat and meet the tug off the bar at that hour, and the volunteer crew would come out with the tug and take charge. I gathered up eight men most of whom were safe men for such an enterprise, and at dusk we set out on foot for the lifestation, eight miles away. It was a stormy, blustery night and we had to cross South Slough in a rickety small boat, which we accomplished without accident. Pitchy darkness had now set in and when we reached the station the waves were beating upon the island with such force that it shook and quivered as if about to be washed away. We could do nothing until the tide was well in, hence employed ourselves in loosening the hatches of the boat house, which was built in a bight of the channel shore and stood on piling above the narrow beach from which we had to lower the boat to the sands. The boat had never before been taken out and the hatches and tackle having been kept painted, were stiff and hard to handle. The boat was a splendid specimen of that class of craft, and with its cargo of necessary equipment, was heavy. By midnight we had the boat on the beach with life-line, cannon to shoot the line, life preservers etc. all stored and ready to push off so soon as the tide should serve. It was yet four hours before we could expect the tug to heave in sight which would be about daylight. We could do nothing but wait and think of the imperiled men 20 miles away. The storm was gradually increasing and the roaring of the surf and the shaking of the island was calculated to disturb weak nerves. The clouds were flying overhead like frightened gulls and occasional gusts brought snow and rain. The surf was thrown completely over the island and even dashed against the lenses of the light (lighthouse lantern panes) almost 100 feet above low tide. As the time grew near for manning the boat, our faces shown by the light of the lantern, exhibited no levity.

"Desmond, the keeper of the station and ex-officio captain of the crew, appeared to be nervous and frankly admitted that our undertaking was a perilous one. Charley Getty, George Wilson, Andrew Jackson and the other whose names I have forgotten were men of experience and good judgment and I was the only one who had never had any experience in the surf. My initiation promised to be more than ordinarily interesting. I had confidence in the "boys" and while not wholly placid, I put on the best face I could and would not have balked under any circumstances. As the time drew near, we examined the lashings, put on our life suits, assumed the stations assigned to us and "stoodby" ready to receive orders. We were instructed to stand at our places with our oars in the sands to steady the boat and when the word should be given, to drop to our seats and shove off. The boat's nose was kept on the sands and its stern out toward the channel. Just to the south of us not over 75 feet away, was a dike, reaching out into the channel, cutting it half in two and standing from ten to 20 feet high. Over this dike the water was rushing like Niagara; as the tide rose and the boat began to float, she would rise to the swell until all hands were put to their best efforts to hold it. Then it would sink back until it rested on the sands again, only to repeat this up and down motion time and time again. We were drenched to the skin, the channel was a seething mass of foam and the roaring surf drowned our voices except when raised to the highest pitch. Charley Getty and the captain each manned a steering oar and sat in the stern. I had the port bow oar and the others were arranged in their places when the command was given to, "shove off." I shall never forget that wild plunge.

"The seething water caught us and hurled us with the force of a catapult under the suspension bridge that connected the island with the mainland, and out into the roaring surf beyond the island. The water was breaking in 30 fathoms and waves were rolling tumultuously. Great combers glowing with phosphorescent light seemed miles in length. As a huge breaker rose before us the order to back on our oars was obeyed with alacrity and we'd back away from it until it broke, and then rush forward again into the rush and swirl.

"Thus for two hours we backed and filled among the breakers that are known the world over for their violence and volume. The cannon (line throwing gun) broke its lashings and threatened to make a hole through the bottom of the boat in its wild plunges from one side to the other. Two men were ordered to haul in their oars and secure the gun. They could hold it but could not lash it and the crew was weakened by the loss of the two men from the oars. The captain turned us toward a bight in the island for the purpose of running ashore and trimming the ship.

"As we neared the shore the port bow oar was ordered to stand by, to take a line ashore. That order was for me. I drew in my oar, caught up the line, and, standing in the bow made ready to jump so soon as I should feel the boat strike. The moment came just after a great roller had drawn back to sea and the succeeding one was coming in. I plunged forward into the water waist deep, only to be caught by the incoming roller which was not less than 10 to 15 feet high. It caught me up and threw me not less than 50 feet. I was completely submerged but fortunately retained presence of mind enough to hold on to my line, and throwing myself on my back dug my heels into the sand, throwing myself head first toward the shore. The return of the breaker left us high and dry on the beach and all hands were ordered to secure our cargo.

"The tug had not yet come in sight and as we were again on the island and not far from the station, the captain made an excuse to go there for something. We put everything in trim and waited for the captain, (Des-

Members of the U.S. Lifesaving Service practice rigging breeches buoy to make rescues from vessels in peril along Oregon shores in days of yore. Oregon Historical Society collection.

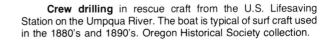

Crew drilling in rescue craft from the U.S. Lifesaving Station on the Umpqua River. The boat is typical of surf craft used in the 1880's and 1890's. Oregon Historical Society collection.

The Coast Guard's Cape Arago Light Station, showing the lighthouse and other buildings on the eroded islet, south of the Coos Bay entrance. The old lifesaving station once stood on the bank of the small sandy beach below the dwelling to the left of the foot bridge. U.S. Coast Guard photo.

mond) knowing that the tug would soon whistle for us. After half an hour and no captain, I took another man and went to the station to ascertain the cause of the delay. We found him snugly ensconced behind the stove, and in answer to us he declared that all the money in Christendom would not induce him to go out into that surf again. Here was a problem. A man who claimed to have been at sea all his life and who had been entrusted with the responsibilities of life-saving keeper, on the first occasion of his services being called for, and in the most critical moment, showing the white feather when his crew of volunteers were clamoring to do this act of generosity and mercy. We begged, argued, entreated and finally threatened, but all to no purpose. Going out again we saw the tug about a mile away, and from the steam from

her whistle we knew she was blowing for us. We secured another (smaller boat) from the lighthouse keeper, a boat that leaked badly, and sent two men off to the tug to announce the situation and to ask the captain to send the tug's boat in with the crew that had volunteered and we would meet them with the lifeboat. The proposition was refused. The trip out in the small, leaky boat, in such a surf was a very hard, dangerous mission, but those two men were brave men, and it was our purpose to take the lifeboat out to them ourselves, when with astonishment we saw the tug deliberately turn and disappear over the bar.

"It looked like a shocking piece of cowardice all round. We knew, however, that the captain of the tug was no coward, but up to this day there had been no

An early photo of the Cape Arago lighthouse islet, showing the first and second lighthouses to grace the landscape. The initial one is in the far background, abandoned because of erosion. The second one, in center, a frame structure was replaced by the present lighthouse built in 1934. The footbridge was also rebuilt.

satisfactory explanation offered."

The mission was accordingly scrubbed.

Watson was of the opinion that James Desmond should have gone to prison for his refusal to man the surfboat, but as it turned out, after several days' investigation the boat keeper, was merely relieved of his position and replaced by a seasoned and able keeper named William Abbott.

The local newssheet branded Desmond as follows:

"There is no excuse, and it is only a pity that our laws cannot reach him and hang him for the lives of the men who were sacrificed through his pusillanimity and cowardice."

Meanwhile back at the wreck scene, the survival of those on the *Tacoma* rested with the people of Gardiner. Where an outright show of cowardice had been displayed by the boat captain at Cape Arago, a hero was being born in the name of John Bergman. Despite overwhelming odds he directed rescue operations from the beach, and was willing to go one step further than any of the volunteers who aided him. Throughout the second and third days, a small dory-like craft was repeatedly launched into the savage surf, but each time it capsized spilling its occupants into the chilling surf. Time after time, Bergman ordered the craft righted, bailed out and relaunched. Always encouraging his cohorts, he would point to the wreck, just 400 tormenting yards away where occasionally over the noise of the howling wind the terrifying screams of the perishing could be heard. Both frustrated and exhausted, Bergman seemed possessed of superhuman strength. With little food in his stomach and hours

without sleep, his driving determination finally paid off on the third day when the rescue craft managed to negotiate the surf by virtually standing on end. Pulling on the oars, the men gave it their all through the tempest at last reaching the sorry pile of wreckage. Pitiful survivors watched grimly, praying with all their inner beings that God would spare them. Suffering terribly from cold and hunger, they stood like frozen statues, hoping.

In a miraculous piece of seamanship the dory, bucking like a Brahma bull, managed to work in on the lee side of the reef. So anxious were those waiting, that they made a stampede for the craft as it came alongside. Had not first assistant engineer J. K. Grant kept order with his pistol the craft would have swamped. It was a tense moment; some were taken, some left behind. Every man not at an oar had to bail constantly. With Bergman on the steering sweep, the rescue craft came in through the breakers, volunteers on the beach wading out to their armpits to assist. Women stood ready to receive and nurse the gaunt survivors, ten in all.

No sooner was the first mission accomplished than Bergman and his recruits were on their way out through the surf for more survivors. The craft was successful in picking up another group, but on the way in, tragedy intervened. Before the eyes of those on the beach, a giant wall of water snatched the rescue boat, flipped it into the air, then dropped it rudely into the trough, its people flung out to fight for survival in the troubled sea. Those from the ship, terribly weakened by exposure and hunger, could struggle no longer. Again volunteers waded into the surf to lend a hand. Among those pulled in was first assistant engineer Grant. He was placed gently on the sands above the driftwood line and covered with blankets. Pale and drawn, eyes like hollow sockets, his heart finally gave out.

Still on the battered wreck, nine waited their turn to be rescued.

Continuing to standby offshore was the *Sol Thomas* seeking a chance to get a line to the wreck, but that opportunity never came.

Thursday morning arrived. The storm had abated for a few hours but was only gathering new breath to fill its powerful lungs. The seas continued massive and treacherous, a threat to any who would challenge. A second tug arrived on the scene, the *Fearless* skippered by Capt. James Hill, which had steamed north from Coos Bay. Aboard were many prominent maritime men who had come to render advice for saving the perishing. Included were John Kruse, shipbuilder; and Captains Falk, Nelson and Bendergard of the *Mary & Ida, Gotoma* and *Wing & Wing,* respectively.

Due to her deep draft, the *Fearless* was unable to get any closer to the wreck than the *Sol Thomas*. It was ironic, however, that just six years later, on Nov. 20, 1889, Captain Hill, his crew and the *Fearless* would all perish in this very same marine graveyard.

For those who clung to their miserable perches aboard the *Tacoma*, three days and four nights had passed without food or warm clothing, in totally adverse weather. The nightmarish experience must have been such that even death would seem welcome. And death it was, for no other rescue craft were to reach the side of the wreck until the last shred of human life had flickered and died.

On the other hand, 18 survivors owed their lives to the courage and stamina of John Bergman and his volunteers. Had it not been for the cowardice of one James Desmond, the lives of the unfortunates might have been spared. Every calamity produces its heros and cowards, and in this incident there were extremes of both.

In the wake of the tragedy all attention was turned toward Captain Kortz, erstwhile master of the *Tacoma*. Why had he not remained with his ship in true sailor fashion, and how had he allowed his command to get so close to shore? One could not label him a coward for he had earlier distinguished himself in the rescue of many passengers from the big sidewheel steamer *Great Republic* which had stranded at the Columbia River entrance just four years earlier (1879). Further he was a highly respected navigator and pilot.

At the subsequent hearing he testified that the ship's compass was defective causing the *Tacoma* to pursue an erroneous course in weather which blotted out all landmarks.

The *Coos Bay Times,* however, was as critical of Captain Kortz as it had been of Desmond. The entire populace was stirred by the newspaper account which read:

"...at four p.m. on Monday, he (Kortz) and the officers took observations and supposed that they were 28 miles offshore. The Captain then ordered the course changed to south by east, three quarters east, and that's all he (Kortz) knows about it. One thing is certain; a terrible mistake has been made, human life has been sacrificed unnecessarily. While the exact cause may not be known, it should be known that 28 miles offshore, 6 miles north of the Umpqua, with a shore trending easterly, and a northern ocean current, is too near for a steamer to bear east of south in a fog . . . we cannot but believe that the captain was either recklessly careless or unpardonably ignorant. He ran ashore with plenty of water west of him; the case is prima facie against him."

A lighthouse had been placed at the entrance to the Umpqua River by Uncle Sam as early as 1857, first on the Oregon Coast, but unfortunately the tower was built on sand and with the river freshets and the scouring effects of the tides, the foundation was undermined and the structure, in 1861, came tumbling to the ground. From 1861 till 1894, the government frowned on a re-

placement despite constant agitation by maritime interests of the area and of their weak political representation. All through that "dark" period, many navigation charts continued to show a lighthouse at the location, lacking any notation of its destruction. Whether or not the presence of a lighthouse could have prevented the loss of the *Tacoma* remains problematical, but some vessels wrecked in the vicinity are known to have been misled by either the lack of the light or by the erroneous navigation charts.

Nine years after the loss of the *Tacoma,* Capt. John Bergman then in charge of the U.S. Lifesaving Service's new Umpqua Station at Gardiner, was recognized for his brave deeds. Presented the coveted gold lifesaving medal, he became a legend in his own time. The members of his volunteer boat crew in the *Tacoma* rescue mission were also cited for their bravery.

If nothing else good came out of the tragedy, the *Tacoma* wreck did much toward allotting government funds for the lifesaving station on the Umpqua.

Captain Bergman retired in Florence, Oregon after a long and illustrious career. He passed away at the ripe old age of 92, having outlived his Swiss wife, who had borne him seven children, and having married twice after that. At his funeral services the words that accompanied the awarding of his gold medal were read again, Coast Guard pallbearers proudly carrying his body to its final resting place.

And speaking of last rites—what were those of the ill-fated *Tacoma*? At an auction two weeks after the wreck, a company representative won the bidding for the spoils at $500, but little of any value was recovered. So went the dream ship of the H.S. Crocker & Co. whose brand new vessel had been chartered out for Pacific coastal service. The vessel never earned a single dollar for her owners or operators; the elements had won a clear cut victory in both lives and property.

One of the most bizarre and least publicized shipwrecks along the Oregon coast involved the loss of the superior British merchant clipper ship *Atalanta,* and most of her crew, in the late fall of 1898. There was no chance for the making of heros or cowards in that disaster but a near clean sweep for the ocean which swallowed most of the traces, sparing only three lives and a few pieces of wreckage strewn along the beaches.

Let us go back to the beginning. The *Atalanta* was loading grain at Tacoma, a cargo that was destined for Dalgoa Bay, South Africa. The vessel was one of the most beautiful of her type afloat, and perhaps the last of her breed ever built. Turned out in 1885 by Duncan & Co., shipbuilders at Port Glasgow, Scotland, this true clipper boasted an iron hull and a great spread of sail replete with a main skysail and double topgallant yards. She could carry 2,500 tons on a net register of 1,752

U.S. Lifesaving surfboat tests the bar swells of the Coquille River (early 1900's) bar as men on the little steam engine atop the jetty trestle look on. Many old time shipmasters considered Coquille bar one of the most dangerous on the coast.

tons, a good payload for a ship of clipper lines. Proud owner of the *Atalanta* was Ninian Hill, a man who took fierce pride in his fleet. Handpicked was her skipper, Capt. Charles McBride, a true English seafaring salt, excellent navigator and one who demanded a "shipshape and Bristol fashion" decor at all times. The clipper was maintained like a luxury yacht and its spit and polish condition would have made the most particular housewife blush with envy.

Appointments were the finest—hand polished hardwoods in her cabins and saloon and more brass than the ships of the royal navy. Nothing had been spared to make her the pride of the seas. Any blue water sailor would have been proud to have been a part of her crew, and certainly no one handled her with more pride than Captain McBride. He had been known to sail his graceful steed right up to dockside under canvas, thumbing his nose at tugboat skippers who had steamed out of port to dicker for a towing fee.

At dock in Queenstown in one instance, the port admiral and his flag lieutenant came down to inspect the vessel. When told she was manned by a crew of 30 men, he exclaimed:

"In the Royal Navy she would have 300, but they could not have kept her better!"

Not only was the *Atalanta* handsome, but she could sail rings around most of the sailing ships of her day. To her credit was the logging of 950 miles in three days while running her easting down. On another occasion on a passage from Cardiff to Singapore in 1886 she made 320 and 325 miles on two consecutive days. Every fast sailing vessel with a sporting master was anxious to challenge her to a race, captain and crew often making siz-

able wagers on the outcome. In the majority of cases, the *Atalanta* either came out the winner or at least among the top three. Some of her memorable voyages included an 80 day passage from New York to Melbourne, and a similar voyage from The Start (England) to Melbourne. She also logged a 37 day trip from Shanghai to Tacoma.

It was early in October, 1898, when three full-rigged ships from England were at Tacoma loading wheat for South Africa. In those years, Tacoma and Portland were the largest West Coast grain ports. The former was having a bonanza, having catered to a record 53 vessels loading for foreign ports in September of the same year. The trio of English square-riggers were the *Imberhorne, Earl of Dalhousie* and the *Atalanta*. All had reputations as swift merchantmen. Many waterfront wanderers spent hours gawking over the graceful lines of the *Atalanta*, and commenting about her figurehead, a beautiful maiden of the sea. Originally, the owners had intended using her as a troop carrier between England and its colonies, thus providing more than the usual number of accommodations, although passengers were seldom carried. The vessel measured 265 feet in length with a beam of 40 feet and holds 23 feet in depth.

For 30 years Captain McBride had been in the employ of Ninian Hill & Co. and was considered their most able shipmaster. At age 52, he was in the best of health.

Capt. H. A. Lever of the *Imberhorne*, Capt. David Thompson of the *Earl of Dalhousie* and McBride were friendly rivals and inasmuch as the three ships were loading at the same port for the same destination, it followed suit that a race would ensue, and as usual McBride made the challenge. The others eagerly accepted and with a toast and a hardy handshake the arrangements were made. McBride knew he would have a handicap inasmuch as the *Dalhousie* would sail two weeks before his ship and the *Imberhorne*, one week, but still with the utmost confidence he wagered he would get to South Africa first, despite the handicap. Details were worked out at the Tacoma Mission known as Seaman's Rest. Make no mistake about it, such races were taken with the utmost seriousness. Fierce pride rode on the line with both shipmasters and crews.

Word of the forthcoming race quickly spread along the waterfront, into the local newspaper and to virtually every household. Excitement ran high.

On Oct. 26, the *Earl of Dalhousie*, loaded with 25,428 bags of wheat, weighed anchor outbound for Cape Town. On Nov. 3, the *Imberhorne* departed with 31,385 bags of wheat headed for the same African port.

McBride grew anxious, but had to wait on some last minute repairs and some extra canvas. Also, the ship was short a few hands in the foc's'cle which necessitated the nefarious work of boarding house crimps to fill the empty berths.

Second officer Duncan Houston and seaman Henrik Jacobsen went ashore the evening before departure to visit the mission, and to bid farewell to the hostess, asking that she might write them at their African destination of Dalgoa Bay.

Finally on Nov. 11, the *Atalanta* sailed with 23,967 sacks of wheat, towing out to Cape Flattery behind the steam tug *Tyee*. The tall ship spread her canvas like the wings of a phoenix, gracefully leaning to the wind, pursuing a southwesterly direction. The breeze was brisk giving promise of an excellent start.

On the following day, a weather front moved quickly in with ominous storm clouds. The glass dropped fast and voluminous seas began lashing the Washington and Oregon coastlines. Offshore the *Atalanta* dipped her nose into the brine and moved along under storm canvas.

Came Nov. 17. All around was a seething mass of white spume shooting skyward from liquid mountains that rose to unprecedented heights and then dropped into deep troughs, like bottomless pits. The vessel raced on in pursuit of her two rivals. Come Hell or high water, Captain McBride was determined to win the race, but then, even the most capable of shipmasters can err, and a fatal mistake is a final mistake. In this case, disaster!

On Nov. 19, bold headlines in Pacific Northwest newspapers carried the terse message that the *Atalanta* had been wrecked and that only three of her crew of 27 had survived. Had it not been for those survivors the world might not have known of the sudden and tragic demise of the clipper ship. Clinging to a battered ship's boat, fighting against overwhelming odds, Francis McMahon, John Webber, and George Fraser made the beach through thundering surf, one with no apparel except a cotton shirt. After recuperating on the beach under a driving rain, the trio managed to walk to the home of a nearby farmer who gave them succor, and got out word of the regrettable tragedy.

The *Atalanta*, skirting too close to the hostile outcrops of the central Oregon coast struck a hidden reef, west of Big River, four miles south of Alsea Bay, (16 miles south of Yaquina Bay) and about a mile offshore. Breaking in half forward of amidships, the masts were carried away and the decks swept clear.

Captain Clark and his surfmen from the Yaquina Lifesaving Station, hours later, arrived on the scene but there was nothing they could do except transport the survivors to Newport.

Seaman Fraser, one of the survivors recalled that when the *Atalanta* got amid the breakers all hands were summoned, first officer Charles Hunter frantically spreading the alarm by shouting down the hatch for all below to get topside fast and not to bother with their clothing. Among the first to hit the deck was McBride. Immediately he bellowed,

"Put the wheel hard up, square the yards!"

But, nobody gave much heed to the order. The captain turned to the officer of the watch.

"By God, Hunter, where are you bringing us?"

McBride's words were barely audible over the howling wind. Combers lifted the ship three times bringing her down hard, the mizzenmast aback and dead square. Once again McBride shouted an order;

"All hands lay aft, we're going to wear ship!"

According to Fraser's account...."I got ahold of the main brace and all of us started to pull. We squared the main braces, but the next moment the ship struck and shipped a sea forward of the main rigging. Second mate Houston then shouted, 'Clear away the boats, that's our only chance!' "

"We jumped upon the boat skids to clear the port boat," continued Fraser. "I had no knife and asked seaman Brook Williamson to throw me one . . . we cut the cover forward and the two of us tore it off . . ."

Following was a nightmare, all the men running to the mizzen rigging, for now the vessel was shipping water all over. Before Fraser could gain the poop, he was swept across the deck, grabbing a stanchion until the sea had spent its force. Then he climbed hand over hand into the mizzen rigging. As the ship lurched to port, he climbed to the crosstrees and held fast as the vessel righted herself and listed to starboard. Fraser then crawled along the crosstrees to the port rigging. At that moment the combers lifted the wreck and slammed it down hard, and there she settled, the impact causing her to break apart just forward of the mainmast which in turn came crashing down taking the mizzen along with it.

Fraser recalled being thrown rudely into the churning vortex swimming frantically to the main hatch cover floating nearby. The heaving seas tossed wreckage about, one piece hitting him on the head. Still, he reached his goal. Another seaman tried to climb onto the hatch cover with him but it lacked sufficient buoyancy to hold them both, so Fraser swam to another hatch cover. At almost the same time, a battered lifeboat floated by half full of water. With herculean effort he managed to climb in, coming eyeball to eyeball with seaman Webber struggling up on the other side of the craft. The two then managed to haul McMahon aboard, but without the aid of oars and amidst a wild sea spread with pulsating wreckage, they had no way of helping perhaps a dozen shipmates clinging to the rigging of the fallen mizzenmast. One seaman hung to the cam rail and another clutched a davit, fighting desperately to keep from being swept away.

The lifeboat drifted clear of the wreck, its three occupants making a desperate effort to keep from swamping. They managed to rip the tops off the air tight tanks using the plate to propel the craft till the winds carried them toward the beach. After a devilish ride through the breakers the men were roughly deposited on the wet sands.

McMahon's account told of his being on the port watch when the *Atalanta* stranded. He recalled Captain McBride running toward him, tears in his eyes, sobbing. "My boy," he repined, "we are lost...I can't swim but two strokes."

McMahon remained near his skipper after they were thrown into the sea. The Old Man grabbed some fallen spars and was struggling amidst the wreckage as the other drifted away, treading water from one piece of debris to the next. About that time, Webber and Fraser managed to pull him into the lifeboat. McBride soon vanished beneath the waves, probably caught in a pincers between the spars.

Mournful cries for help came from first officer Hunter and the others scattered about the mizzen rigging like victims of a spider web. One by one they disappeared from sight. The man who clung to the davit was the last to go. As his strength finally gave out he let out a death wail, broke his grip and dropped into the foamy brine, never again to be seen.

As the sea covered traces of its dastardly act the brevity of life was never more apparent. Imagine the thoughts flashing through the minds of the victims hanging there between Heaven and Hell waiting to meet their Maker.

At the subsequent hearing, McMahon testified he told Hunter on the night of the wreck, about 11 p.m., Nov. 16 that a light sighted must have been, "a landsite because it was so steady." The first officer, however, insisted that it was only a passing vessel.

Could it have been Yaquina Head Lighthouse?

The ship had been on a starboard tack, course, south by east, one half east, McMahon recalled. Throughout Wednesday (Nov. 16) the *Atalanta* had sailed south by west, but the shipmaster had become irritable because of the aggravatingly slow progress, and course was accordingly changed.

Webber placed the blame for the wreck squarely on Captain McBride for his drive to make up time in the race rather than to remain in safer waters. He claimed the desire to cut out unnecessary water and not following the safety of a general three degrees west course after casting off from the tug at Cape Flattery had placed the vessel in jeopardy.

All three survivors remembered McBride's terse words when he darted up from below at the time of the stranding. In essence he placed the blame on the officer of the watch, when exclaiming, "By God, Hunter, where are you bringing us?"

The survivors, however, held the captain at fault, he having been the one who set the course.

It was 16 hours after the wreck that word reached the Yaquina Bay Lifesaving Station, there being no telegraph at Alsea Bay. Notification was received at 6 p.m.,

Nov. 17, Captain Clark, keeper, and his crew immediately going into action. There being no road connecting the two bays, the surfboat skipper borrowed a team of horses from a local farmer which was used to pull the cart, bearing the boat and equipment, along the beach. The horses, tired from a day's work in the field, just plain gave out about half way to the Alsea. With several miles yet to go the surfmen became the beasts of burden by pulling the surfboat and line-throwing equipment. Though almost exhausted they kept on till reaching the scene of the wreck four miles south of Alsea Bay.

But alas, it was all in vain, for the breakers still rumbled at unprecedented heights. It would have been suicidal to run the surf. After all the time that had passed it would have been a miracle if any additional survivors remained. The wreck had been pulverized and the spectators were in accordance with the wisdom of the keeper's decision.

Found among the wreckage that littered nearby beaches was the *Atalanta's* logbook, its writing still legible and containing the last entry which read like the ship's obituary:

"Nov. 17, 1898, 1 a.m., Cape Foulweather is concealed by fog and there are heavy sheets of rain."

Captain Kenny, Lloyd's agent and surveyor at Tacoma who knew Captain McBride well, could not believe that a man so well versed in the ways of the sea would have let his command get so close to shore.

"This was an extraordinary latitude for a wheat carrier to be in," he insisted, and at first thought the vessel might have been mistaken for one of two German square-riggers also carrying the name *Atalanta*.

Four months were to pass before the master of the *Imberhorne* and *Earl of Dalhousie* were to hear of the loss of the *Atalanta*. Though the tragedy was over the memories lingered on. Three bodies washed ashore several days later after the wreck but were so badly mutilated that they could not be identified.

At the hearing presided over by British vice consul James Laidlaw, Captain Smith of the *Cape Wrath* and Captain Brush of the *Poseidon,* their final conclusion surprisingly did not point an accusing finger at the late master of the *Atalanta*. It read:

"The ship Atalanta somehow broke off her course and ran on the reef in the night."

That simple conclusion did not coincide with the testimony of the survivors who cited reckless navigation and the fact that the master of a ship is always responsible for its fate. The fact that the *Atalanta* was deeply laden may have been one of the reasons she broke up, though it was hard for the experts to explain how such a well found vessel could break up so quickly.

Also brought out at the hearing was the fact that six

members of the crew had been shanghaied at Tacoma. Two of the survivors, Fraser and McMahon, both testified that they were abducted, the latter that his advance $35 had been taken from him by an infamous Tacoma boarding house bully named Dave Evans. He further told of being laid out cold by a knock on the head and that he was carried aboard ship. Fraser said he was "worked over by an ex-prize fighting runner before being taken aboard."

The latter piece of testimony did much to throttle the illicit operations of the boarding house which had long preyed on seamen. It further promoted the humanitarian work of the Seaman's Mission.

A different light was placed on the wreck by the residents of the Alsea area. One young lad named Charley Bobell said all he could see through the murk were the masts. Spotting a survivor in a life preserver, he waded out in the surf but could not reach him. When the wretched individual was finally pulled ashore he was exhausted and dying. Though Bobell had been taught artificial respiration by his father, those present would not let him touch the victim until the coroner arrived. Shortly after, the man succumbed and was buried on a sand hill next to the grave of a black man who had earlier washed up on the beach.

For years, a ship's wheel marked the spot, but finally disappeared with the ravages of time. Whether it was the wheel of the *Atalanta* was never ascertained.

Though it was not mentioned in any other report, young Bobell claimed that "All were very drunk," but whether he was referring to the survivors or just making an irresponsible statement that the wreck was due to drunkenness, was never revealed.

Captain McBride was asleep in his cabin when the vessel struck and it is doubtful that he or his first officer would have tolerated drunkenness at the height of a storm. Whatever the condition of the ship's complement, nothing could reverse the fact that of the 27-man crew, only three survived. Some of the bodies drifted several miles southward to Ten Mile Creek.

Local settlers reaped a harvest from the spoils, including two barrels of whiskey, hogsheads of fresh meat and salt pork. Other mementos found resting places in homes and museums, grim reminders of that regrettable hour in the late fall of 1898 when the *Atalanta* reached her last port — a port of no return.

Oregon's most coveted commercial sailing vessel was the full-rigged (clipper) ship *Western Shore* of 1,177 tons, built at North Bend, Oregon in 1874. Though her career was brief she was perhaps the finest vessel of her type ever built on the Pacific Coast, once logging an all-time record voyage from Oregon to Liverpool in 97 days. R. W. Simpson drew the sail plan, A.M. Simpson designed the hull, and John Kruse constructed the vessel. Reproduced from a painting by W. S. Stephenson, courtesy of Grace Kruse Dement. The vessel was wrecked at Duxbury Reef, Calif., in 1878.

On the crusty fringes of Boiler Bay, named for the ship's boiler seen in the upper center of the photo. It is all that remains of the steam schooner *J. Marhoffer* which while on fire, drifted into the bay May 18, 1910 and became a total loss. Note the beachcombers in the lower right hand corner.

CHAPTER SIX
BARS, JETTIES AND THE
ARMY CORPS OF ENGINEERS

A LOOK AT THE MAP of the United States will reveal that Oregon has the straightest coastline of any major maritime state in the union. Most access to harbors is through bar openings, and good commercial portals are few in number, demanding constant maintenance. Without jetties and properly maintained bar depths, nature's forces would win the battle and marine graveyards would be far better stocked than at present.

Synonymous with improved navigation on the Oregon coast is the Portland District Army Corps of Engineers. A century ago, the work of the District consisted of small, simple, almost quaint efforts to improve navigation, according to Col. Robert L. Bangert. He cited the pulling of snags from river waterways, cutting bars 17 feet deep with primitive bucket dredges or dynamiting rocks out of the Columbia River as representative of work done in the early years. By comparison today, the agency maintains all of the main ocean bar entrances and jetties with federal funds and has tackled the building of massive complex dams on the Columbia and Willamette rivers plus a host of navigational projects that run annually into the multi-millions of dollars. That branch of the service has given yeoman output to the state of Oregon.

The Corps traces its origin to the earliest days of the republic, when on June 16, 1775, the day before the Battle of Bunker Hill, George Washington created the first engineering unit in the Army. Its services did not become active on the Oregon coast till 1866 when Congress initiated a series of River and Harbor Acts which made the Corps responsible for the development and maintenance of all officially designated federal waterways, including Oregon's ten major coastal rivers. Early works included fortifications as well as public works and the construction of lighthouses. Fort Stevens was constructed just south of the Columbia River entrance in 1863-4. It was ineffectually shelled by a Japanese submarine during World War II, making it the only U.S. continental fort to be fired on in the last 17 decades.

To date, the Army Engineers have constructed 22 jetties on the ten major Oregon rivers, plus accompanying navigation channels on eight of them. Total length of these jetties is 28 miles. Individual lengths range from 6.6 miles on the south jetty of the Columbia River entrance to .24 miles on the north Chetco project in southern Oregon. These jetties contain nearly 26 million tons of rock and concrete fill which if stacked on a football field would tower skyward more than a mile and a half.

Taxpayers have forked over more than $100 million dollars for these Oregon projects, monies well spent, the end product invaluable to the martime industry and the public at large. Commerce, the trade of the world, reaches into every household and to every citizen.

Though Oregon coast projects are only a segment of the Army Engineers' Portland District program, it is the segment that is dealt with in this chapter. The growing importance of the Columbia and Willamette rivers as navigational waterways led to the establishment of the Portland District in 1871. Without improvements on these rivers, the development of commerce in the region would be halted. Major Henry M. Robert, the first Portland District Engineer, most remembered for his publication of Robert's *Rules of Order,* was directed to establish an office in Portland and resume work under the authorization, ''Improvement of Rivers in Oregon.''

Going back even further in history, the first engineers sent by the military to Oregon Territory were at the beginning of the 19th century. It is the Louisiana Purchase which links the history of Oregon and the activities of the Corps of Engineers. Shortly after negotiations for the Purchase had been completed, President Thomas Jefferson appointed two Army Captains, Meriwether Lewis and William Clark, to lead an expedition across the uncharted continent to the mouth of the Columbia River. Basic aim was to find, ''the most direct and practicable water communication across this continent.'' Until that time little was known of the Pacific Northwest since Captain Robert Gray's discovery of the river in 1792. The vast extent of the land spreading to the north and west of the mouth of the Missouri to the Pacific Ocean was a mystery to American citizens. Tales from trappers who had dared venture west and legends of the Indians formed the total sum of intelligence on the area until the intrepid Lewis and Clark made their epic trek to Oregon. Beginning in the spring of 1804, the expedition progressed up the Missouri to its headwaters, portaged to waters of the Columbia, and canoed to its mouth. The winter of 1805-06 was spent at the mouth of the Columbia, where the party erected Fort Clatsop. The two Army captains put their backgrounds in engineering and science to work not only in forging their way across the wild country but in recording the nature of the land they encountered.

Until 1824, the Corps had worked mainly on military projects. Some public works were done, mainly navigation projects, but the President was as likely to assign the work to private concerns as to the Corps of Engineers.

With the close of the Civil War in 1865, an age of tremendous growth was experienced. On the establishment in 1866 of the authority, ''Rivers and Harbors of the Pacific Coast'', Army Engineer activities in the Far West were on an equal footing with the rest of the nation for the first time. San Francisco was the location of the office, and its authority included all the Pacific Northwest, Brevet Lieutenant Colonel R. S. Williamson being the first district engineer.

Where early Oregon coast work is concerned, the name that stands out above all others is Major G. L. Gillespie. For three years, from October 1878 until July 1881, when he was district engineer in Portland, there was considerable activity and progress. In 1901 he became Chief of Engineers. He played a large part in the supervision of the Cascades Canal and the construction of Tillamook Rock Light Station, one of the nation's greatest engineering feats, plus improvements at Coos Bay, Coquille River and Yaquina Bay.

Mariners of our day seldom stop to think about the jetties that control the river entrances to Oregon ports. Of the ten projects of great commercial value, some were completed before the turn of the century, and though all have undergone renewal from time to time, some of the basic original layouts remain. In addition, the agency today has completed its seventh small-boat basin on the Oregon coast, a breakwater-boat basin at Port Orford. The Engineers are also responsible for the harbor entrance and facilities at Depoe Bay, probably the smallest ''doghole'' in the continental 48, though certainly not the least active.

Following is a list of the major Oregon Coast jetty projects and their completion dates:

Columbia River
    South jetty completed in 1895
    North jetty completed in 1917
    Spur jetty ''A'' completed in 1939

Nehalem Bay: completed in 1918

Tillamook Bay
    Channel to Miami completed in 1927
    North jetty completed in 1927
    Bayocean dike completed in 1956
    Small-boat basin, Garibaldi, completed in 1958

Yaquina Bay & Harbor
    North & South jetties completed in 1896

Siuslaw River
    Jetties completed in 1917
    Channel completed in 1930

Umpqua River
    North jetty completed in 1919
    South jetty completed in 1933
    Training jetty completed in 1950

Coos Bay
    Jetties completed in 1928-29
    Channel dredged to 24 feet in 1937

Coquille River
    Jetties completed in 1908
    Entrance channel completed in 1933

Rogue River
    Jetties completed in 1960

Chetco River
    Jetties completed in 1957

Diplomacy, always a factor in Corps of Engineer planning has to be even more profound today what with the emphasis on environmental status. Every project must be looked at from two sides — one the vast offshore waters of the Pacific, and the other in the estuaries of the coastal rivers. In other words the commercial value of a project in any river must be considered in the light of what damage it might do to estuary life. Sometimes the Engineers have to grit their teeth. The coastal region embraces two distinct marine environments, and many marine species move between these two ecosystems at different stages in their development. Estuaries perform a unique and often vital function in the life cycles of a large number of plants and animals. An estuary includes all the area where ocean salt water mingles with fresh water. Here the tides pump in rich supplies of nutrients and oxygen from the ocean while the fresh water flow removes waste materials. In many places, solar radiation penetrates shallow tidal waters to allow abundant vegetation growth. The result is a unique feeding and spawning ground for many forms of marine life that are important links in the food chain.

Some 217 square miles of the Oregon coast are occupied as estuaries, a valuable ecological asset. But, the two problems come face to face here, and often the Engineers have hard decisions to make, as much of this same area contains important commercial harbors and recreational areas. A proper balance is called for where nature and man-made use of these unique ecosystems must be carefully considered.

And how is this done? An example of how efforts are actively taken to accomplish this is the Corps dredging program to keep Oregon's coastal harbors open to commercial and recreational navigation. All proposed dredging activity is carefully reviewed by federal and state environmental and fishery agencies, and is open to the general public whose voice in the matter is encouraged.

Wherever possible, the dredging material or spoils are utilized to provide or enhance wildlife and marine life habitat. Special procedures are followed to minimize the impact of dredging on the natural environment. In addition, the Engineers are always involved in research, locally and nationally, and administer a permit program to protect coastal and river environments. The authority given to that body originated with the River and Harbor Act of 1899, which allows no dredging or construction in navigable waters without permission of the Secretary of the Army, and that act handled with tact and authority is still valid after nearly 80 years. Original intent was aimed at navigation right-of-way, but now extends to environmental considerations. Today, any public or private concern wishing to build or dredge in coastal or river waters must apply for a permit for approval or disapproval.

In the early to middle 1800's, navigation from the ocean into the Oregon coastal rivers was extremely dangerous and often impossible, and as proof the main bar entrances along the Oregon coast claimed many ships. Each river deposited large quantities of sand and sediment at their respective mouths and would build up hazardous spits or bars that literally crawled across the entrances, making official charts for one year erroneous

for the next. Channels constantly changed, and the toll in lives and property was legion. It demanded skippers with nerves of steel and a sixth sense to risk bar crossings, expecially with ships of sail where the winds were a basic factor. The portals which catered to the greatest volume in commerce naturally claimed the most ships back when the bars were in their raw condition, the best example being the Columbia River entrance.

Many coastal mariners in the early years were of the opinion that the Coquille River bar was the most hazardous especially when a sailing vessel lost the wind while in transit. The difficulty at the Coquille was shifting sand and rock obstruction. The survey completed in the summer of 1878 was performed by Assistant Engineer Channing M. Bolton. He learned from the pilot at the Coquille, Captain Parker, that:

"The sands shift so rapidly that I cannot rely on information from one day to the next, but have to make a thorough examination of the channel before each trip."

A request was made for $164,000 to build two training walls two to three thousand feet long, to run parallel to each other along the deepest section of the existing channel to deep water. The plan was designed to increase velocity due to the contraction of the channel to keep it scoured to a depth of 12 feet.

Work continued under Major Gillespie in 1880 after the plan by Major Wilson was revised. Within two years the jetty had reached a length of 850 feet and by 1886 was 2,000 feet long. Two years later, the $215,000 jetty was completed. By 1908, a second jetty was finished.

The survey made under Major Wilson at Coos Bay in 1878 showed that obstructions to navigation were caused by shifting sands and by unpredictable tides. A detailed chart was made of the entrance, and plans called for construction of two jetties to cost $972,000. The Board of Engineers accepted the findings but ruled that only one wall would be built at a cost not to exceed $600,000. Work got underway during Major Gillespie's tenure in 1879, but it was found that the floor of the bar was too rocky to permit pile driving. Thus timber cribs were built to hold the heavy rock. After two years, only 700 feet of the cribbing had been put in place. Gillespie called for more funds in 1881. He stated:

"...if better water in the lower harbor and more direct channel over the bar can be maintained all the lumber interests bordering the bay will be increased in value, the mills will be kept running throughout the year...the improvement will be of benefit to all southern Oregon, for at the present time this is the only port south of the Columbia River from which there is a regular steamer line south, and from which lumber is shipped in noteworthy quantities. It is possible to built up here a very important trade, not only with San Francisco, but with the islands of the Pacific which give a demand for lumber, and the various kinds of excellent timber.''

Spectacular surf—the Coast Guard motor lifeboat *CG 44303* on practice maneuvers off the Umpqua River on the central Oregon coast. Official Coast Guard photo.

Work dragged on until completed in 1889, due to slow receipt of funds and damage to the jetty and tramway caused by excessive seas. But Coos Bay was to emerge as the most important port on the Oregon Coast. The total jetty project was not completed until 1929, and the bar was deepened to 24 feet in 1937.

A third project under Gillespie's reign was at Yaquina Bay. Surveys made in 1879, and again in the spring of 1880 called for a 2,500 foot jetty drawn up by Assistant Engineer J. S. Polhemus. The bay entrance had been limited to only seven feet by a sand spit and outer shoals. Gillespie said of the bay:

"If a depth of 17 feet on the bar at high tide can be maintained by improvement, the harbor will become a shipping port of great importance, not only for the products raised in the immediate vicinity, but for a great part of the Upper Willamette Valley, with which it is said that there will soon be a railroad connection."

The plan was approved in July 1880 and in the same

year an initial appropriation of $40,000 was forthcoming. Progress was aggravatingly slow. According to Major Gillespie:

"The village of Newport, in the harbor, is very small and at the time the assistant engineer took charge of the improvement, the single sawmill which the bay possessed was out of order, and had no logs on hand suitable for the construction. In consequence, considerable time was spent collecting logs before any lumber for the scows or timber for the cribs could be obtained, and all the various materials and implements of construction—iron, anchors, picks, chains, crowbars, oakum etc., had to be purchased either at Portland or San Francisco, and sent to the harbor by special boat. These considerations not only made the initial preparation very expensive, but delayed—much beyond my patience—the time of the beginning of the jetty."

The entrance to the harbor (Yaquina) was considered so dangerous that no tugboat captain was willing to hire

Up, up and over, Coast Guard rescue craft noses solidly into a whopper off the Oregon coast. Such craft are self-righting and sometimes do a 360 degree roll, a nightmare experience for any crew. Official Coast Guard photo.

out and assist the work, so a tug had to be purchased in San Francisco.

The exceedingly strong and variable currents at Yaquina Bay presented the party with the greatest imaginable difficulties. Work in boats became impractical, and the assistant engineer (Polhemus) elected to build the jetty from the shore outward. He stated that,

"... the stone for the purpose has to be delivered by a tramway 2,500 feet long, starting from a wharf erected in a sheltered spot on the inside of the harbor. This plan necessitates the handling of the stone four times before it reaches its final place in the jetty, but I see no other way of accomplishing the desired end."

This method was used for the next seven years by Polhemus until the initial south jetty project was completed in 1888. Actually the north and south jetty program was not completed until 1896, and as difficult as it was, became the first double set of bar jetties on the Oregon coast.

Gillespie was still district engineer when the initial important work on the Columbia River bar was begun. The River and Harbor Act of 1878 had authorized an examination at the mouth of the Columbia to determine the nature and cost of permanent developments. The good major reported the following year:

"It is impossible to give an estimate of the extent to which commerce will be benefitted by this improvement. Should an improvement be adopted for the harbor which will give an increased depth of water over the bar and enable vessels drawing 22 to 23 feet of water to cross without danger at all stages of the tide, the commerce of the whole Northwest will be increased beyond the capabilities of anyone to estimate at the present time."

Even in the 1876-78 period total value of exports crossing over the Columbia bar amounted to nearly $20 million. Gillespie stated:

"The citizens of Astoria are anxious that some extensive improvement should be undertaken in hand to in-

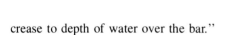
Quarrying rock for the Coos Bay jetty, rebuilt in 1965. Portland District Army Corps of Engineers photo.

Rocks weighing from two to 30 tons went into the construction of the Columbia River north jetty. Tug *Samson* herds rock barges.

crease to depth of water over the bar."

With the mouth of the river in its natural state, the tides and currents from the ocean, plus the natural current of the Columbia itself, could alter almost overnight the entrance to the river. Charts dating back several decades showed that two channels existed at the mouth of the river. The difficulty lay in the fact that of these channels, neither was of sufficient depth nor dependable enough to guarantee safe bar transit, especially during adverse conditions. Only the most foolhardy of skippers dared cross without the aid of a pilot or a tugboat; in fact, in the 1878-81 period several vessels became victims of the bar. Channel depth changed abruptly, and the 17 to 21-foot depth was never certain for a long period of time.

In 1880, Gillespie submitted a plan for an 8,000-foot jetty at the river's south entrance. This, compared with the other Oregon jetties, was almost three times as long, and the cost was estimated at $4,750,000, which in those years was mighty big money. It really shook the Congress when such funds were requested. The project was designed to obtain a secure, deep channel by concentrating the current of the river and the tidal action of the sea. The request was denied by the board of review. Oregon interests were furious and clamped on the pressure until the plan was reviewed by the board at the order of Congress. The west was being opened, and a blueprint even more grandiose than Gillespie's was adopted. Citizens had sent evidence of the large number of shipwrecks, while authorized maritime interests presented the commercial value of river commerce. The mammoth south jetty was completed in 1895 and the north jetty in 1917, and up until the 1930's it was the largest project undertaken by the Portland District.

The massive Columbia River jetties of the 1970's have been rebuilt many times and the present 48-foot bar depth on the Columbia is far beyond the dreams of the early Army Engineers. Back in 1884-85 when the south jetty project was in its infancy, men were hired, materials were ordered and delivered, offices, shops, a wharf and a dock were constructed and an approach trestle from the beach completed. A quarry site for the rock was chosen and housing and mess facilities installed. Then the final survey was made, but the 1886 appropriation was a mere $170,000. Two years were to pass until Congress coughed up $500,000. Still more money, much more was needed and thus it took ten years and $4 million to complete the jetty. When finished in 1895 it measured 30 feet at its crest and from 80 to 90 feet along the base. The bar depth was about 31 feet.

Though the bar depth gradually increased to 36-37 feet at the entrance, shoaling problems demanded a second jetty. The decision was made to proceed with construction of the north jetty to bring the project depth to a reliable 40 feet. Cost of the 2½ mile jetty was to be about $6 million. Actual construction was started in 1914, with Kern & Kern as general contractors under the direction of the Army Engineers. The job was completed in 1917, and the survey proved right, the bar depth gradually exceeding the planned 40 feet. When completed, the Columbia River jetties were the largest in the world, and for the first time, there was an almost sure guarantee of safe transit provided all of the prevailing rules were followed.

After completion of the north jetty, District Engineer Lt. Col. C. H. McKinstry reported:

"The improvement has made it possible for the largest vessels operating on the Pacific Coast to enter and

Construction workers at the rock unloading site during construction of the Columbia River north jetty. Grace Kern photo.

Self-dumping rock train used in the construction of the north jetty of the Columbia River about 1916. Courtesy Grace Kern.

leave at all normal stages of tide in any weather except during the most severe storms. Bar-bound vessels, once so common, are now, on account of improved conditions, rarely to be seen.''

Portland marine interests with the improvement of the bar demanded the deepening of the Columbia and Willamette to the Rose City's door and this project through the years has been a major endeavor. Without a deep river channel all vessels would have to unload part of their cargoes at Astoria.

All of the bar projects on the Oregon coast presented difficulties for the builders and often winter storms did irreparable damage. In addition, when large funds were requested for bar projects in the early years, the Engineers found that many of the solons in Washington D.C. were totally ignorant of the maritime needs of the West Coast. Whenever the word Oregon was mentioned many thought only of Indians and were reluctant to pass sufficient funds to complete projects. In 1880 when Major Bolton recommended that $200,000 would have to be spent for the jetties at the entrance to the Coquille, the political giants raised their eyebrows.

''Where's the Coquille?'' said one.

''Never heard of the place,'' exclaimed another.

The major explained that without the aid of the jetties the Coquille, portal to vast stands of timber, was extremely dangerous. Through the work of some tireless individuals, $20,000 was squeezed from Uncle Sam to begin the project.

The first commercial schooner crossed the Coos Bay bar in 1852 with great difficulty. The initial vessel to bring cargo across the bar was the *Cynosure,* skippered by Captain Whippy, in 1853. He send out a boat crew to seek the proper channel, but the rough seas capsized the craft and its occupants were all drowned. The *Cynosure* finally got across the bar with its supplies for the newly opened Randolph mines.

Casualties were numerous at the entrance to Coos Bay, second only to those of the Columbia River bar. Between the 1850's and 1880's many well known commercial carriers came to grief, the *Cohansa, Jackson, Cyclops, Noyo, New World, Fearless, D.M. Hall, Ida Rogers, Gussie Telfair, Charles Devens* and *Energy* to name a few. Some of those imprisoned vessels were refloated, but most ended their days ensnared by the tentacles of sand.

In 1856, the schooner *Quadratus* was totally wrecked in an unfortunate episode that claimed a mother and child, and an A. M. Simpson Lumber Co. official. Four years earlier, the USRC brig *Captain Lincoln* was driven aground a few miles north of Coos Bay carrying a detachment of soldiers. The vessel sprang a leak in heavy seas before coming to her final resting place. The survivors set up a camp where they could carefully watch the actions of the Indians. Naming the place Camp Castaway, they awaited their fate.

The ill-fated vessel had sailed from San Francisco Dec. 28, 1851 with C Troop of the First Dragoons under command of Lt. H. W. Stanton, destination Port Orford. Instead, the ship was driven northward of her destination by a persistent storm, grinding to an unscheduled stop on Jan. 3, 1852.

Camp Castaway existed about four months before the troopers abandoned and marched southward along the beaches. The Indians though curious, remained passive during the entire operation.

The above and numerous other marine disasters led to early efforts for bar and navigation improvements along the Oregon coast. The fickle temperaments of the bar entrances were a serious blockade to the growth of waterborne commerce and in many cases, shipmasters refused to risk crossings except under the most favorable conditions. The answer in most cases was in the construction of jetties, the express purpose being to concentrate and accelerate waterflow at the mouth of a river. This concentrated waterflow scours out shallow sand deposits and stabilizes the river channel. Combined with periodic dredging, jetties provide a safe route from ocean to river. Construction begins generally with a bed of rocks placed on the ocean floor. Larger boulders are placed atop this bed to form the main body of the jetty. Boulders get progressively larger toward the jetty's seaward end where wave action is the most powerful. Here rocks up to and over 30 tons each are used to resist the perpetual onslaught of the sea. Prior to the 1950's, jetty rocks were hauled to placement site by rail dump cars. Today they are hauled by dumptruck and placed by large movable cranes. Some of the older jetties still have the remains of the wooden trestles which supported the little steam engines that rolled on the rails pulling rock-laden dump cars.

Although jetties stabilize and deepen river channels they do not entirely solve the problem. Each river continues to pour tons of sediment downstream toward the ocean. In order to keep the bar channels and harbors clear, dredging is essential. A navigation channel provides a deepwater path through the river bar and upstream to the port area. Each year from May through October, government dredges move 18 million yards of sediment from coastal river channels. Dredging is accomplished primarily with two types of vessels, both of which vacuum sediment off the bottom with a powerful suction device. The dredgers are filled with internal compartments which handle dredged material and later dump it at sea or in deepwater areas. Pipeline dredges, often operated by private contractors, transport the dredged material through large pipes to deposit sites on shore.

A hopper dredge acts as a huge vacuum cleaner sucking dredge material off the harbor bottom. The suction comes from large dredge pumps which then route the material through discharge pipes into hoppers where the excess water runs off and is piped back to sea. The hoppers are sealed off from the rest of the ship so they can be opened along the ship's bottom to deposit the material in pre-selected deepwater areas.

An example of what can happen to an Oregon bar entrance when jetties fall into disrepair and dredging is discontinued, is readily seen at the Nehalem Bay entrance. When the jetty project was completed, in 1918, there was sufficient lumber and salmon interests to war-rant its maintenance. However, as the years passed, much of the basic industry on the bay declined and so did government funds for repairing the jetties and dredging the bar channel. Where once commercial lumber schooners and small freight boats crossed, one today can almost walk across the entrance at extreme low tide. At this writing efforts were being made to renew interest in rebuilding the jetties so flattened by pounding seas that they appear like scattered, rotten teeth. The controlling bar depth is a mere five feet and the channel changeable.

Alsea Bay bar on the other hand never was granted funds for jetties, but a half century ago small coastal steamers could negotiate the channel on high tides. Today the entrance has a shifting bar with a depth of around six feet. With a rising tide, the *Pacific Coast Pilot* says the bar fills in with sand and the full effect of the tide cannot be counted on. Sometimes even small pleasure craft hit the bottom. In the case of the Alsea, it is believed the logging activity upriver through the years has caused slides on the river banks during periods of heavy rains. Without natural growth, silt has washed down to the river mouth building up against the tidal action.

Seagulls can walk across the entrance of the Yachats River but descendants of the pioneers can remember when a 40-foot commercial craft was able to cross the bar.

The Oregon coast attracts millions of visitors annually and many camp and fish at the numerous parks along the shoreline, several of which abut the bar jetties.

The seaward end of any Oregon jetty is often swept by waves that pose a real danger to the novice trespasser. A single ocean wave can generate a force of 20 tons and woe be to any person atop the jetty when the surf is running high and creaming the rocks.

Bar entrances on the Oregon coast from north to south are, Columbia River, Nehalem Bay, Tillamook Bay, Siletz Bay, Depoe Bay, Yaquina Bay, Alsea River, Siuslaw River, Umpqua River, Coos Bay, Coquille River, Rogue River and Chetco River. A breakwater port is maintained at Port Orford.

At this writing, the Portland District is operating three hopper dredges, the *Biddle, Harding* and *Pacific** on Oregon coast projects. In 1977, the Corp's largest hopper dredge, the 525 foot *Essayons*, was sent around from the East Coast to redredge the mouth of the Columbia River to its project depth of 48 feet. A large silt up had lessened the depth to 44 feet, too big a job for the District's largest dredge. It was the first time the queen of the Army Engineer fleet was needed on the West Coast in 20 years, she having originally established the 48 foot bar depth.

By comparison, the smallest hopper dredge is the *Pacific,* a 180 foot craft with a hopper capacity of 500 cubic yards, ideal for maintenance work on the tricky

Siuslaw bar, as well as at the Tillamook bar, Umpqua bar, Coquille, Rogue and Chetco rivers. She is small enough to work where her larger sisters seldom go. Not only the smallest in the Portland District, the *Pacific* is also the oldest, having been built in 1937.

In 1857, the Corps of Engineers developed the first successful seagoing hopper dredge. Today the agency operates 15 hopper dredges in coastal and inland waterways of the U.S. Hydrographic survey vessels with complex electronic equipment are used to perform survey work to determine depths in project areas.

Now, with a brief knowledge of the jetties, bars and of the responsibilities of the Corps of Army Engineers, Portland District, let us take a backward glance at some interesting cases of ill-fated ships that might have been spared with bar and channel improvements in the early years.

Ships, like people, take on personalities. Some are successful, some failures, some have lenghy careers, others drop quickly from the scene, some are breadwinners, others floating coffins.

The lumber schooner *Phil Sheridan,* a coaster, had been trading along the Pacific Coast from the time of her completion at Little River, Calif., in 1869. Built for C. Brown of San Francisco at a cost of $20,000, she did the majority of her trading along the redwood coast and southern Oregon, usually with a minimal freeboard under overloads of lumber. For the first few years of her service life she made good money for her owners, but her good fortune suddenly took a nosedive when on Sept. 14, 1876 while crossing foggy Umpqua River bar, before the advent of jetties, she locked horns with the much larger steamer *Ancon,* narrowly averting going to a watery grave.

After costly repairs, came December 1878 and her crew was gathered excitedly at the taff rail, viewing the overturned hull of a sailing vessel, floating derelict at the whims of the tides and currents off the Rogue River entrance. The *Sheridan's* skipper ordered a closer examination and to the surprise of the observers it was found to be a sistership, the schooner *Johanna M. Brock,* built to the same specifications as the *Sheridan,* at Little River, by the same builder, Tom Peterson. Apparently she had capsized off the Rogue on December 10 after her cargo shifted in heavy seas. No sign was found of her seven man crew, the wreck finally grounding south of the river entrance.

Seamen of old were a superstitious lot, and not without exception was the crew of the *Sheridan.* On arrival at Little River, flag at half-mast, Dec. 29, 1878, the schooner brought the tragic news of her sistership and missing crew.

The jinx continued. A few months later, the *Sheridan* again grounded while crossing the Umpqua bar. This time she was hung up for a few days, but fortunately the

Rail trestle over Columbia River north jetty with pile driver seen in center background. Courtesy Grace Kern.

seas remained moderate. Finally pulled free, the schooner, after repairs, was back at work again but always an uneasiness was apparent among her crew. Time and tide, however, erased most of the fears of the past until the fall of 1886, when the *Sheridan* collided with a steam schooner off Cape Mendocino. Again she survived, coming out second best. Then, on Sept. 15, 1887, as if drawn back to the place of her initial mishap, she foundered off the Umpqua River, the crew managing to escape before the last vestige of the vessel vanished beneath the sea. Not many tears were shed at her passing.

Another of Tom Peterson's creations, the schooner *Alice Kimball,* built at Little River in 1874, had a service career similar to that of the *Phil Sheridan,* and was totally lost on the Siuslaw River bar Oct. 12, 1904.

Scores of early lumber schooners were wrecked on the Oregon and northern California coasts. Another of the Tom Peterson schooners, the *Uncle Sam* was lost with her entire crew, the derelict crashing ashore March 4, 1876 off Cape Foulweather, (Oregon) reputedly the victim of a severe coastal storm. No trace of her crew was ever found. Ironically, the ill-fated sailing vessel, named for Uncle Sam, was wrecked during the 100th year of our nation.

One of the first to give an analysis of Yaquina Bay and bar was Captain Collins of the schooner *Juliet.* While master of the vessel, he sailed too close to shore in 1852, and just north of the river entrance came to grief. Though he and his crew escaped they were to spend a considerable time in the area before help came. In the interim Collins had an opportunity to survey the area and to salvage a portion of the cargo from the wreck. He labeled the Yaquina, a fine river, navigable for vessels drawing six to eight feet of water, but labeled the inlet to be a bad one. There were then no settlers in the area and the skipper imagined the wreck to be about 30 miles south of the Columbia River, a totally erroneous position. Perhaps that is why no commercial vessel entered the river until the *Calumet* in 1856, four years after the wreck of the *Juliet*. The former was bringing supplies for Fort Siletz.

The *Juliet* which had been headed for the Columbia River from San Francisco when wrecked, presented a difficult situation. The only way for Collins to get word to a white settlement was by Indian runner.

He hired a redman to carry a message several miles inland. It read:

"We have many Indians around who are annoying but disposed peaceably. The portion of the cargo saved is valuable and we wish not to leave it for the plunder of the Indians. In the summer season a portion of this may probably be got off the beach, but at present it is necessary for us to leave; and whoever this shall reach will confer a great favor by coming or writing with what information they may have. Write the bearer by all means and if horses can be had, bring them six or seven in number, and oblige many persons.

I sign for all,
...J. Collins."

The letter eventually found its way to a pioneer newspaper, and was published. The pilot boat from Astoria was dispatched, but the erroneously stated location prevented her from finding the wreck site.

After several months, Captain Collins received instructions for an overland route to Corvallis and word that assistance was forthcoming in saving his cargo. In the interim, on April 6, he had written a second letter for the Indian runner to carry. It read:

"The *Juliet* was wrecked on the morning of 28th of Jan. and since, about one quarter of her cargo has been saved in a damaged condition. The portion saved belongs equally to the different shippers by that vessel, and is at present under charge of the first officer and one seaman. There is no doubt but that it may be taken off in the summer season, but with little difficulty."

Collins' description of Yaquina Bay in its raw state is a far cry from the existing condition with two well maintained jetties and a sufficient bar depth for handling log ships and LNG carriers.

With the completion of the Oregon Pacific Railway between Corvallis and Yaquina City in 1885, and with the inauguration of a passenger steamship service from San Francisco to Yaquina Bay, the central Oregon coast made a bid to attract business and commerce away from the Columbia River, namely the ports of Portland and Astoria. The new steamship line offered passage from Yaquina City to the Golden Gate for only $14 by virtue of cutting off 40 hours from the regular 3½ day voyage from Portland to San Francisco. The grandiose plan to break the Portland monopoly showed great promise at first, but fate intervened, disaster striking in December of 1887 when the SS *Yaquina City* ran aground near the south jetty, (still under construction) and became a total loss. There were fortunately no casualties. Again the

following year, her running mate, the SS *Yaquina Bay*, on her initial voyage north got out of the channel while crossing Yaquina bar and was carried into the breakers where she too was battered to pieces.

A properly dredged channel, and a north and south jetty would have prevented the two disasters.

Cries of barratry and subversion having been instigated by Portland maritime interests were rumored but no proof forthcoming that the ships were purposely wrecked. Instead, the company continued to decline in the face of the overwhelming setback. Poor management and financial problems by the rail-steamship enterprise followed, and the firm went into the hands of the receivers, the railroad being sold in December of 1894 for $100,000. Yaquina City's dream of controlling North Pacific commerce rapidly faded, the port falling into ignominy, yielding to neophyte Newport and Toledo.

As earlier mentioned, perhaps the most feared of the Oregon bar entrances is the Coquille. Even today with maintained jetties, the controlling depths are only nine feet in the channel entrance, and seven feet to the lumber wharf at Bandon. When the bar is rough, ships have been known to almost pitch up to a perpendicular posture. Many have regretted a decision to attempt the crossing without expert guidance, especially under adverse bar conditions.

A lighthouse was established at the inner end of the north jetty in 1896 but was abandoned in 1939 in favor of navigation aids on the south jetty. The long abandoned structure, witness to several shipwrecks, has been established as an historic site.

In the opinion of several commercial fishboat and pleasure craft operators, Tillamook, Umpqua or Rogue bars, under rough bar conditions, are the most dangerous on the coast.

Despite the presence of jetties, dredging, navigation aids and other precautions, accidents due to human error can and do occur. One unfortunate disaster occurred off the Columbia River bar on Sept. 13, 1976.

The 42 foot charter fishboat *Pearl C.* radioed for assistance off the Columbia River entrance about 1 p.m., Sept. 13. Water was reported in her bilges and she was having a rough time of it. A 44 foot Coast Guard motor lifeboat from the Cape Disappointment station was dispatched to the scene, but because of defective navigation equipment was unable to locate the stricken vessel, lying south of the river bar, until 6 p.m. Immediately a towline was placed aboard the charter boat but because the Coast Guard skipper was fatigued after long hours of duty in angry seas he reasoned his alertness insufficient to try towing the *Pearl C.* across the heavy bar. He accordingly, called the station for a replacement vessel. When the second 44 footer arrived, the tow was transferred and the three craft headed in. Between buoys 6 and 8, the charter boat suddenly began to heel over and started going under. Unfortunately, neither the Coast Guardsmen nor the skipper of the *Pearl C.* had ordered those aboard the ill-fated craft to don lifejackets. Two of their number, Robert Rowan and Douglas Jewett were carried into the sea, struggling for survival. The *Pearl C.'s* skipper, William Cutting (of Ilwaco) and seven other sports fishermen never had a chance. All eight went down with the vessel. One of the 44 footers jockeyed in to assist the survivors, and an immediate call was sent out for additional assistance.

USCG helicopters from Clatsop Airfield were soon airborne; the cutter *Modoc* also responded. An all-night search was undertaken but the net result was the finding of a single body, Bernice Winegar of Utah, recovered at 4:30 p.m. on Sept. 14.

From the standpoint of loss of life it was one of the worst charter fishboat mishaps recorded. The manner in which the rescue was handled and the unfortunate outcome prompted Coast Guard officials to conduct an immediate investigation and hearing. Public opinion was additionally negative. The investigation was conducted by Philip A. Hogue, head of the newly formed National Transportation Safety Board.

Mike Campbell, skipper of the second 44 footer on the scene, testified that after taking over the tow of the *Pearl C.,* he considered the wisdom of not towing the vessel across the choppy bar until conditions improved. However, when he saw that progress was being made against a strong ebb tide, he decided to continue onward. Only minutes later, the fishing craft rolled to port and capsized, snuffing out the lives of the unfortunate eight.

"I looked back," Campbell testified, "and it appeared that more white water than I had ever seen was going across the stern of the *Pearl C.* She just started listing to port and continued to the point that her mast was touching the water."

Campbell's testimony was somewhat contradicted by fireman Richard Hansen, a crewman on the rescue craft. He said, "the *Pearl C.* was rolling on the waves from the time the rescue boat started the tow, not just before it capsized."

The two did agree, however, that the capsizing of the craft was totally unexpected.

"There was no time," stated Hansen, "she was really running bad."

Campbell said a "sneaker," (an unexpectedly large wave) may have caused the sinking. When asked why he thought the *Pearl C.* sank, Campbell said,

"I don't know for sure, but it just happened to be the combination of the tide and the swell conditions, and the fact that the *Pearl C.* was taking water over the stern and possibly inside the vessel."

He further testified that he was under no pressure from his superiors to bring the ill-fated craft in the night of Sept. 13. In similar cases he told of having awaited

calmer waters and an improvement in tidal and bar conditions. He further admitted that his alternative would have been to come about and seek refuge from the strong current and "wind chop" in the lee of the south jetty.

The decision was his to make.

After the *Pearl C.* capsized, Campbell recalled both engines on the towing craft died due to the fact that the 200 foot towline had become entwined in her propellers. He could see the outline of the charter boat's hull in the murk but did not actually see it go down. Campbell's boat was able to pluck one survivor from the water, the other being rescued by the second 44 footer.

Before the investigation and hearing were concluded, Coast Guard officials had to concede that though its search and rescue operations were usually at a high degree of efficiency, on this occasion several unfortunate inconsistencies had occurred.

Jim Colt, handling the initial 44 footer that went to the rescue, admitted that neither the radar nor radio-direction finder on his motor lifeboat *44304* were in working order the afternoon of Sept. 13. The long search missed the *Pearl C.* on the first sweep by from ten to 16 miles, and was conducted to the north of the Columbia River Lightship instead of to the south. One of the survivors of the tragedy said he had, before the fishboat foundered, radioed a heading in relation to Saddle Mountain, a prominent landmark in the Oregon Coast Range. Despite the fact that Colt had been at the Cape Disappointment station 22 months, he had never heard of Saddle Mountain, and even if he had, he testified that the shoreline was "basically a blur." He further said that when the initial towline was put aboard the *Pearl C.* no order was given for the occupants of the craft to don lifejackets. Colt said he figured the skipper of the charter boat to be a professional and responsible for seeing that his passengers were equipped when the vessel was in an emergency.

About his fatigue, Colt stated:

"I was tired and I was wet and I had lost my edge. Your reactions are not as quick or maybe your eyes get a little blurry. I thought it would be safer this way."

Thus it was that the second 44 footer joined the rescue effort.

It was just one of those days for the Coast Guard, a day marked with negligence, carelessness and a portion of bad fortune. If one lesson was learned, it was the importance of wearing life jackets in any emergency.

Coast Guard rescue craft are called on to perform some very dangerous tasks especially around bar entrances where the sea and surf always pose a threat to any craft in good or bad weather. The seaworthy motor lifeboats are designed to roll completely over and come back to a righted position, and for the man who lives through the 360-degree roll, it's a nightmare experience never forgotten. Several rescue craft have flipped in

Oregon coastal waters, usually after getting broadside to the breakers on rescue missions. To learn what it's like, let us consider a first-hand account that comes from the files of the Umpqua River Coast Guard Station. The swells on the Umpqua bar and its offshore waters are perhaps the most spectacular on the coast.

Following a long and demanding three hour training session in the surf, the crew of the self-bailing, self-righting Coast Guard motor lifeboat *CG-44303* were very tired. Having undergone training in some spine-tingling runs through fantastic surf, the new trainees had never dreamed that such wave action existed. It was designed by nature to condition men for the real thing, should an emergency arise.

Exercises over for the day, all hands rejoiced as the boat's coxwain, who was also the officer-in-charge of the station, headed back across the bar. The surf had been steadily building and was inundating the jetty rocks. The brisk October breeze excited the waters and as the combers hit shallow bottom they mounted like liquid mountains. The well-experienced skipper was not necessarily concerned, as he had experienced the vagaries of the rough bar numerous times, and he figured the rougher the swells the better equipped his crew would be for rescue missions. The neophytes, green around the gills, were wondering why they had chosen such duty. Little did they know what was about to come. Mounting far behind the boat's wake was a giant sneaker. Like a seismic wave it rose suddenly to 20 feet and then without warning cascaded over the fantail. The startled helmsman tried to gain control by backing down on his engines, but the propellers, out of water, fanned only air. Broadside to the massive swells the craft began heeling over. Fear masked the faces of the small crew. Towering over them, a great wall of water rained down with crushing power. In the flashing of an eye the lifeboat was on her side at 90 degrees. Nothing was left to do but clutch anything solid, and then just pray.

"Hang on!" shouted the skipper frantically, hoping that all he had taught his crew had soaked in.

Some had a chance to strap themselves into position, but the others had only time to take a stance. The *44303* was going completely over. Knees bent for cushioning effect, the men pushed upward with every bit of strength they possessed, bracing themselves solidly between the safety grab rails and the deck. Desperately filling their lungs with air they suddenly felt themselves upside down under the weight of tons of water, frigidly cold and swirling madly. Lungs began to burn and the pressure was like it would crush them. There was that terrible compulsion to break free rather than follow instructions. Better judgment told them that if they hung on long enough the boat would right itself. But those terrible moments seemed an eternity. But, hang on they did, for as their instructor had warned, to let go risked being chewed up by the fast spinning propellers.

The experience can not be adequately described unless one has gone through such a trial. As the boat rolled, one of the crew was in the cabin and was fortunate enough to have a large air bubble pass over his head allowing him an extra breath of air. The others had to either wait to breathe or drown. Finally, just as the builders had guaranteed, the boat righted itself.

Ironically, the diesel engines kept purring through the entire ordeal, the twin screws still spinning. Needless to say, many prayers had gone up to the Lord before the adventure was over. Undamaged, the motor lifeboat continued on to her station her once green crew seemingly having aged ten years. They would long remember that training cruise of Oct. 12, 1969. As for the boat's skipper, a chief petty officer who had pioneered in that type of craft, it was the fifth time he had rolled a boat over and before his career ended while at the Yaquina Bay Coast Guard Station, he had undergone the experience nine times without suffering any adverse effects. The man in question was none other than cigar-smoking Coast Guard Chief Tom McAdams who put in 26½ years of Coast Guard service, retiring at age 47 to become a commercial fisherman. In June of 1977, he was awarded the coveted Coast Guard Legion of Merit Medal for his valuable services and for the saving of scores of lives. His knowledge of motor lifeboats and of surf conditions was considered second to none. He was chosen as a subject for the Charles Kuralt national CBS television program, *Who's Who*.

McAdams' successor, Chief Daniel Sutherland, while stationed at the Coos Bay Coast Guard Station helped put a record in the *Guiness Book of World Records*. It happened while on a 52 foot Coast Guard motor lifeboat, one of only four of her type in the nation.

Said Sutherland: "it was the only time a 52-foot Coast Guard lifeboat had turned 360 degrees, capsizing and righting itself in rough seas." And it happened twice in rough seas that night in November 1971.

"It's quite a boat," he insisted, "It'll take you to hell and back, if you can hang on."

In June of 1965, a Coast Guard 44 footer struck the south jetty of the Umpqua bar. The craft didn't do a flip, but three men and two women received injuries.

One of the more tragic events in Coast Guard history involved a multiple accident off the Columbia River bar on Jan. 12, 1961. During the attempted rescue of the troubled troller *Mermaid*, three motor lifeboats were lost, the 50 foot *Triumph*, plus a 40 and a 36 foot rescue craft. Five Coast Guardsmen paid with their lives and two fishermen perished, bringing the toll to seven.

Modern Coast Guard motor lifeboats and surfboats, foot for foot, are perhaps the best balanced craft afloat. And well they need to be, for the unbroken expanse of ocean from the Orient to the Pacific Northwest is wide open all the way leaving nothing on which the waves can snub their noses for 5,000 miles. When they reach the bar entrances on the Oregon Coast following storms at sea, they build up to great heights before spilling and expiring on the shore.

Cape Disappointment station in the lee of the Columbia River's north entrance is the busiest on the West Coast with the Westport CG station at Grays Harbor not far behind. The Umpqua station at Salmon Harbor (Winchester Bay) logs more than 350 assistance calls each year, even though not in a heavily populated area. The first self-righting lifeboat was assigned there in 1964. Station personnel have rescued 500 persons that might otherwise have drowned. For the most part, the rescue craft cater to distress calls from commercial fishing craft, charter boats and pleasure craft as do most such stations today. In the bygones, before modern innovations in navigation, commercial cargo vessels hugged the Oregon shores and many were wrecked, necessitating the services of the shore-based rescue craft. Today, deepsea traffic remains well offshore except when entering coastal ports, and the number of major shipwrecks has been greatly reduced.

From the days of the old lifesaving service, inaugurated in 1871, through the advent of the first powered lifeboat on the West Coast in 1908, to the day the Coast Guard took over coastal search and rescue work in 1939, great strides have been made. Though the formidable coastwise cargo and passenger fleets of yesteryear have vanished, and though innovative radio and radar equipment that sees through inclement weather have become standard instruments, the name of the game is still the same. When man is in peril on the sea the Coast Guard motto reads, "You have to go out, but you don't have to come back."

Appearing like a pre-historic animal, this steam-operated conveyance boasted two claws that handled the largest jetty rocks, some of which weighed several tons. No, it isn't a modern rig, but was used in the building of the Columbia River north jetty and is here mounted on a rail car near the quarry site about 1916.

Empty barges being towed back to the Fisher quarry site for another load of jetty rock, about 1915. Courtesy Grace Kern.

Launching of a rock barge on the Columbia River for the firm of Kern & Kern of Portland, six decades back.

Tug Samson bringing in rock-laden barges to be unloaded onto rail cars for transport to the Columbia River north jetty construction site. Jetty was built from 1914-17. Courtesy Grace Kern.

Crossing out in heavy weather over the Nehalem River bar (1916) before the jetties were constructed. The steam tug is the *Geo. R. Vosburg*, workhorse of the area. For a time, the town of Wheeler carried the name of Vosburg. The tug was almost lost in 1912 after stranding on the south spit of the Nehalem. Mayer photo.

Barge *Port of Nehalem* (Nehalem) seen in 1914 loading at the Wheeler Lumber Co. mill for the Columbia River. The tug *Geo. R. Vosburg,* not seen in the photo, was standing by to tow the barge north. Mayer photo.

CHAPTER SEVEN
REGRETTABLE MARINE DISASTERS

MARITIME TRAGEDIES, both major and minor have been numerous along the Oregon and Washington coastlines.

The morning of May 4, 1880 dawned as a typical spring day on the North Pacific. A gentle breeze was fanning the ocean, ideal conditions for commercial fishing. Virtually every small fishing boat in the area was trolling for salmon or dragging for bottom fish. Boats were spread out over a 35 mile area north and south of the entrance to the Columbia River and Willapa Bay.

Unknown to anyone but God, a phenomenal freak of weather was in the making. The occupants of the estimated 250 fishing craft, most of which were under sail, were completely oblivious to what was about to happen.

Without forewarning, a powerful wind of hurricane force suddenly came out of nowhere changing the peaceful ocean waters into massive, seething billows. Showing no mercy, winds of more than 100 mph contorted the sea's face and made playthings of the small fishboats. Pummelled, tossed, turned, capsized and swamped, one by one they disappeared from view, terrified fishermen thinking that the end of the world had come. Thrown into the swirling mass of liquid fury to fend for themselves, death to most came quickly. Blasts howled like a thousand banshees wailing a death knell for all in their path. The shore was blotted out by the great ridges of pulsating brine.

Though the majority of severe storms that batter the Northwest coast come from a southerly direction, and seldom in the spring, this sudden fury was unlike anything before experienced. With herculean force it came up "like thunder cross the bay" from a northwesterly direction, most places along the shore being little ruffled by the strange occurrence. Localized, it was a freak, furious mini-hurricane of unprecedented celerity destroying everything in its path. Had it swept across the land there would have been mass devastation. For those unfortunates caught in the vacuum there was no escape, almost like the time when God flooded the earth.

For 30 minutes the brutal punishment continued until virtually the entire fleet had been eradicated. Never before and never since has such a strange contingency of weather been witnessed off the Columbia River. It was like a series of "twisters" in formation sweeping over the ocean. That half hour of indescribable chaos ended almost as quickly as it had begun. The air became totally still and the seas grew calm just as when Jesus told the great tempest, "Peace, be still!" But the outcome was not the same as that day 2000 years ago, for in this case estimates of the dead ran from 200 to 325, some claiming the latter figure as conservative. More than 240 fishboats were destroyed.

So shocked were friends and neighbors of the deceased that a shroud of gloom hung over the area for weeks. The stark reality of the catastrophe was renewed in the hearts of the landsmen when the beaches were covered with the mute evidence — dead bodies, splinters of wood, nets, troll poles and other fishing gear. The sea soon covered over the traces without the slightest show of remorse.

In all the annals of Pacific Coast marine history no single peacetime tragedy has taken a heavier toll in lives with the possible exception of the disaster that befell the Canadian Pacific liner SS *Princess Sophia,* which in a blizzard on Oct. 25, 1918 slipped off Vanderbilt Reef in Southeastern Alaska and plunged to her doom with 343 souls. There was not one survivor with the exception of a bedraggled canine who could only repine of the experience with a mournful howl.

Another heavy loss of life occurred at Port Chicago, Calif., ammunition loading dock at the height of World War II, when on July 17, 1944, the freighters *E.A. Bryan* and *Quinault Victory* were blown sky high after the former's 5,000 tons of ammunition ignited. Some 325 were killed and scores injured. Both ships were totally destroyed and in addition, a Coast Guard fireboat and

five guardsmen perished. Damage was visible ten miles away.

Other disastrous shipwrecks along the Pacific Coast with heavy loss of life included the SS *Pacific* which foundered southwest of Cape Flattery Nov. 4, 1875, claiming 275 persons, sparing only two. The SS *Brother Jonathan* went to the bottom off Northwest Seal Rock. *Valencia* in 1906 crashed on the hostile west coast outcrops of Vancouver Island with a loss of 117 lives. The British naval vessel *Condor* vanished somewhere off the Northwest Coast after departing Esquimalt B.C. for Honolulu in December 1901 taking her entire crew estimated from 104 to 140. The bark *Star of Bengal* was wrecked on Coronation Island, Alaska, Sept. 20, 1908, with 111 deaths, mostly Oriental cannery workers. The SS *Columbia* was in a collision with another vessel near Point Delgada, Calif., July 21, 1907, where estimates of the dead ranged up to 88; the burning of the HMS *Grappler* in Seymour Narrows, off Valdez Island B.C. on April 29, 1883, took between 72 and 88 persons, mostly Orientals. The SS *San Juan* plunged to her grave after colliding with the oil tanker S.C.T. *Dodd* Aug. 29, 1929,

Sea Lion Caves said to be the world's largest sea cavern, the haunt of hundreds of the Stellar variety of mammal, the largest bulls weighing as much as 2,000 pounds. The cathedral beauty of the 1500 foot long cavern boasts blends of green, pink, red and purple rock formations. From a photo by Mel Anderson.

87 perishing.

pler in Seymour Narrows, off Valdez Island B.C. on April 29, 1883, took between 72 and 88 persons, mostly Orientals. The SS *San Juan* plunged to her grave after colliding with the oil tanker *S.C.T. Dodd* Aug. 29, 1929, 87 perishing.

And so the chronicle of death ships goes on and on.

Along the Oregon coast with its numerous shipwrecks through the years, horrendous death tolls have fortunately been limited to a relatively few vessels. The largest marine graveyards are around the entrances to the Columbia River and Coos Bay.

One of the larger losses of life in Oregon waters involved the sinking of the SS *Francis H. Leggett* which foundered in tempestuous seas about 60 miles southwest of the Columbia River on Sept. 18, 1914. Bound for San Francisco from Grays Harbor, the cargo-passenger vessel spared only two persons to tell the tragic details. Sixty-seven others went to a watery grave. Bodies were washed up on Tillamook shores for weeks, intermingled with huge amounts of lumber and railroad ties. One home at Manzanita was completely built from salvaged cargo.

Lord Byron once wrote of a shipwreck:

"Then rose the sea to sky the wild farewell—Then shriek'd the timid and stood still the brave—Then some leap'd overboard with fearful yell, as eager to anticipate their grave."

Such an epitath might well have applied in the case of the ill-fated SS *General Warren,* one of the most portentous shipwrecks to occur on the Oregon Coast.

We find the *Warren* in the winter of 1852 loading at a Willamette River berth in the bustling little Oregon seaport of Portland. The 309 ton sidewheel steamer had been in service for eight years after being launched in Portland, Maine for the Portland Steam Packet Co. She carried passengers along the New England coast until beckoned around Cape Horn when her owners heard the shrill call of California gold. Thus in 1849 she came west packed to the gunwales with passengers and assorted cargo. After a strenuous voyage with frequent stops for fuel, and often beset by furious gales, she finally made San Francisco, joining a vast fleet of vessels that had converged on the port from nearly every corner of the world. Most of the vessels were abandoned almost before their anchors were dropped, passengers fighting with officers and crew to get ashore first. Many had never used shovels, picks or axes, let alone knowing the rudiments of mining gold. They thronged bars, restaurants and hotels anxious to learn more about the "diggins" and how they might get there. Little else seemed to matter.

As multiple thousands of people poured in, the harbor became like an isle of lost ships, hundreds being left to rot and decay while their occupants joined the daily cries

More than a million candlepower beams out from the 80 year old British-made lens in the lantern of Heceta Head Lighthouse on the central Oregon coast. This thought-provoking photo was taken by Lt. Dave Jones of the U.S. Coast Guard in 1977. The lighthouse was long ago automated. Tower was built in 1893-94.

on the San Francisco streets, Gold! Gold! But while lustful men went out of their heads over gold, it was the wise merchants and shipowners who provided the vessels that carried supplies and afforded transportation which for the most part showed a greater profit over the long run. Though it was difficult to get personnel to man the ships, somehow they kept going and the tremendous demand for goods forced an inflationary spiral the likes of which has seldom been seen.

Among the steamers that remained in operation was the *General Warren.* Placed on the Pacific coastwise run carrying both passengers and cargo she was kept busy, so much so that her maintenance and drydocking was neglected. One of her frequent ports of call was Portland. On this certain voyage she was loading grain at the Rose City, but it was the middle of the miserable, wet winter of 1852, and only a moderate number of passengers had embarked for the voyage south.

Captain Charles Thompson was in command of the ornate packet, and Capt. George Flavel had been engaged as pilot. Dropping her lines, amid a fair crowd of well-wishers on the rain-covered wharf, farewells were exchanged, the vessel sliding into the stream and slowly slithering down river to the confluence of the Willamette and the Columbia. Paddles thrashing the water and a pall of smoke pouring from her stack, she moved along under an overcast sky creating a somewhat melancholy scene. The somber atmosphere failed to deter a reasonable gaiety among the passengers.

A few hours later, the steamer passed Astoria, and by late afternoon was headed toward the Columbia River bar. The glass had begun to drop, the sky black and more threatening than before, a typical January setting. Much to the discomfort of her passengers the steamer pitched and rolled over the bar swells, paddlewheels sometimes emerging clear of the water. Once across and into open sea, the pilot schooner *Mary Taylor* stood by to pick up Pilot Flavel. With final adieus and a blast of the steamer's whistle, Captain Thompson set a course to the southwest against a stiff southerly breeze.

With darkness approaching, little progress was made, the clouds dropping a leaden canopy and letting loose with torrents of rain driven in almost horizontally on ever-increasing winds. The shipmaster conferred with First Officer Ed Beverly and both admitted grave concern over the growing fierceness of the weather, already blowing gale force. Staring into the murk, the quartermaster tightly gripped the ship's wheel, his eyes glassy from the reflection of the binnacle light.

The dining saloon was virtually empty, most of the passengers having taken to their staterooms with uneasy stomachs. Captain Thompson shunned rest. He had a premonition about the gale, his long experience at sea having given him an insight into weather. As he observed the ship's acrobatic tendencies he ordered slow ahead, just enough to keep her head into the wind. Some of the storm canvas had already been ripped to pieces. Creaking in every joint, the *General Warren* reminded one of its namesake just before he gave his life in the Battle of Bunker Hill.

Something told the skipper to reverse course and re-cross the bar into sheltered waters. But then the pilot was long gone and the river entrance a seething mass of white fury all the way from Cape Disappointment to Point Adams. Additionally, a strong current was running with the tide. White spume only was visible in the inky, storm-filled night. Thompson's better judgment told him that any attempt to reach sheltered waters would have to wait till daylight. The plunging vessel, despite her deadweight, was raising her forefoot repeatedly out of the water, and would then dive until the whole forward half would be lost under tons of brine.

Up the tube came the engineer's voice:

"We're taking water down here!"

Pumps were working to capacity, but wet grain had broken loose in the holds and was choking the outflow.

Frightened passengers were in the passageways fearing the worst. The stewards tried to calm their fears but most demanded a confrontation with the captain. All through the night the steamer fought for survival in a great, roaring battlefield. Increasing in violence with each hour, the gale had a staggering malice from which there was no escape. Shouldering each onslaught, the vessel shook and staggered under tons of green which smote the upper deck and raced a torrent down her whole length. Suddenly there was a sickening, cracking sound heralding the crashing of the foretopmast to the deck. All hands were summoned to clear the debris, all the while the wind screaming and clawing at the standing rigging, the loud roar of the boarding seas filling every heart with fear.

Staggering like one inebriated, the *General Warren* threw her people around like ten pins, causing cracked ribs, cuts, bruises and mal de mer. The thrust of the seas was like a mighty army zeroing in on a solitary target. The big walking beam writhed in its fittings, the paddlewheels turned in uneven pattern. Broken dishes and loose pans made a shambles of the messdeck as a volley of profanity came forth from the cook's mouth. As sea water leaked into the engine and boiler rooms, soaked seaboots tramped through the pilot house with reports of the steamer's worsening condition.

As the vessel settled lower in the water the agony of her slow rise under the crushing weight of the sea caused the shipmaster great concern. It was as if the whole ocean was avid to swallow its prey, each wave a shocking reality, spray rattling like loose gravel, stinging exposed skin. Red eyes were inflamed from the salt sting. The gauntlet of green water was outlined against a livid sky which at last had begun to lighten slightly in the east. To the surprise of most, they were to see the dawn of another day, their staggering steed though still afloat, faltering and groaning to the tune of the gale screaming insanely.

Fear-stricken passengers could contain themselves no longer. En masse they rushed the pilot house demanding that Captain Thompson take them back to Astoria. Only after he told them that he too, wanted to get back inside the bar were their demands quelled. Already he had ordered signal flags raised calling for the pilot's return. The pilot boat, however, was bar-bound and as the storm raged on, it was not until 3 p.m. the following day that the *Mary Taylor* reached the steamer's side. Under the most adverse of conditions, and to the muffled cheers of the passengers, Pilot Flavel reboarded the *Warren* from a small boat, greatly endangering his life.

Whatever ray of hope the passengers had for relief was dampened when the pilot told them he was unwilling to risk taking the vessel across the bar in her damaged condition; not until conditions improved. But, the rejected refused to take no for an answer. Flavel was just as adamant. As the condition of the steamer worsened and water began pouring in below the waterline, Captain Thompson told the pilot that his ship could not remain afloat much longer. The panic-stricken passengers again made a run on the pilot house taunting the pilot, shaking fists and accusing him of cowardice. Agitation mounted till it became as fierce as the storm.

Outnumbered to the man, the pilot finally relented,

"Very well if you insist," he warned, "I'll take you in, but I refuse to be responsible for what might happen!"

After signalling the wallowing pilot schooner to stand by, the *Warren*, down by the bow, swung awkwardly about, seas slamming into her superstructure. Passengers huddled in the main cabin for protection. Sinking lower and lower in the water the seas now had a free sweep of the ship until there was hardly a dry place.

In the interim, the relentless winds refused to abate one iota, the pilot boat being driven far from the steamer. Flavel insisted on dropping the anchors, but the captain and the passengers kept up the pressure demanding that the vessel be put aground at the nearest possible location to prevent her sinking. Flavel begrudgingly gave in to their demands.

"I never realized what a worthless tub she is," he uttered.

Then without further delay he ordered the wheel hard up and set a direct course for Clatsop Spit. The low-riding, slow-moving steamer responded sluggishly. The engine was nearing its last revolutions as water rose around the boilers and steam began to hiss. Oily brine sloshed over the grates.

Darkness came on again making the aspect of survival even more frightening. By 7 p.m., amid the breakers the steamer struck with a grinding thump on the outer spit, immediately the sea beginning its mission of destruction. As the combers barrelled into the ship's stern, timbers started to split, steam lines ruptured.

Above the howling wind, Captain Thompson ordered all hands forward for whatever protection was available from the onslaught. Both he and the pilot wore grave expressions of almost total despair, but neither betrayed their feelings, trying to encourage the wretched shivering, soaked passengers. The officers and crew knew that the steamer was doomed and that her complete demolition by nature's forces was but a matter of time. Still, one hope remained. Though the lifeboats had been either smashed or damaged, one was still in usable condition. The captain called for volunteers with the hope they would be able to run the gauntlet of the wild seas and bring help. Response was slow for most felt their chances of survival were better by remaining with the wreck. Thompson insisted that Flavel, because of his experience with bar conditions, be the one to take charge

The Oregon coast's first official woman lighthouse keeper, Mrs. Mabel E. Bretherton, was assigned to her post at Cape Blanco in 1903.

of the boat. Those joining him were Edward Beverly, first officer; Wm. Irons, second officer; two seamen and five passengers. The choice was a genuine risk at best. Without hesitation, the men leaped into the boat which fortunately was at the lee side. The falls were cleared and the craft struck the uprising sea with a smack, sinking deep into a cavity. When it rose, tackle blocks were unhooked, and they pushed off with the oars. It was a hair-raising moment, but providence intervened and kept the boat from being smashed like an eggshell against the bulk of the steamer. Those at the oars pulled with their every ounce of strength and managed to get free. Flavel urged them on against virtually overwhelming odds; it was an epic fight of men against the elements. Their boat was so small and the sea so great. With the wind and current at their backs they made a remarkable three hour run across the bar using sail for the final run to Astoria. Coming alongside the anchored bark *George & Martha,* (Capt. C. Beard, master) they pleaded for immediate assistance. No sooner had they told their tale of woe, than a whaleboat was provisioned and a fresh crew headed out over the bar in search of the shipwreck victims.

The outbound mission was far more difficult than the

inbound, the craft having to battle against adverse winds and seas.

Meanwhile at the wreck scene, Clatsop Spit had a solid grip on the *General Warren*, holding her firm while the breakers made an all-out attack. Sweeping seas crushed the wheelhouse and deck house, the stack was canted to one side, the paddlewheels broken and the masts leaned precariously. Men and women disappeared overboard without trace, without cry, like figures wiped from a blackboard with a single imperious stroke. The rudderpost was driven up through the fantail and the rudder snapped off. Davits and stanchions were bent in weird angles, steam continued to rise from deep in the ruptured engine room.

As waves deluged the steamer's carcass like giant vacuum sweepers, those remaining alive struggled desperately, but there was no place to go, the spit being inundated and the ship breaking apart beneath their feet. Agony and despair were never more emphasized than at that very moment. Still no help in sight.

Suddenly, it was all over. Cries faded on the wings of the wind, all struggling ceased, the wreck was pulverized and the cruel surf ground its victim into the menacing sea sands.

By the time the whaleboat reached the scene of the wreck virtually nothing remained except pieces of wreckage and a few corpses floating face down in the water. The valiant endeavor had been all in vain. Dog-tired, the boat crew returned to Astoria with the grim news.

Some 42 persons had perished, the only survivors being the ten who initially got away in the lifeboat. For days the beaches were searched in the odd chance that there might be other survivors, all efforts proving unfruitful. Among the bodies that drifted ashore was a young married couple, hands tightly locked together, in death as in life.

Captain Thompson was lost with his ship, having done his best, his only crime having been to allow the *General Warren* to cross the bar with a gale in the making.

Among other tragic Oregon coast shipwrecks was that of the SS *Santa Clara* which stranded at the south entrance to Coos Bay bar Nov. 2, 1915. Despite a persistent rescue effort, 21 persons were lost. Nor has the wreck of the SS *Alaskan* been forgotten though she foundered as long ago as May 13, 1889 off Cape Blanco, 31 perishing in that incident.

In our age there has been much emphasis on oil transport and tanker disasters. Though the emphasis was not as great several decades back because of little stress on environmental damage, similar problems sometimes met with disastrous results.

The episode in question involved the Associated Oil Co. tanker *J.A. Chanslor*. The date was Dec. 18, 1919.

Oil in modern times is what keeps industry turning and the mammoth tankers that roam the high seas, some over 500,000 deadweight tons, and as long as five football fields, would have made the *Chanslor,* by comparison seem little larger than a lifeboat. Of 4,900 tons, with an overall length of 378 feet, she was a standard-sized ocean tanker of her day and was skippered by an able master, Capt. A. A. Sawyer. Carrying a crew of 38, more than most of the highly-automated supertankers of today, she generated 2,000 horsepower with her single steam engine compared to better than 40,000 horses in supertanker steam turbine plants.

Built in 1910 at Newport News, registered at San Francisco, the *Chanslor* was a trouble-free vessel well suited to Pacific coastwise and offshore operations. Back in 1919, few got excited over oil spills, as they were relatively few. None could visualize the day of the supertanker a half century later, nor of such horrendous mishaps as that of the *Torrey Canyon* which spilled her guts off England, polluting the frenzied waters of the Atlantic with 700,000 barrels of black crude. By comparison, the *Chanslor's* full capacity was about 30,000 barrels. And it must be borne in mind that the *Torrey Canyon* when wrecked in 1967 was far smaller than the big supertankers of today.*

A half century ago many homes and business buildings were still heated by coal, though oil was the desired commodity. A conversion was taking place across the country. One never guessed in those times the world would one day face an oil shortage nor did any in the industry ever contemplate a partial return to coal as a source of energy, let alone the capturing of solar and nuclear energy.

One thing in the transport of petroleum that has remained constant is the concern for the safety of those who man the ships. Safety first is still the fast rule on every tanker. Each crew member is subject to far greater danger than in other forms of merchant shipping due to the volatile nature of the cargoes, and every precaution is taken to prevent strandings, collisions and conflagrations. Unlike in the *Chanslor's* day, modern tankers are equipped with innovative electronic navigation gear that can see through the thickest fogs. Radar screens scan a given area while depth sounders probe the depths and outline the ocean bottom contours. Still, with every conceivable warning system, accidents do occur and the vigilant human element is still necessary even in the face of automation miracles.

In the days of the *Chanslor,* merchant ships still navigated close to shore on coastwise runs and the element of danger was far greater. Navigating from a standard compass and depending on coastal lighthouses and foghorns was much different than remaining ten to 12 miles offshore with guidance from radiobeacons and loran systems.

With 30,000 barrels of California oil stowed in her

*The supertanker *Amoco Cadiz*, 229,000 tons, spilled 69 million gallons of oil off the Brittany Coast March 16, 1978.

Fleet of Flowers at Depoe Bay. This annual celebration honors those who have gone down to the sea in vessels and have not returned. A fleet of commercial and charter fishboats prepare for the parade out to the ocean as hundreds of onlookers peer down from the Depoe Bay Bridge. This unique bay is perhaps the smallest commercial harbor in mainland U.S.A. Flower wreaths are dropped on the ocean surface as a memorial.

in'ards, the *J. A. Chanslor* crept along the Oregon coast under a thick veil of fog and moderate to heavy seas. It was a miserable winter day, the wind and currents carrying the vessel closer to shore than she had a right to be. The coastline was shrouded by a thick, wet blanket and the world seemed to close down around the tanker and her company of men. Captain Sawyer eyed the compass and then peered to starboard into a world of nothingness. The sonorous wail of the ship's whistle sounded like a funeral dirge.

Without warning the tanker lurched violently. There was an indescribable grating of steel and rock in combat. She reeled and rocked, shuddered and groaned, twisted and turned. Rivets popped as if fired from a machine gun, a torrent of water roared into the engine room where the plates were ripped wide open below the waterline. In her death throes she buckled like an accordion, men trapped in a vice, sliding down perpendicular steel walls, scraping over barnacle-encrusted rocks, pounded under tons of frigid liquid, like the butt end of a giant waterfall. Impaled firmly on a rock buttress, the ship's bow was

forced upward, the strain amidships taking the burden. It cracked wide open, massive breakers charging in for the kill.

Sawyer didn't have time to issue an order, yet alone a chance to lower a lifeboat. The crewmen not swept into the maelstrom were imprisoned inside the twisted compartments. Death was swift for 36 souls but miraculously Captain Sawyer and two of his crew, lungs about to burst, popped to the surface, struggling amidst a wild array of wreckage and thick gooey oil. As the tanker was torn asunder, the three survivors clung desperately to pieces of wreckage being jostled about in a cruel sea polluted with great masses of oil. Despite every card stacked against them the wretched invididuals somehow managed to kick and squirm until heaving breakers caught them in a twisting roll and washed them ashore. All three lived to tell of the tragic event.

Ironically, when the fog lifted, the lofty form of Cape Blanco Lighthouse loomed into view over the shattered wreck. Its light had been unable to pierce the shroud that had covered the shore.

Tug "Tatoosh", with hawser fast to S.S. Washington. Drifting in towards North Head while waiting for the Washington to cut her Anchor Chains.

Trouble on Peacock Spit at the Columbia River entrance. The tug *Tatoosh*, right, attempts to get a towline aboard the steam schooner *Washington*, broken down and drifting helplessly toward North Head. This was one of the few incidents when a vessel was saved from Peacock Spit. The date was Nov. 17, 1911. The river entrance has been greatly altered since this photo was taken.

For days, only the forepart of the tanker remained visible to mark the grave of the 36 who perished; then it too was swept away leaving no evidence of the tragedy. Cries went up to better safeguard coastal shipping by forcing traffic lanes farther westward, but several years were to pass before navigation innovations would be able to do what a beacon and foghorn were unable to do. Today, by using the proper precautions, regardless of adverse weather, there remains little excuse for vigilant navigators of merchant ships to become ensnared on the coastal outcrops.

The *Chanslor* was just one of a number of ships whose obituary involved Cape Blanco, where many a brave soul lies asleep in the deep.

Where the word bizarre is concerned, few incidents can eclipse the wreck of Southern Pacific Railroad Co.'s SS *Czarina* involved in a chilling disaster on Coos Bay bar. The fatal day was Nov. 13, 1910 and the 220 foot cargo vessel was outbound over the bar, her holds filled with lumber, cement and coal destined for San Francisco. With Capt. C. J. Dugan in command, the *Czarina* carried a crew of 23 and one passenger, a young 20 year old man named Harold Willis, who had boarded at Marshfield (now Coos Bay) for return to his studies at the University of California.

Storm warnings had been posted before the departure of the *Czarina*. They, however, were not heeded, inasmuch as the iron-hulled vessel had breasted many gales

since her completion in 1883 at a British shipyard in Sunderland. She was one of the most rugged merchant ships on the coast and considered one of the more seaworthy, despite her age.

Captain Dugan and First Officer James Hughes were both in the pilot house as the vessel headed for the bar. Southerly winds were already howling, and the sky looked like the top of a circus tent. The *Czarina,* riding low in the water with a near capacity cargo, responded slowly to her helm. The quartermaster held the wheel tightly to keep her in the proper channel. Rain rattled like gravel against the wheelhouse windows. Below, the black gang shoveled coal into the hungry boilers and made repeated checks of the valves. The voyage had begun like many others as a routine run down to San Francisco, except that nature was about to unveil her sinister plot to destroy the *Czarina*.

Solidly on the bar, the swells became mountainous. The deep-laden ship poked her nose into each comber and came up like a wet dog shaking itself, water pouring down the slanting decks and through the scupper holes. Straying slightly from the channel, the vessel struck bottom near the south jetty. Obeying a quick command, the helmsman spun the wheel hard to starboard. The great force of the bar swells caught the steamer in irons and catapulted her toward the north jetty. The steering apparatus appeared to fail, responding in a most unusual manner.

Well aware of his dangerous position, Captain Dugan, in desperation, ordered the bos'n to drop the anchors to hold their precarious position. Out of the hawse pipes rattled the giant hooks, but whatever momentary comfort they might have afforded was short-lived, the flukes unable to hold the ship in the tempest. Huge breakers lifted the entire bulk as if it were a drift log.

"Full ahead!" Dugan shouted down the tube, virtually deafening the engineer. Despite the engine's best it wasn't enough to keep the *Czarina* from being rudely driven on the shoals alongside the north jetty. From then on it was a one-sided battle. All mobility was lost, the screw beating itself to a halt in the sands. One after another the seas boarded, sweeping the decks and flooding the midship housing. It was a desperate scene. Ashore, news of the stranding spread like wildfire. Hundreds rushed to the beach to watch the death of a ship.

As the seas hurried their work of destruction, the Cape Arago Lifesaving Station was alerted and her eager surfmen prepared to render assistance. All the while liquid battering rams knocked out bulkheads, carried away lifeboats, cowls, stanchions, and crushed skylights. Accommodations were flooded, bulkheads twisted and torn. With no rescue boat in sight, the crew was forced into the shrouds, or to cling to the masts to keep from being swept into the maelstrom.

Beach equipment was set up on the shore opposite the wreck. Attempts were made to launch the surfboat, but every try was futile, the breakers insurmountable. Frustrations built to a fever pitch, but there was just no way to reach those wretched souls. The Lyle gun was fired repeatedly but each time the line dropped into the sea, short of the mark. Meanwhile the gale raged on. Just before night came on, fires were kindled as a ray of hope for those on the wreck and to give the would-be rescuers a hint of warmth. With the last ray of light the shivering crowd took a last look at the shipwreck victims who appeared like insects entwined in a spider web. Wailing cries were drowned out by the roaring wind and mighty surf. Then night closed in solidly with its incessant cold rain that cut to the marrow. Those on the wreck began falling from their perches one by one, strength ebbing from their blue bodies. Suffering was indescribable.

By dawn's early light only a half dozen men still clung to the shrouds, among them the passenger Harold Willis, whose father had arrived from Marshfield to anguish with the other spectators. Despite the inclement weather, the crowd again swelled to watch the funereal scene unfold. The endurance test continued until the last victim gave up the struggle and dropped into the churning vortex. Came the sudden reality that all were gone and the wreck a worthless hunk of scrap metal.

But, one who fell from the shrouds somehow endured the surf, held afloat by his lifejacket. Though he had lost consciousness, and the will to fight longer, he remained buoyant and was carried up on the beach. Identified as First Assistant Engineer Harry L. Kentzall, he was rushed to the local hospital and eventually recovered, following long and tender care. He was the sole survivor and he like Job of old could repeat, "And I only am escaped to tell thee."

Among the 24 who perished were Captain Dugan and his first officer James Hughes. The chief engineer, Henry Young was also among the victims, and first reports said it was he and not Kentzall who had survived.

The maritime world was shocked by the *Czarina* disaster, especially by a news photo showing the victims clinging to the shrouds in their final hour of agony. Public outcry demanded reasons why the vessel had crossed the bar into the teeth of a gale. Poor judgement in unnecessarily challenging the Pacific storm was evident. The vessel could have waited it out in safe haven inside the bar, but a decision was made and that decision proved fatal.

The situation was very similar in the loss of the States Line freighter *Iowa* on the Columbia River bar a quarter century later. In command of Capt. Edgar Yates, she crossed the bar at midnight, Jan. 12, 1936, squarely into a 76 mile-an-hour gale. Rudely thrown onto Peacock Spit the freighter was hastily demolished and her entire crew of 34 perished.

Man's greatest efforts are puny measured by the eons of time. Here, the once proud British bark *Peter Iredale* displays her encrusted remains. Wrecked Oct. 25, 1906, she has been playing hide-and-seek with the shifting sands ever since. She lies in her grave off Fort Stevens State Park just south of the entrance to the mighty Columbia River and has been denoted as an historical site.

Fighting a losing battle against the elements. Tillamook Rock and its lighthouse breast the fury of the Pacific. The old sentinel dating from 1880, abandoned as a lighthouse in 1957, and now owned by a private individual, is slowly succumbing to time and the elements. Ed Delanty photo.

Last of a once large fleet of lightships that marked perilous marine navigation areas along the coastlines of America. The *Columbia River Lightship*, on station in 210 feet of water off the entrance to the river, will someday be replaced by a large ocean buoy as have the other Coast Guard lightships. Official Coast Guard photo.

Former Columbia River Lightship, the *No. 93*, was photographed from a Coast Guard aircraft several years ago. This is the view that a high flying gull gets when swooping down to get some of the morsels thrown overboard by the lightship crew. Coast Guard photo.

CHAPTER EIGHT
EXCERPTS FROM THE WAR YEARS

IN THE ENTIRE JAPANESE NAVY during World War II none harassed the Pacific Northwest coast more than did Commander Meiji Tagami, master of the far-ranging submarine *I-25*. Much of his mischief was done off the Oregon coast. This dedicated, persistent naval officer, had he been fighting for the allied cause would have been highly honored for his daring, cunning and aggressiveness.

A World War II B25 bomber crew was decorated for the sinking of a Japanese submarine off the Oregon coast on Christmas morning 1941. That submarine was reputedly the *I-25,* whose executive officer said following the war, had pumped its bilge oil off the Columbia River five days before the alleged bombing. The "sinking" has been the subject of a debate ever since the war, but in all likelihood, the American airmen received their decorations for a ghost submarine that wasn't really there. The aircraft later flew in the Tokyo raid led by Gen. James Doolittle.

At any rate, the *I-25* was not sunk and she was to return to the Northwest coast to carry on her submarine war.

Neither cruel or vengeful as were many of his counterparts in the Nazi U-boat fleet, Tagami never shelled lifeboats bearing survivors nor took undue advantage of the victims of his submarine. Trained in both conventional and psychological warfare, some of his acts in the early years of the conquest were most unusual and some even questionable. His navigational skills were exceptional and seldom did he take unnecessary risks. Tagami, unlike many in the Japanese submarine service survived the war and was well and hearty when the surrender documents were signed aboard the battleship *Missouri* on August 14, 1945.

Six Japanese submarines departed the land of the rising sun in May of 1942 assigned to reconnaissance patrol off the Aleutian chain. From this squadron, *I-25*, carrying a collapsible float plane, and her sister sub *I-26* were detached to continue on to the Kodiak area which the former submarine surveyed from May 27-30. The twin underwater marauders then proceeded south to take up positions off the Washington and Oregon coasts where they engaged in torpedo attacks on American and British (Canadian) vessels as well as in shore bombardments. Both sailed for their homeland the end of June, but during their initial visit the following acts of hostility occurred.

Bagging the first victim was the *I-26* which successfully attacked and sank the SS *Coast Trader* on June 7, 43 miles west of Cape Flattery, while the *I-25* on June 19, torpedoed the British (Canadian) freighter *Fort Camosun* off the Washington coast, leaving her for dead after punching a 30-foot hole in her hull. The crew abandoned, and to all intents and purposes the vessel should have gone down, but remained afloat. It was the vessel's maiden voyage out of British Columbia ports. As fate would have it, she was intercepted by an allied towing craft and brought into port to undergo a major piece of surgery.

Satisfied with his effort, Tagami next decided to engage in a little psychological warfare. Boldly attacking Fort Stevens at the south entrance to the Columbia River on the night of June 21, 1942, he was responsible for the first enemy action against a continental United States fort since the War of 1812, and though little if any damage occurred it caused great concern in the military ranks. The *I-25* remained just out of the known range of the fort's old 12 inch mortars, installed in 1898, with a range of about eight miles. Shortly before midnight, the Japanese commander gave the order to begin firing, having taken his bearings from the beacon at Tillamook Rock Lighthouse, the only navigation aid fully lighted at the time of the bombardment. Some ten to 15 shells fired from the deck gun whizzed through the darkness, one striking near a ten inch battery, but fortunately causing no damage.

Excitement was at a high level, militiamen wondering if an all-out attack would follow. They were ready. Unknown to the Japanese the newly installed fort guns were six inch Navy Barbett's, radar-guided with 360 degree traverse control and steel shields. They had been tested both at Fort Stevens and at Fort Canby at the north entrance to the Columbia and had a range of 17 miles. Their installation was part of the considerable coastal defense work accomplished by the Portland District Army Engineers.

But alas, the night before the attack, a rather wild party was allegedly held for the Army brass. The officer of the day had not sobered up and was in no condition to handle the tense situation. Though his men, in true Yankee fashion, wanted desperately to return the fire, the drunken CO was in no frame of mind to arrive at a course of action. In the interim the submarine silently stole away in the night to a place well out of range of any shore guns.

There was no excuse for what had happened, for the night before the attack on Fort Stevens the companion submarine *I-26,* under the guise of night, surfaced off the west coast of Vancouver Island and fired away at lonely Estevan Lighthouse and the nearby radio station. That attack lasted 40 minutes off and on, shells landing in front of the lighthouse and on the hills above, doing little damage. The keeper had presence of mind to immediately douse the light.

It was the first attack on Canadian soil by a foreign power since Canada had achieved dominion status in 1867.

The Fort Stevens contingent should have been on total alert; instead, the fortress, which had never fired a shot in anger from its inception, was destined to remain pacifist. And, to this day, phased out and maintained as a public state historical site, it has yet to fire at any would-be enemy.

After the shelling, a military plane was dispatched from a field near Astoria to investigate what appeared to be a possible target five miles west of the fort, but a two-hour search produced no results. Clever Tagami, always on the safe side, was in the cradle of the deep and had no plans to surface until night again returned.

Before sailing back to Japan, the two submarines sailed southward performing some additional psychological minor bombardments on California coastal installations, including some oil fields near Santa Barbara, the purpose, more to create panic than to inflict serious damage.

America's reverse psychology effort was manifested in the daring Halsey-Doolittle bombing of Japan, originating from a carrier in the Pacific April 18, 1942, an act which caught the Japanese War Ministry by complete surprise and gave the Yankee cause a boost.

Again in mid-August 1942, the *I-25* with Tagami still in command, departed Yokosuka, with a new twist to the war of nerves. Her float plane was equipped with six special type incendiary bombs designed to ignite giant forest fires in the timber-rich areas of Oregon state. Landfall was made off Cape Blanco two weeks later, followed by a wait for the desired weather conditions. Forests of southern Oregon were tinder dry, ripe for burning, when the plane took off from the sub on Sept. 9. It flew inland to an area near Mt. Emily, nine miles northeast of Brookings. There, two incendiary bombs were dropped. Due to the alert action of a forest ranger both blazes were spotted and immediately squelched before they could spread.

Again on Sept. 29, the plane was dispatched on an incendiary mission, this time the target being east of Port Orford. Again, vigilant spotters located and quickly extinguished the flames.

Instigators of the nefarious plot had envisioned huge conflagrations sweeping over Oregon, not only destroying the forests but also the towns and cities in their path. Either the Japanese were ill-advised or had underestimated American surveillance, for at best their efforts were folly, producing nothing but harassment. Ironically, Commander Tagami must have accepted the pilot's false report that the fire-bombing missions were successful, though he cancelled a planned third flight it was learned after the war.

America had its eyes on the West Coast, and military preparations increased in anticipation of major enemy action. The mouth of the Columbia was mined by the Coast Artillery as it had been during World War I. The mines were deadly types, four feet in diameter and anchored at the bottom of the river by steel cables and weights. They could be detonated either by contact or by electric charge, and woe be to any enemy submarine foolish enough to attempt entry to the river.

The Portland District Army Engineers were also responsible to a large degree for radar installations set up on the Oregon coast. They were located at Shore Acres (south of Coos Bay), Gold Beach, Oceanside, Cape Perpetua (later moved to Yachats), Neskowin, Tillamook Head, Fort Stevens and at locations in southwestern Washington.

Several lookout towers were spread along Oregon's coastal ramparts, and mammoth searchlights were installed at the mouth of the Columbia to aid artillery batteries in case another offshore shelling occurred.

After the float plane's second mission, Tagami elected to turn his attention back to the more practical goal of sinking enemy merchant ships. Taking up position once again off Cape Blanco, submerging by day to avoid coastal air patrols and rising like a gray ghost at night, the *I-25* prowled the shipping lanes. Five days later, just before dawn, a tantalizing object was spotted. A bearing was taken and the submarine silently slipped under the surface. Through the periscope at firing range, about 50 miles north of Blanco, an oil tanker lay dead in the water. The time was 6 a.m., the target having become motionless so repairs could be performed on her troublesome main engine. Had her master, Capt. D. W. Davidson, known what was about to happen he would have kept moving, regardless of the problem.

There was a light chop from the northwest. Visibility was excellent despite the fact that dawn was just beginning to break on that fourth day of October 1942. The tanker was the SS *Camden,* operated by Keystone Tankship Corp., whose owner was Charles Kurz & Co. of Philadelphia, one of a fleet that carried Shell Oil products.

On the trackless ocean, the only other ship nearby was the Union Oil tanker *Victor Kelly* steaming seven miles north of the *Camden.* Two lookouts scanned the sea from the aft gun platform and two others stood guard on the bridge. Undetected, the submarine moved to a firing position. Always the cautious one, Tagami had no intentions of letting this juicy morsel slip away. Taking a final bearing, he alerted his torpedomen.

"Down scope," he ordered.

"Fire one!"

Five seconds later the command:

"Fire two!"

The missiles catapulted from the tubes at rapid speed, the commander having fired from the maximum range to avoid any retaliation. The first torpedo missed the tanker by a scant five feet.

"Torpedo! Torpedo!" cried a voice from the ship's bridge wing.

Within seconds the second torpedo struck with a resounding blast, ten feet from the stem, ripping open a mammoth hole in the bow section. Immediately smoke and flames erupted in the forepeak tank. The gunnery crew stood at their battle stations as fuel oil burned furiously around them. Down by the head, the stern

section rose, the propeller becoming airborne. The decks were awash, clear back to the bridge. Men scurried to-and-fro contemplating a third explosion. The radioman got out a distress call while the gunnery crew searched the sea for a sign of the marauder, trying to get off a shot before the tanker took her final dive.

In the confusion that followed, a messman was observed swimming away from the wreck without a lifejacket. He drowned in the chilling waters.

Shortly after 7 a.m., the boats were lowered, and within 20 minutes two of them were pulling away from the mortally wounded *Camden.* Fortunately their adventure was short-lived, for two hours later the neutral Swedish motor vessel *Kookaburra* (of the Pacific Australia Direct Line) spotted the two bobbing lifeboats and rescued the survivors at 10:50 a.m., taking them to Port Angeles where they were put ashore the following day.

Leaving the scene of her victory, the *I-25* cautiously crept away. The ill-fated *Camden* which had been en route to Puget Sound from San Pedro with 76,000 barrels of petroleum products, refused to sink. The day after the attack, the Grays Harbor tug *Kenai* spotted the floundering tanker, got a line aboard and began towing her slowly toward the Columbia River. When off the entrance, the tanker was down so low in the water that a bar crossing could not be risked. Instead, it was decided to continue the tow to Puget Sound. After wrestling with her unwieldy charge for nearly a week, the *Kenai* found herself 60 miles off Grays Harbor. There, the dying vessel suddenly burst into flames, her last act before plunging to her final resting place in 52 fathoms, position, 46°46′38″ N. 124°31′15″ W.

When interviewed following the loss of his ship, Captain Davidson recalled that he had been under torpedo attack in the same location off the Oregon coast three months earlier on June 23, but escaped unscathed. In that incident two search planes were unable to find any trace of an enemy submarine.

Fresh from the kill of the *Camden,* the *I-25* waited for another tanker to come in view of its periscope. Tagami wasn't disappointed. The very next day, ripe for the altar of sacrifice, came the 6,800 gross ton Richfield Oil Co. tanker *Larry Doheny,* Portland-bound out of Long Beach with 66,000 barrels of fuel oil. It was night, the vessel blacked out and steaming along at a steady ten knots. Lookouts were posted forward and aft. Radio silence was maintained. There was a moderate swell fanned by a strong ocean breeze, and though no moon was shining, visibility was again good.

Like a prowling wolf, the *I-25* rose from her watery lair, pursuing a southerly course while recharging her batteries. From the conning tower Oriental eyes scanned the surface with nighttime binoculars. The hydrophones were manned, but the submarine was not equipped with

No copters in those days. A boat crew attempts to land at Tillamook Rock in 1934 after a howling gale did much damage to the facility, including sweeping away the derrick boom used in landing keepers of the light.

radar. All at once there was great excitement aboard. Another potential target had been spotted. Figures moved hastily about. The conning tower and decks were immediately cleared for action, the hatch cover secured behind them. Shortly, with a rush of water a deadly torpedo headed in the direction of the tanker.

At precisely 10:07 p.m. a dull thud shook the *Doheny,* followed by a loud snapping noise. Flames leaped into the sky, great orange fingers dancing against a rigid black backdrop. The missile struck No. 2 tank on the port side forward ripping out a 12 by 14 foot hole. The entire starboard side, severely weakened, began to buckle. Other tanks ruptured and oil spewed onto the main deck, immediately igniting. Within a few minutes the tanker was aflame from stem to stern.

Capt. Olaf Breiland, master, eyed the situation with horror. The intensity of the blaze drove the radio operator from his transmitter before he was able to dispatch a distress signal. Flames crept up to the ammo storage area near the bridge where two .30 calibre machine guns were located. Suddenly there was a huge explosion. Screams were heard from trapped victims.

"Abandon! Abandon!" shouted the skipper trying to be heard above the roar.

Within 15 harrowing minutes of the attack, and with extreme difficulty, the charred boats were cleared away. One of the deck gun crewmen, intent on revenge, remained by the 5-incher at the peril of his own life hoping for one shot at the submarine. With flames all around, he was at last driven from his post, leaping into the ocean where one of the lifeboats stood by to pick him up.

In the confusion, there had been no way of counting casualties. The company of the tanker had consisted of 46 men including the armed guards. Now that the lifeboats were free of the furiously burning tanker, a tally showed six unaccounted for, five of whom were believed consumed in the flames and another having drowned after jumping overboard. All through the night the lifeboats wallowed near the tanker in a sea of black oil, the heat so penetrating that it kept the survivors warm at a considerable distance. Explosions were audible as fresh pockets of fuel oil ignited, the flames reflecting weird images on the ebony sea, choking billows of smoke belching skyward. Frustrated, silent and anxious, the survivors conversed little, most with burns and all spattered with oil. Throughout the night they remained nearby the burning ship hopeful of rescue.

Like a haunted castle in mediaeval times, abandoned Tillamook Rock Lighthouse stands her vigil in solitude. Photo by Ed Delanty.

On the following morning, the lumber steamer *Coos Bay* hove in sight and moved in for the rescue. The watch was doubled during the operation, searching for a periscope, but the *I-25* was well hidden in the depths. After taking the survivors aboard, the freighter searched the area for several hours for others that might have survived and then continued on her course.

The 430 foot *Larry Doheny* slipped under the surface at 11:10 a.m. a charred pathetic form, ending 21 years of service.

Steaming into Port Orford, the *Coos Bay* debarked the tanker's survivors who in turn were treated, released, and reassigned.

The war went on.

In the interim, the *I-25,* getting low on fuel and ammunition returned to Japan for resupply. There, she was sent out to more pressing needs in the Pacific theater, never again to come back to the Pacific Coast.

Allied forces were beginning to strike back.

Other merchant ships destroyed at the hands of Nipponese submarines off the West Coast during the early war years included the tankers *Emidio* and *Montebello,* lost off the California coast through the action of the *I-17* and *I-21* respectively, while the *I-19*

was credited with torpedoing the freighter *Absaroka,* which like the *Fort Camosun* refused to sink and was towed to port. Several other allied merchantmen received damage, but for the most part, the Japanese Navy elected not to keep up pressure on Pacific Coast shipping. The reason has always been a mute question. Certainly an all-out effort such as was carried on by the German U-boat pack in the Atlantic could have reaped havoc and have greatly throttled the allied strikeback.

Japan's hopes for destructive psychological warfare on the Pacific rim was likewise misguided, the greatest fiasco of all coming as late as 1945 when some 9,300 paper war balloons were launched into the air from northern Honshu, designed to drift with the air currents across the Pacific and land on American and Canadian soil. Each carried 25 to 65 pounds of incendiary and anti-personnel bombs. From them, Japanese warlords visioned the burning of great sectors of North America. Many of the strange conveyances, 33 feet in diameter, unmanned, drifted over the Oregon coast. Most fell harmlessly into the Pacific short of their goal, but 90 are known to have landed in various locations in Alaska, Hawaii, Canada, and as far east as Michigan.

U.S. military intelligence feared a much more sinister

plot such as poisonous gasses or lethal bombs, and accordingly clamped a tight security on the discovery of the balloons. However, they were basically non-destructive, the bombs and incendiaries failing to ignite. Curious civilians at times tinkered with their strange payloads instead of alerting military experts trained to disarm them. A woman and five children were the only known victims. A balloon, with an attached bomb landed at Bly, Oregon on May 5, 1945 and when an attempt was made to detach the explosive, it went off, killing all six.

McChord Air Base near Tacoma had as one of its standing assignments the shooting down of any of the strange Japanese balloons. Not difficult to spot, they were filled with a lighter-than-air gas and a rectangular electronic control device about two square feet which automatically released sandbags as the balloon lost gas in its flight over the ocean, thereby controlling altitude.

The reader may be wondering about the fate of the Japanese submarines I-25 and I-26. The former vanished with her entire crew in the southwest Pacific after harassment of targets in the Antipodes. Tagami, however, was not then her commander, having been reassigned to other duties. The I-26 was lost in the Battle of Leyte Gulf, but only after inflicting heavy blows against the allies. Among other strikes, she was credited with the torpedoing of the aircraft carrier USS Saratoga, southeast of the Solomons August 31, 1942, and then on Nov. 14 sank the USS Juneau near Guadalcanal, one of the most tragic chapters in U.S. Naval history. The cruiser virtually disintegrated, nearly all of her 700-man complement perishing, including the five Sullivan brothers.

The hectic days following Pearl Harbor prompted much action along the Oregon coast. The state's geographical nature, with numerous sandy beaches, to all intents and purposes would be the likely area for a Japanese invasion. Although most navigation lights and many shore lights were extinguished on the night of Dec. 7, 1941, a general blackout was not ordered till 24 hours later. Tillamook Rock's beacon continued to burn, but Coastguardsmen covered buoy lights with a black cloth material.

It is alleged that the Cape Disappointment lighthouse beacon was ordered extinguished at gunpoint by an Army officer, the keeper refusing to do so having received no such orders from his immediate superiors. The irate military officer threatened to blast the lens to bits unless his order was carried out. It was.

Several days later, vessels were given permission to show lights of reduced visibility, and blue stern lights became standard equipment on many cargo vessels.

The blackout was responsible for a major shipwreck at the entrance to the Columbia River. The 420 foot Matson freighter Mauna Ala grounded Dec. 10, 1941 on Clatsop Spit after having been ordered to return to the West Coast while en route to Honolulu with a full cargo of Christmas goods. Unaware that the coastal aids to navigation had been extinguished, shipmaster Capt. C. W. Saunders was proceeding at dead slow off the darkened river entrance. Ship's officer O. S. Anderson picked up a blinker signal, difficult to decipher but which he thought was a command to halt. When no further messages were received, Captain Saunders ordered "full ahead," expecting to spot the lightship. Instead, the 7,000-ton vessel piled up at 6 p.m., 2½ miles south of the position of the blacked-out lightship.

Coast Guard lifeboats managed to remove the crew of 35, there being no casualties.

A subsequent hearing conducted by the Bureau of Inspection and Navigation ruled "the blackout of navigational aids, lights, and silencing of radio beacons at the mouth of the Columbia River under wartime restrictions caused the wreck of the Mauna Ala, which stranded on Clatsop Spit Dec. 10, 1941."

The vessel and most of her cargo were a total loss.

One extremely alarming event that occurred during the war years ended on a somewhat humorous note. A wing of Canadian fighter planes returning from exercises, mistook the Columbia River entrance for the mouth of the Fraser River. Civilian air observers immediately reported unidentified fighter planes fast approaching. The alarm spread rapidly and the military scrambled the Portland group and alerted all air units in the Pacific Northwest. It was at first thought to be a Japanese strike, but there were some mighty red Canadian faces when their planes were intercepted by the American squadrons. Needless to say, certain officers in the Canadian air force were given a few additional lessons in the geography of the Northwest coast.

A tight cork was kept on all Oregon coast activities. This writer having enlisted in the Coast Guard was one of many dispatched from boot camp to beach patrol assignments on the Oregon coast in the early months of the war. All beaches were searched around the clock by both Army and Coast Guard units, either from lookout towers or by "sand pounders" on foot. As organization progressed, walkie-talkies and patrol or attack dogs became constant companions to the beach walkers. Some shore areas had barbed wire strung to repel would-be invasions, the rusted wreck of the bark Peter Iredale, having reposed on the beach near Fort Stevens since 1906, was intertwined with it. Both that fort and Fort Canby on the opposite side of the river were beehives of activity. Hardly a day passed without reported sightings of enemy submarines, planes, agents or flotillas, most of which proved fabrications but which had to be checked out. Anxieties and fears prompted many imaginations to run wild.

Military forces responded rapidly to reported sightings of submarines, and as was earlier told, the crew of a B25 bomber was cited for the sinking of a Japanese submarine off the Columbia River, which in all probability never happened. Persistent reports of both German and Japanese agents landing from submarines by night at various places along the coast were a concern. A reported sinking of a Nazi U-boat off Pacific City and of a Russian submersible by a Japanese submarine had little factual foundation. Many retaliatory blows were struck by allied naval forces against the enemy in the Pacific theater, but despite many claims, post-war records showed no "official" sinkings of Japanese submarines along the Oregon coast during the conflict, discounting the single B25 claim.

The writer was involved in one incident that received no small amount of concern. It happened like this:

The place was Tierra del Mar Beach, north of Pacific City, then the location of a Coast Guard station, from which patrols were sent out to three different beaches. Due to strictly enforced war restrictions all communications with headquarters were in code. On a routine night patrol we were burdened down with the usual equipment—rifles, sidearms, walkie-talkie and a patrol dog. To protect the innocent, we will refer to my partner as Joe.

It was a late fall evening and the truck left us at a wilderness spot from where we had to walk about a mile to the beach. The trail ended at a high bank from which a switchback path led down to the sands where our long trek would begin.

All across the nation appeals had gone out for dog owners to donate their pets for the war effort. Demand was generally for German shepherds, Doberman pinschers and similar breeds that could be properly trained for patrol and attack purposes. So in demand were the canines that the quotas could not be filled. Thus, the restrictions as to types of breeds were relaxed and in certain cases dogs of the hunting variety were accepted. Most of the animals assigned to Pacific City were proper types, but somehow a pointer had slipped in and out of the K-9 Corps training school. How he ever graduated remains one of the great mysteries of the war, but there he was, big as life and twice as stupid. It took little knowledge to know that hunting dogs made extremely poor war dogs, their noses concentrating, for the most part, on the scent of birds and animals, instead of humans.

Such a dog was "Pluto," properly named for his Disney double. Always the last to be assigned, coastguardsmen did their best to stay clear of him if at all possible, for though huge for his breed, he had an insatiable desire to go out of his head whenever there was a bird to be pursued, and if a patrolman happened to be on the other end of the leash it was tantamount to being on a pair of water skiis towed by a runaway power boat, or better yet hanging on to a spooked horse. Orders,

however, were for a patrolman to keep his dog under control at all times and never turn him loose except in the most dire emergency. The canine was the total responsibility of the handler.

Ornery and disobedient as ever, Pluto was giving my partner and me the full treatment. It was dusk; below the sea cliff lay six miles of beach. Suddenly the dog caught sight of a flock of sandpipers swooping along the ridge, and he was off to the races with me on the other end, just as if Snoopy had grabbed Linus's security blanket. The strength of that canine was unbelievable and it took 15 minutes to get him partially calmed down. The two of us decided that perhaps if we let him loose for a few minutes he would run his legs off and settle down for the long beach patrol. That was a mistake.

Nevertheless, we violated the rule and set him free. Like an express train, tongue down to his knees he returned to the chase running back and forth, changing pace each time the birds reversed their flight. For some reason that evening there was a great number of seabirds flying along the crest of the 60 foot bank, as if they had come in to avoid a storm at sea. The sandpipers seemed to know they were dealing with a dumb brute who couldn't get out of his own way. The chase continued for another five minutes at astounding speeds. Suddenly Pluto stopped. Panting furiously, he leaned far out over the cliff, biting at the birds in flight. A gust of wind caught his hind quarters, and over the bank he went, head first.

"He's gone over!" exclaimed Joe excitedly.

Taking off like a shot we peered over the ridge. No sign of the dog.

"He must have bounded off that narrow ledge and bombed straight down to the beach," said I, "We're in big trouble if anything's happened to that GI hound."

Adjusting our equipment we made knots down the switchback trail. Once on the beach we pursued different directions.

"Over here!" I shouted to Joe, "Over here!"

At first we thought Pluto was dead having made a nosedive into the sand. Releasing him gently from his self-made excavation, we could see blood flowing from a gash on his brow.

"He's still breathing," sighed Joe feeling the dog's pulse. "Pretty weak though."

"What do we do now?" asked I, "Six miles of beach to walk before we meet the midnight truck.

"How about a message on the walkie-talkie?" suggested Joe who had the instrument strapped to his back.

"All well and good," I returned, "but what code message fits the occasion?"

Getting down behind a stump and using the low beam of our flashlight we searched the code book.

"Here's one," said Joe, "Patrolman Injured."

I looked at him quizzically.

"Its the only one in here that even comes close," he announced.

After cogitating over the matter we decided to send the message. Twice it was repeated.

"Over! Over!" exclaimed my partner, but no recognition was received.

"They won't confirm," said Joe.

"How are we going to get the pooch to the other end of the beach," I asked Joe, "He's limp as a dishrag."

"What about a stretcher?" suggested my cohort.

"A what?" I returned.

"I've got some rope; we can lash some driftwood pieces together. Better than dragging him," reasoned Joe.

With no other alternative, we hastily searched the driftwood line and collectively found some pieces that met our needs. Assembling our makeshift conveyance we lashed the dog securely and then lifted it coolie-fashion and mushed on down the beach into the growing darkness.

The air grew chilly and an occasional star poked its light out from mottled clouds. Our night guide was the white-flecked foam line of the incoming tide. The hours passed drearily, the dog getting heavier and heavier. Rest periods became frequent. Once, we heard Pluto give out with a sickening moan, as if he was in great pain.

Shortly afterward, Joe kicked something on the beach that had a tinkling sound. Stopping to pick it up he discovered an ancient barnacle-covered whiskey bottle that had drifted in on the tide. Pulling out the stubborn cork, he shook it.

"Wow!" he grimaced, "That's potent stuff. Just a swallow left, why not give the mutt a swig. Might revive him."

Before I could answer, Joe had Pluto's head braced under his hand and was pouring the evil smelling fluid into his jowls. The dog gave a sudden jerk. Gulping once, he relaxed and fell into a contented sleep.

Hoisting the stretcher to our shoulders once again we resumed our safari. The area was sparsely populated and a total blackout was in effect. When finally gaining the end of the beach, 15 minutes before rendezvous time we were both exhausted and hungry. Sitting down on a log, contented to be relieved of the extra burden, we listened to the surf pounding. A light breeze was blowing. Suddenly Joe jumped up.

"Did you hear that?"

"What?" I asked.

"Listen! It sounds like soldiers walking through the sand."

"Sure does," I whispered, hand cupped to my ear, "Sounds more like a whole regiment."

As the sounds grew louder we heard noises like the movement of heavy equipment.

"Could it be an invasion?" my partner asked.

"Two rifles and a dormant dog against a landing party. Pretty awful odds," said I.

Ducking low as possible behind the drift, we both kept praying our ears were playing tricks on us.

"I better send another message," insisted Joe wrestling with the walkie-talkie.

Both of us felt petrified. The only thing due was the small truck that was to pick us up, a sound with which we were well acquainted. Was this the long-rumored Japanese invasion of the Oregon coast? Were there landing craft nearby unloading men and equipment?

As Joe was about to send his Mayday message, I detected some words in English.

"Hold on Joe."

Again we listened intently. There were commands followed by more marching feet, heavy engines and what sounded like a plane overhead.

"Halt!" Who goes there? Stand and identify yourselves!" rattled a hoarse voice from seemingly out of nowhere. As we rose slowly from our prone position, what seemed like a brilliant searchlight blinded our eyes. Out stepped a high-ranking Army officer flanked on all sides by a vast contingent of militiamen. Representatives from three branches of the service had flooded the area and none of them were Japanese.

After meekly identifying ourselves, the spokesman bellowed, "Your code message, 'Patrolman injured! . . . Where are the invaders? The extent of your injuries?"

"Ouch!" muttered Joe, "I think we're in hot water."

Our communication was taken to have meant an invasion, or at least some kind of enemy action in which injuries had been sustained. A red alert had gone out, and battle-ready troops most of whom had been roused from deep sleep had converged at the rendezvous point, en masse.

Joe and I looked at each other, faces as red as the alert, small lakes forming under our armpits. Trying to explain our dilemma was like flying an airplane in reverse. We presented Pluto to the authorities in his stupor. Reviving momentarily, the dog managed a large belch and then fell back to sleep.

When our account passed through the troops I thought we would be tarred and feathered on the spot. Oaths and cursings filled the night air. There was dead silence in the truck all the way back to Pacific City. While the dog received hospitalization, the two of us went before the commanding officer for a severe reprimand, a cut in rank and weeks of peeling spuds.

Because of strict war secrecy the story remained hushed but probably involved one of the larger defensive forces assembled on the Oregon coast to thwart a possible invasion.

As for Pluto, he recovered, but I heard later he was

bugled out of the service on a Section 8.

Another withheld but true war incident occurred off the Oregon coast in 1944. Involved was a 125 foot Coast Guard cutter, one of the service's smaller ocean going vessels which at the time was working in conjunction with two Navy minesweepers, escorting a small convoy from Alaska to California.

The cutter, with but two racks of depth charges mounted on her fantail was the only vessel in the flotilla equipped to fight submarines. Total complement of the twin-screw, diesel-powered steel cutter was 54 men. Bunks were stacked in places five high, below deck forward. Aboard was a Coast Guard gunnery officer who had received one of the nation's highest war decorations for his part in capturing a vitally important German radio station in Greenland. Reassigned to the cutter for more peaceful duty, he had grown extremely proud of his decorations, and perhaps his fame may have been a little much for him to handle. Not taking away from this war hero's valor, but he was known to have frequented the deck in working apparel with battle ribbons attached, and the rumor went around the ship that sometimes he even sacked-out with the decorations intact.

Though many Coast Guard vessels had performed admirably in the war effort, this vessel's chronicle contained no great accomplishments, mostly just workaday routine patrol work. The scene was set. The cutter escorted the small convoy southward well off the Oregon coast, moving at the speed of the slowest vessel, which happened to be a medium-sized cable ship, which at best managed about six knots.

Just at the break of a cold dawn, the warning signal reverberated through the cutter. On the bridge the sonar was pinging loudly. There was a flurry of activity as all hands leaped from their bunks. Signalmen were waving flags and blinker lights were flashing. The convoy was on full alert — a submarine had supposedly been detected. Deck guns were manned, some by men clad only in battle helmets and long underwear.

Most of the other vessels had only the minimum in deck armament. All eyes were on the cutter as she alone was equipped to depth charge underseas marauders. Racing out from the fleet at her full 15½ knots, she cut a neat pattern. The sonar's excited heartbeat left little doubt that something was down there, and no allied submarines were reported in the area.

The grizzled skipper, a 25 year veteran of the service who had come up through the hawse pipe, stood by the man at the wheel directing the vessel's course toward the target. When the desired position was reached the engines were ordered stopped. He wanted to be sure of the right place to bomb. Everything was quiet except the sonar and the sloshing of the sea as the vessel drifted forward. The crew, at their battle stations, cold and shivering stood statuesque, waiting, listening, watching.

All set for a direct kill. Could this be the highlight of the skipper's career and honors for the cutter? Everyone was tense.

"Full ahead!" snapped the C.O. The message was repeated and the cutter fairly leaped out of the water as she trembled from stem to stern, like a horse at the starting gate. Swinging in a wide arc she moved in for the kill. The decorated gunnery officer stood like Napoleon alongside the depth charge racks ready to give the order.

Moaning and groaning in every joint, banking steeply on the turn, the ship breezed down depth charge alley. At the precise moment, the gunnery officer raised his arm in an erect military manner that would have rivaled General McArthur himself.

"Drop one!" he shouted eying the blueclads under his authority.

The charge rolled off the rack splashing into the frothy wake.

"Drop two!"

One after another the cylinders rolled down the tracks, over the stern and into the ocean. Everybody had their hands clamped over their ears waiting for the loud reports, watching eagerly for the geysers of water to erupt. Would there be upheavals of diesel oil and wreckage?

All dozen charges were dropped and unfortunately there were no others in the magazine.

But alas, there were no blasts, no geysers, no pieces of wreckage, no oil. The convoy moved slowly onward and the cutter came to an embarrassing halt, the sonar still pinging madly, indicating the submersible to be directly underneath the ship. All attention turned to the gunnery officer who incidently had not forgotten to wear his battle ribbons. His face was scarlet. He was fidgeting. Never in his illustrious career had he been in such a position. This highly-decorated individual in the excitement of the moment had not ordered his men to set the depth mechanism for the charges to detonate. All plummeted to the bottom of the ocean perhaps to lay there dead till the end of time.

Fortunately, the submarine failed to fire its torpedoes and gradually faded from the sonar's range. Without more depth charges the chase ended, and with full daylight there was no chance the submarine would surface for a battle with deck guns.

Down the drain went the moment of victory for the ship, her CO and for the gunnery officer. Another anti-submarine surface vessel joined the convoy off the northern California coast and the cutter limped back to her Grays Harbor base like a whipped puppy, the battle ribbons noticeably absent from a certain officer's tunic. Whenever thereafter the subject came up in the officer's mess, the man in question would simply repine,

"Maybe it was just a large whale."

And I ought to know. I was there.

Work underway on the Yaquina Bay south jetty under the direction of the Portland District Corps of Engineers. Left, background is the city of Newport, and center background the artistic Yaquina Bay bridge. A Corps dredge is at the center of the photo.

A seagull eye view of the Rogue River bar in July of 1969. One of the newer jetty projects, it serves the maritime needs of the Gold Beach-Wedderburn communities. U.S. Army Corps of Engineers photo.

Largest of the Corps of Army Engineers seagoing hopper dredges assigned to the Portland District is the *Biddle*. Much of her dredging work is done on the Columbia River bar. She almost met her demise near buoy 9 at the river mouth August 9, 1977 when in a collision with the Matson container carrier *Hawaiian*. The accident occurred in a heavy fog and the dredge received a huge gash in her starboard side, the drag head being jammed into the hull, flooding two compartments. Pumps kept the dredge afloat, the tugs *Betsy L.* and *Salvage Chief* towing her to Portland Drydocks for a $2.5 million repair job. Nobody was injured in the incident.

Busy workhorse of the Corps of Engineers, seagoing hopper dredge *Harding* heads out for a new assignment on the Oregon coast.

Smallest of the seagoing hopper dredges assigned to the Portland District Corps of Engineers is the *Pacific*, 180 feet in length with a hopper capacity of 500 cubic yards. Built in 1937, she is ideally suited to work on the more restricted bar and river areas.

VIEWING OREGON'S SALTY COAST

A PORTFOLIO OF CAMERA STUDIES

BY

DENNIS C. MAVITY

Dennis C. Mavity who supplied several photos for this book, is staff photographer for the Newport News Times. With a varied background in news, magazine and commercial photography, he has also been an editor of periodicals in Missouri and Oregon, and for eight years did press photography for a firm which supplied newspapers in the San Fernando Valley. Winner of many awards, his latest is the Oregon Newspaper Association's 1976 award for the best spot news photo for a weekly newspaper.

Looking down from Cape Foulweather, south, along the Oregon coast under a sparkling sun. At the center of the photo is the Inn at Otter Crest.

Great fireball. The sun hovers over a quiet ocean and a sleepy coastal community in central Oregon.

Like the gateway to Paradise, the Pacific puts on its finest show in this scene south of Depoe Bay.

Looking south from Beverly Beach toward Yaquina Head, mottled clouds hovering over the ocean present a mood of loneliness.

The central Oregon coast presents many fascinating scenes for the photographer. Here, the sun reflecting on the ocean plays a prank as it reflects back to the lens and drops a massive diamond among the rocks below.

Camera magic. Filters create a serenade almost like stardust falling from the Star of Bethlehem. Actually the sun's reflections afford the effect as they flash back at the camera lens.

Appearing more like a bed of red hot coals on an island in the South Pacific, this is an Oregon ocean scene near the Devil's Punchbowl. The sun is casting its light from partly cloudy skies.

Under lofty Cape Perpetua, two beachcombers stroll the sands, framed between lofty snags.

In their sunset years, these gnarled spruce trees have lost
the battle to erosion as the winter breakers undermine their roots.

Storm flags were flying at the Depoe Bay Coast Guard Station, but this boat put to sea just the same. The geyser in the background is the famous Spouting Horn which is putting on a show as the growing seas send breakers shoreward to sweep the outcrops.

Standing defiant against the ocean surges as it has for countless ages, this big hunk of hard basalt holds firm on the beach at Seal Rock.

Driftwood signpost near Otter Rock. The Pacific on this occasion was living up to the meaning of its name.

Clinging to the slopes of Cape Foulweather, the Lookout gift shop. This area was to have been the location of the Yaquina Head Lighthouse, but geographical confusion in the early 1870's placed the lighthouse in its present location.

In the Marine Gardens area near Otter Rock.

Driftwood graveyard—silvered bones of once proud trees lie intermingled on the shores of Alsea Bay, carried in by the winter storms.

Alsea Bay looking toward Yaquina John Point named for the
valiant Indian leader who believed that all man should be free.

Perfectly framed in a marine setting at Port Dock #3 Newport, a solitary commercial fishboat is seen from the seawall supports.

If only these rocky sentinels could speak what a story they would have to tell. This summer scene was taken at Harris State Park near Brookings.

Looking upward through the opening of the Devil's Punchbowl, a freak of nature chiseled out by the persistent elements. As seawater rushes in, the briny froth turns to a witch-like brew.

Sand, surf, trees and monoliths are all featured in this ocean
scene near Otter Rock in the shadow of Cape Foulweather.

Like the battered remnants of a segment of the French Foreign Legion, this driftwood fence stretches along the sand dunes of Bayshore on the ocean front north of Alsea Bay.

When Capt. James Cook sighted Cape Perpetua in 1778, he gave it a wide berth, preferring to stay well clear of such rocky lava basalt outcrops as are seen in this photo.

Numerous sea vistas present themselves in the Cape
Perpetua area. Thousands of tourists come to visit annually.

On the ocean fringe of lower Cape Foulweather, about
three miles south of Depoe Bay.

Not far from the Inn at Otter Crest is found a most unusual contour of rocks along the ocean front. This is part of the Marine Gardens area where the pounding ocean surf sculpts with the hand of a madman.

Nature's deterrent against erosion on sandy beaches. Stiff, coarse yet graceful, shore grass digs its roots deep into the sand and holds the line against encroachment.

Trail to the beach at Marine Gardens—beautiful all the
way.

Looking westward on a clear day you can see forever. The world's greatest ocean kisses the Oregon coast for nearly 400 miles.

Segment of the vast commercial fishing fleet that homeports at Newport.

Seemingly lifting their arms to pray, part of the Newport trolling fleet is silhouetted against sparkling Yaquina Bay.

Resembling a sewing circle, fishboats meet bow to bow
as if discussing their exploits at sea.

Like driftwood gargoyles, these strange nature-carved figures peer intently toward the artistic Alsea Bay bridge which connects Waldport with the north side of the bay.

This weird photo was taken through the rain-smeared windshield of a vehicle just below the Yaquina Bay Bridge at Newport. It might be titled "an inebriate's view of the Oregon coast."

A study in architecture and the natural elements which appear to blend together here in perfect harmony.

Though appearing as if ice had spread its cold grip over the Pacific Ocean and Yaquina Bay, it was merely a sunny November day, no snow, no rain. Fact is it seldom snows on the central Oregon coast.

What began as a routine surf rescue drill turned out to be the real thing. As a result, some rare photos were captured of a Coast Guard motor lifeboat actually flipping and making a 360 degree roll. Dennis Mavity was on the Yaquina north jetty and recorded the entire sequence. The *CG-44300,* a 44 footer and the 52 foot *Victory,* a larger Coast Guard lifeboat were involved. The drill, in charge of Chief Tom McAdams aboard the latter, is told in the series of four photos. Here the two vessels are seen wallowing in high surf near the Yaquina jetty.

Suddenly a "sneaker" catches the *44300* and over she goes. Designed to self-right, it was a nightmare experience for the men who made the trip through Davy Jones' locker.

Perhaps the nation's most picturesque lighthouse—
Heceta Head. Since 1894 it has beamed its light seaward and
continues to be one of the greatest contributions to the scenic
Oregon coast.

Oregon's "Jonathan Livingston Seagull" candidate; this lovely creature soars through the air with the greatest of ease.

Pete the seagull is a pretty special guy around Yaquina Bay. He likes people, and for the most part people like him, as long as he doesn't leave his calling card in the wrong place. Pete's a pretty wise old guy and has been around for a fair share of years. Some gulls live as long as 50 years, and the way he's posing you'd think he was the mayor of Newport.

Look at that one in the middle showing off with his balancing act. Two feet for beginners.

139. **Come on in,** the water's fine. Seagulls frolic with a wary eye out for a tasty morsel.

Posing like a professional model, this contented seagull looks almost as good right side up as upside down. He must be "reflecting" on his qualities as a bird.

Grace personfied. The remarkable seagull in flight.

Primping under the November sun, these mallard ducks
are happy in their habitat in one of Oregon's coastal estuaries.

Headless seagull? No, it just appears that way, but notice that landing gear.

"**If I had the wings** of a seagull, I'd fly above all the works of man, look downward and shake my head."

Ocean surf ballet dance. This phenomenal photo at Agate Beach speaks for itself.

Man's greatest efforts are puny measured by the eons of time. Here, the once proud British bark *Peter Iredale* displays her encrusted remains. Wrecked Oct. 25, 1906, she has been playing hide-and-seek with the shifting sands ever since. She lies in her grave off Fort Stevens State Park just south of the entrance to the mighty Columbia River and has been denoted as an historical site.